Covered Wagon Women

Diaries and Letters from the Western Trails 1864–1868

Volume 9

Edited and compiled by
KENNETH L. HOLMES

Introduction to the Bison Books Edition
by Sherry L. Smith

University of Nebraska Press
Lincoln and London

♾

First Bison Books printing: 1999
Most recent printing indicated by the last digit below:
10   9   8   7   6   5   4   3   2   1

Library of Congress Cataloging-in-Publication Data
The Library of Congress has cataloged Vol. 1 as:
Covered wagon women: diaries & letters from the western trails, 1840–1849 / edited and compiled by Kenneth L. Holmes; introduction to the Bison Books edition by Anne M. Butler.
p.   cm.
Originally published: Glendale, Calif: A. H. Clark Co., 1983.
"Reprinted from volume one . . . of the original eleven-volume edition"—
T.p. verso.
"Volume 1."
Includes index.
ISBN 0-8032-7277-4 (pa: alk. paper)
1. Women pioneers—West (U.S.)—Biography.   2. West (U.S.)—History.   3. West (U.S.)—Biography.   4. Overland journeys to the Pacific.   5. Frontier and pioneer life—West (U.S.)   I. Holmes, Kenneth L.
F591.C79   1996   978—dc20   95-21200   CIP

Volume 2 introduction by Lilian Schlissel
ISBN 0-8032-7274-X (pa: alk. paper)
Volume 3 introduction by Susan Armitage
ISBN 0-8032-7287-1 (pa: alk. paper)
Volume 4 introduction by Glenda Riley
ISBN 0-8032-7291-X (pa: alk. paper)
Volume 5 introduction by Ruth B. Moynihan
ISBN 0-8032-7294-4 (pa: alk. paper)
Volume 6 introduction by Linda Peavy and Ursula Smith
ISBN 0-8032-7295-2 (pa: alk. paper)
Volume 7 introduction by Shirley A. Leckie
ISBN 0-8032-7296-0 (pa: alk. paper)
Volume 8 introduction by María E. Montoya
ISBN 0-8032-7297-9 (pa: alk. paper)
Volume 9 introduction by Sherry L. Smith
ISBN 0-8032-7298-7 (pa: alk. paper)

Introduction to the Bison Books Edition

Sherry L. Smith

A diary is an intensely personal document, an individual soul's daily rendering of events and emotions. Most diarists expect no one, with the possible exception of family members, will ever read the words they put to page. Such thoughts are for private rather than public purpose. Yet, if that diary survives over time and if it is linked to a migration as momentous as the European-American sweep across the North American continent, it becomes the source and substance of history itself. It becomes a public account whose value transcends the individual life that shaped it. It becomes a communal document, which provides insight into the writer's time, place and historical context.

What a time 1864–68 was in this nation's history. The diarists presented in this volume lived through and, in some cases, participated in three of their century's most momentous events—although they rarely made an explicit connection between their individual actions and the broader context. And who could blame them? How many of us pause at the end of the day to connect our commonplace toil to historical context? Yet it is in making those linkages that these women's diaries hold, in part, their interest and value for historians.

First, of course, these women and their families took part in perhaps the most quintessential American experience: migration. Of course this was not simply a nineteenth-century affair. For millennia, people had been moving into and around the American continents. Long before Europeans stumbled upon the Western Hemisphere in 1492, the ancestors of Native Americans walked the land, seeking havens to establish homes, raise families, or find security. Although the pace would pick up when Europeans entered the picture, the essential pattern of movement, dynamism, and change was already in place.

The European newcomers did not understand this, of course. They presumed momentum was solely theirs and that Native Americans existed in a time warp, of sorts—outside of historical processes. Indians, according to nineteenth-century common knowledge, were changeless, not only incapable of a past but also of a future. It would have come as a surprise to the women whose works are offered here to see themselves presented as an extension of Indian behavior patterns. Nevertheless, they were.

Connections to European migration and immigration would have been easier for the women to make. By the time they climbed into their covered wagons, the land that had become the United States had witnessed over four centuries of such activity. Most of their predecessors departed from European and African shores, but others came from Pacific Islands, China, and other Asian points of embarkation. And once in the New World, the immigrants did not necessarily stay put. African slaves had little control over their destinies or destinations. As human beings transformed into commodities, they found no respite or security in the marketplace of flesh. Immigrants from Europe and Asia exhibited greater freedom to move and move again, to search out the best chance for themselves and their descendants.

New generations, in turn, took up the standard, linking movement with opportunity, penetrating into, or at least across, the heart of the continent as the years passed. By the 1860s such migration was commonplace. In fact, the reader who looks to these diaries for insight into *why* these women and their families moved will find no explicit explanations. It is as if the answer is too obvious, the motive too routine to require articulation. Still, the journey across the nation's wide expanses was not so ordinary as to remain unrecorded. The women's journals reveal, in fact, the extraordinary stamina and fortitude, both physical and emotional, such treks demanded of participants.

They also demonstrate the family networks which proved so crucial to a successful migration experience.[1] Far from operating alone, families reached out to one another across wide distances, as they had for centuries, encouraging the initial move and providing a warm and welcoming hearth once their emigrant relatives arrived at their shared destination. Nineteenth-century Americans may have venerated the individual, but they mostly operated in the context of family, group and community.

While the women's journeys coincided with the ongoing American saga of migration, their experiences also corresponded with another powerful theme of their century—the transfer of dominance over the Great Plains from Indians to Americans. This tale climaxed in the 1860s when, as historian Elliott West put it, "two cultures acted out two compelling visions in a land that could support only one."[2] Vibrant horse cultures, living off the grasslands' bounties, could not coexist with a culture bent on mining gold, growing wheat, raising cattle and building railroads across former buffalo commons. Perhaps the collision between cultures was not inevitable, but no one at the time seemed capable of imagining an alternative to conquest. Neither side, according to West, seemed able to use "their prodigious imaginations to picture how varied peoples and dreams might occupy the same place."[3]

By the 1860s some Native Americans and Anglo-Americans resorted to warfare, raiding, and violence as the conflict over control neared its end. Several of the women whose diaries are presented here walked right into—and through—what became for Plains Indians a life-or-death struggle over their way of life. And although several diarists noted the occasional burned-out ranch or stage stop in northeastern Colorado (part of Cheyenne reaction in the wake of 1864 Sand Creek Massacre) and expressed anxiety about their own safety, here too they failed to make the connection between their individual actions and the larger picture.

Of course, none of these women intended to plant her family on the Plains. Their destinies rested at the far edge of the continent: California, Oregon, or Idaho. They were, after all, just passing through. Yet even transitory passage carried an environmental price, as horses and other stock consumed precious grasses. More significantly, trailing across this mid-section portended final capitulation of the entire geographical space to United States jurisdiction. Nation building came later to the center, the "jumped over" area, but it came nonetheless. Perhaps nothing better symbolized this than the completion of the first transcontinental railroad in 1868, the year of the last diary printed here. The late 1860s, in fact, not only doomed the Plains Indians' hegemony over the region but also signaled the beginning of the end for covered wagon travel itself. Modernization took many forms, but none more symbolically significant than the locomotive engine chugging across the West. Some westward moving families continued to carry their belongings in wagons into the twentieth century, but the future rested firmly in the power and promise of the railroad.

The third crucial national story that coincided with these women's journeys was the Civil War and Reconstruction. Of these events, which threw the country into four years of terrible bloodletting followed by more years of turmoil, violence, and political upheaval, the women, again, wrote nothing. Ruth Shackleford mentioned rumors of "rebels" ahead as she traveled through Iowa in 1865 but nothing came of it. Three years later, Shackleford and Harriet Bunyard noted the presence of "Negro" soldiers in Reconstruction Texas, but neither woman seemed to understand that these "buffalo soldiers" signaled early efforts on the part of the federal government to begin integrating African-American citizens into all aspects of American life. Such a thought, in fact, would probably have horrified Bunyard, who upon passing Fort Chadbourne announced she "expected to find people living there but the only inhabitants were a few colored soldiers [and] One Mexican keeping stage stand."

Of course, these women were moving, physically, away from the battlefields of civil discord. National politics loomed far less importantly over their immediate lives than finding sufficient forage for their animals or coping with the inevitable illnesses and deaths that accompanied overland journeys. Still, the West could not evade the fundamental questions raised—and answered—by the Civil War and its aftermath. In that region too, African-Americans would be free to take up both rights and responsibilities of citizenship, as those Texas-based soldiers demonstrated, regardless of Harriet Bunyard's assumption that they were not "people."[4]

For all the linkages historians make between these diaries and their historical context and for all our efforts to discern patterns and point to representative behavior, there is no denying the compelling individuality of each of these documents—or, more accurately, each writer. To be sure, these women had much in common but they also differed from one another in sometimes subtle ways. And that is what makes them not only entertaining but also instructive in a broader sense of that term. Beyond the historical significance, the fundamental human stories lie. At the core of each of these diarists, a personality remains, a complicated woman who sometimes adhered to patterns and predictable behavior (based on nineteenth-century gender roles, for instance) and sometimes did not.

Readers will duly note the predictable behaviors along gender lines, whereby the women looked after children and prepared meals while husbands cared for the animals, made decisions about travel routes, and provided protection from threats—real or imagined. But they will also delight in the unexpected moments that come from encounters with these flesh-and-blood folks. On a rainy June morning, for instance, Clarissa Shipley's husband prepared his own breakfast and then brought one to his wife and children, who had not yet stirred from their cozy wagon beds. Mary Louisa Black willingly forewent Victorian sensibilities about bodily functions when she wrote, "The flux is not so frequent but when I have actions I am puped [sic] out." The touching, considerate gesture of husband to wife and the earthy explanation of a common, but rarely acknowledged, intestinal problem bring these women into clearer focus. Herein they take on shape, not simply as symbols but as people.

Their individual voices come through not so much in what they say, but rather, in how they say it. None of these women engage in significant self-reflection, and none could be accused of self-absorption. What is striking, in fact, is how little they focus on self, emotion, feeling or psychology. Yet they surely experienced deep emotions while "travailing," as Black frequently rendered the word, "traveling." What distinguishes them is how they expressed those feelings. Elizabeth Porter's account offers a staccato, rhythmic accounting of a child's burial one day and the birth of another the next. Only after many entries, wherein she almost roboticly ticks off the deaths of traveling companions as well as family animals who had been close enough to acquire names, she allowed herself, "Feel kind of lonesome all day."

This, however, proved more forthcoming than Mary Black's terse entries which list nothing more than the day's final destination—all she could apparently muster in the wake of her five-year-old daughter's death at the journey's outset. Two months passed before she was able to manage a small joke in her diary. What does this say about this mother's deep grief? What does it also demonstrate about her ability to keep on living?

Not all were reticent, however. Ruth Shackleford's account is expansive, detailed, and descriptive. She paints word pictures of daily camp scenes: "Frank [her husband] has just got through cleaning. Matt has laid down under the wagon to sleep. Ann is in the wagon patching a shirt. My children are all under our wagon in the shade. Mr. Morrison is shoeing oxen." In this way, she draws us into the moment, sits us down next to her, takes us into her life. Further, she is more willing than Black or Porter to convey her emotional state. Early in the journey, her party passed the grave of a forty-year-old woman, a stranger. Yet, Shackleford notes, "It makes me feel so sad to see a lone grave here in this doleful looking country and [to] kneel at the head to read the name. I can't keep from crying, thinking how I would hate to be left on this road." Yet Shackleford, too, succumbs to the numbing experience of frequent deaths as the trail takes its toll on her party. Two months later, as they bury her sister-in-law, then a nephew, and finally a niece, Ruth no longer allows herself the luxury of emotion. Only near the end of the trek does she note, "We all feel more homesick than ever. I feel like I could cry my eyes out."

Each of these accounts makes the difficulty of cross-continental travel abundantly clear. To be sure, the women note occasional scenes of beauty or curiosity. Sometimes they even had fun. But the overwhelming theme in diary after diary revolves around the tremendous cost to body and spirit that the migration required. Each document individually reinforces the impression that the trail experience was not a joyous adventure but one of drudgery characterized by mile after mile of dust, dangerous river crossings, and death by disease or accident. It was an experience to be endured and, hopefully, survived. It was the space between two stationary existences; the bridge from one life to another.

The ultimate goal was home—albeit in a new and unfamiliar place. That longing was nowhere more evident than in Ruth Shackleford's 1865 diary, wherein her fascination with homes and houses of all kinds borders on obsession. As her party passes through settled communities, Ruth time and again offers assessments of various houses. Once beyond what she would consider "civilization," she even begins transforming hills into houses, at least in her imagination. "We passed some of the prettiest hills this evening . . . I counted four in the shape of houses all in a row. The largest one with a smaller one at one end, looked like a church with a cupola." Ironically, of all the families represented here, Shackleford's is the most transient. After three years in California, she and her husband take to the trail again, heading "home" to Missouri.

For the last twenty years or so historians have systematically sought out, published, and analyzed diaries of women overlanders. Such efforts brought out from the shadows the "hidden half," of the story and certainly enriched our understanding of its complexities. They also sparked scholarly debate. Some issues will remain, perhaps, forever controversial. Did women share power with their husbands in the course of migration or merely acquiesce to spouses' dictates? Did women find greater or lesser opportunity at the end of the trail? Are these "pioneer women" heroines who brought "civilization" to the West or villains who helped usher in catastrophe for Native Americans?[5] Most of these issues did not particularly trouble or interest the women themselves. And therein lies one more valuable aspect of these diaries. They remain both static and vital. The words will not change, but future readers can bring their own questions and concerns to them, finding new meanings in the humble, private musings of these women.

NOTES

1. For examples of family migration networks in a different context see John Bodnar, *The Transplanted: A History of Immigrants in Urban America* (Bloomington: Indiana University Press, 1985), 57–71.

2. Elliott West, *The Contested Plains: Indians, Goldseekers, and the Rush to Colorado* (Lawrence: University Press of Kansas, 1998), 336.

3. West, *The Contested Plains*, 337.

4. For more information on African-American soldiers and the impact of Civil War and Reconstruction on race in the West see Quintard Taylor, *In Search of the Racial Frontier* (New York: W.W. Norton & Company, 1998).

5. For more on these issues see Anne M. Butler, introduction to *Covered Wagon Women: Diaries and Letters from the Western Trails, 1840–1849*, vol. 1 (Lincoln: University of Nebraska Press, 1995), and Linda Peavy and Ursula Smith, introduction to *Covered Wagon Women: Diaries and Letters from the Western Trails, 1853–1854*, vol. 6 (Lincoln: University of Nebraska Press, 1998).

Contents

Illustrations

Introduction to Volume 9

Recently we listened in on a conversation between two fiction writers. One of them declared, "The business of a novelist is to create believable characters." This set us to thinking about the business of a historian, and we concluded that was "to DISCOVER believable characters." And that is the case for our publication of this set of books.

When I speak publicly about the purpose of our project, the most common question asked by members of the audience has been, "How do you find these documents?"

In answering such a question we point out that naturally our first places to look are historical societies and libraries. Some of them have been published in some obscure periodical or book. Those of them that are most valuable for our purpose, however, are the ones that have never been recorded before. These are real primary documents. Through publication we are making them part of the fabric of American history.

How thrilling it has been to see the manuscript owner's eyes light up when we point out, "Your grandmother will become part of American history now."

Nowhere is this process evident so much as in this particular volume of our *Covered Wagon Women* series. True, two of the items that follow were originally published in rather obscure historical publications: Carolyn Hopkins Clark's 1866 journal had been published by the Daughters of Utah Pioneers in *Our Pioneer Heritage*, X (Salt Lake City, 1967); Harriet Bunyard's 1868 diary made its appearance in the *Annual Publications* of the Southern California Historical

Society (XIII, 1924). However, the rest of these documents, five of them, all were discovered in our pursuit of these fugitive materials of history:

Clarissa Elvira Shipley's 1864 record of a westward journey to the Idaho mines was discovered when we called in to Radio Station KGO, San Francisco, in November 1981. The announcer was more than generous as we explained to him what we were seeking in the way of letters and journals written as women crossed the continent as a dynamic part of the westward movement. A few days later came a letter dated November 29, 1981, sent to us by Mrs. Fay Toal, of Tracy, California. Mrs. Toal told us she possessed the diary of her great grandmother, Clarissa Elvira Shipley. Mrs. Shipley's diary told of the westward journey made with her husband, Brice, and two little girls, Agnes Arvilla, age 11, and Emma Etta, age 9.

The diary of Elizabeth Lee Porter was located one-half mile from our home in Monmouth, Oregon. A friend pointed out a wooden frame house on Stadium Drive and told us that the lady who lived there had a diary of an ancestor who crossed the plains to Oregon in 1864. This lady was Mrs. Ivy Hamar. We found her most cooperative in making the diary available for our publishing project. Mrs. Hamar died on August 30, 1982, at age 93.

The 1865 diary of Mary Louisa Black was brought to our attention in a letter written by Mrs. Marguerite Black of Jacksonville, in southern Oregon. She said she had heard me on Radio Station KGO, San Francisco, and that she had the diary of her husband's grandmother. She supplied us with a photocopy of the Mary Louise Black journal and has cooperated with our project in many ways. We have asked her to write an introduction and an epilogue to the diary.

The most astonishing tale of all about search and research

is the story of the discovery of the diaries of Ruth Shackleford on a trip to California in 1865, and a return trip to the East in 1868. My wife, Inez, and I were staying in a motel in Santa Barbara, California, in December 1979. While there we got to know James and Gladys Howerton of Lincoln, Nebraska, and told them of our project. One of them said, "We have a diary like that at home." They later mailed us copies of both diaries, real treasures of historical significance.

We are happy to share historical discoveries with all of you.

For those who have not read the introduction to the first volume of this series, we reiterate some salient points which have been used to guide the editorial hand. It is a major purpose to let the writers tell their own story in their own words with as little scholarly trimming as possible. The intent in this publication of primary sources is to transcribe each word or phrase as accurately as possible, leaving mis-spellings and grammatical errors as written in the original.

Two gestures have been made for the sake of clarity:

1. We have added spaces where phrases or sentences ended and no punctuation appeared in the original.

2. We have put the daily journals in diary format even though the original may have been written continuously line by line because of the writer's shortage of paper.

There are numerous geographic references that are mentioned over and over again in the various accounts. The final volume in the series will include a geographical gazetteer, in addition to an index and bibliography to aid the reader.

The scarce and unusual in overland documents have been sought out. Readily available accounts are not included, but they will be referred to in the final volume along with the bibliography. If the reader knows of such accounts written while on the journey, please let us know. Our goal is to add to

the knowledge of all regarding this portion of our history —
the story of ordinary people embarked on an extraordinary
experience.

KENNETH L. HOLMES

Monmouth, Oregon, 1990

The Diaries Letters, and Commentaries

ELIZABETH LEE PORTER
Courtesy, Oregon Historical Society

ANDREW J. PORTER
Courtesy, Oregon Historical Society

Iowa to Oregon, 1864

§ Elizabeth Lee Porter

INTRODUCTION

I was engaged in conversation with a friend a few blocks from our home in Monmouth, Oregon, when he blurted out, "Do you see that little wooden house over there on Stadium Street? Well, Mrs. Hamar, the lady who lives there, has her grandmother's diary of her trip across the plains in 1864."

The natural thing to do was to follow up on that conversation, which I did, and so met the most delightful Mrs. Ivy Hamar who, sure enough, had such a diary. It is in the form of a typescript. Mrs. Hamar told us that the hand-written original had disappeared but that she felt that the typewritten copy was an accurate one. We have since seen a second copy made on a different typewriter by another descendant and feel that Mrs. Hamar was justified in assuring us of the accuracy of her copy. The same approach to spelling and punctuation characterized both of the copies.

Mrs. Hamar has since died, on August 30, 1982, at age 93. Since her death we have gotten to know several other descendants of the Porters and have found them very helpful in editing this diary.

The diary was kept by Mrs. Elizabeth Lee Porter as she and her husband, Andrew Jackson Porter, and their five children began their overland journey in Lacelle, Clarke County, Iowa, on April 16, 1864.

They reached Linn County, Oregon, near the city of Albany, on September 20th. Their destination was the claim of "Uncle" Hugh Lee, a relative on Elizabeth's side of the family. The Lees claimed descent from Richard Henry Lee of Virginia. Uncle Hugh Lee had arranged for the Porter family to move into a house belonging to Samuel and Walter McIlree, a short distance from the Lee claim. A year later the Porter family moved to a densely forested claim in the Coast Range of mountains, some twenty miles west of Corvallis, near the tiny cross road of Nortons. Today, on the Eddyville Road near Nortons is to be found a marker which reads as follows:

NEAR THIS POINT
WAS TAUGHT THE FIRST SCHOOL
IN LINCOLN COUNTY
A.D. 1866
ELIZABETH LEE PORTER — TEACHER

Some hundred feet distant from the above is the following burial marker:

ANDREW J. PORTER
1827 — 1881
ELIZABETH LEE HIS WIFE
1831 — 1898
AT REST

The descendants of the Porters have kept careful genealogical records of the family. The vital statistics of the parents and children at the time they crossed the plains in 1864 were as follows:

PARENTS: Andrew Jackson Porter, father, b. Oct. 26, 1827, Delaware County, Ohio; m. Nov. 8, 1853, Crawford County, Ohio; d. Benton County, Oregon, Jan. 14, 1881.

Elizabeth Lee Porter, b. Nov. 4, 1831, Harrison County, Ohio; d. July 20, 1898, Lincoln County, Oregon.

CHILDREN: James Taylor Porter, age 16 years, b. Ohio.

Mary Jane Porter, age 9 years, b. Michigan.

Ruth Florence, age 6, b. Illinois.

Elizabeth Ann, age 4, b. Illinois.

Lucinda Rosetta, age 2, b. Iowa.

There would be four more children, all born in Oregon.

The State of Ohio, Harrison County...

Elizabeth Lee Porter had been a school teacher since her Ohio days. Above is the hand-written teaching certificate, written in Cadiz, Ohio, Harrison County, on July 24, 1850. She was nineteen years old at the time of its issuance.

The 1870 Federal Census lists Andrew Jackson Porter as a "farmer." That would have had to be in the broadest of terms, for the land upon which the Porters settled was (and is) so densely forested that it would have been hard to imagine what land they farmed. Undoubtedly they were mainly stock raisers of cattle and sheep, utilizing mountain meadows and fire burns scattered through the growth of timber. In reality, the clue to the work of the father is to be found in the last two entries of Elizabeth's diary early in November of 1864:

"Wednesday — 2. Made first rails in Oregon. Made only eighty."
"Thursday — 3. Made rails for Hugh Lee."

Andrew Porter was a rail splitter. The land upon which the family settled was forested heavily with Douglas fir, but more important, the Coast Range contains heavy stands of cedar, from which fence posts and rails were made. Cedar does not rot easily in a moist environment as do other woods. The formal name in the Pacific Northwest is "Western Redcedar." The rail splitter was as common as the blacksmith and the harness maker in pre-automobile town life. The descendants of the Porters agree that the men were loggers, working "in the woods" as was said then. Near the marker for Elizabeth's first school in Lincoln County is a giant cedar tree of robust proportions. Their land was richly dotted with such trees. The family also has a tradition that Andrew Jackson Porter was a surveyor.

ELIZABETH LEE PORTER'S DIARY: CROSSING THE PLAINS, 1864

Tuesday April 26, 1864. Started for Oregon.[1] Came as far as Mr. Morrow's, staid all night, had a good visit, started next morning about eight o'clock.

Wednesday—27. Came to the old Boham Station, very cold, some rain, rheumatism pains very bad in left knee, sore toe, Turk tramped it this morning.

Thursday—28. Only traveled 15 miles, camped west of Afton [Union Co., Iowa], very hilly road all day, nothing happened worth nameing.

Friday—29. Bad traveling, rained last night, traveled 15 miles, cold and disagreeable.

Saturday—30. Came to Nodaway [Page Co., Iowa], camped over Sunday.

Sunday—May 1, 1864. The pleasantest day of the season, quite warm. High wind in the evening.

Monday—2. Quite a wind storm and cold. Came about

---

[1]The starting point of their journey was Lacelle, Clarke Co., Iowa.

eight miles and camped on the Middle Nodaway. Saw the city of Quincy [Adams Co., Iowa].

Tuesday—3. Ice this morning the thickness of a knife blade. Came about 10 miles and camped on West Nodaway, cold wind, evening pleasant.

Wednesday—4. Windy. On our way today, Camped on the Nishimattamy [Nishnabotna] for tonight, pretty stream, expect to lay over tomorrow and buy flour.

Thursday—5. Washed and churned, had a fine shower of rain, still continues to rain.

Friday—6. At the same place, Cloudy and lowrie all day but warm, Grass is growing fine. I hope there will soon be plenty. This is a pretty place to camp.

Saturday—7. Quite a hard rain last night, lowrie to day, Just fixing to start to next camp ground. Wrote to Mr. Morrow, churned and sold 1½ lb. of butter for 35¢. Traveled eight miles, still raining.

Sunday—8. Laying still to-day, had quite a scrape, old Gentle[2] got mired and took two yoke of cattle and ten men to get her out. More pleasant, rained this morning.

Monday—9. Traveled about 16 miles, camped on West Nishimabottamy, good camping ground.

Tuesday—10. Dreadful storm last night, blowed hard. Traveled about three miles, very cold, good camp ground on Silver Creek, 10 miles east of Glenwood [Mills Co., Iowa].

Wednesday—11. Camped for the night on the bottom, five miles from Plattinworth [Plattsmouth, Nebraska]. Bought 400 weight of flour a $2.65, coffee 55 cents, candles 30 cents.

Thursday—12. Got to Missouri River, had to wait about five hours to cross. Got across, came about 2 miles and camped for the night. Splendid springs.

---

[2]This was their milk cow.

Friday—13. Traveled 10 miles, quite warm, camped by a good well of water.

Saturday—14. All prairie today, drove some distance off the road to camp. got a good place, plenty of good water, grass pretty short, expect to travel some tomorrow. Killed a coon this evening.

Sunday—15. Came to Salt Creek [Nebraska] and camped, quite pleasant, beautiful crossing Stone Bottom.

Monday—16. Staying at Salt Creek today, very fine weather. Baked and churned.

Tuesday—17. Traveled 10 miles, uncommonly warm and dusty. Cattle very tired.

Wednesday—18. Traveled 14 miles, quite warm, camped at ranch, folkes planting corn. Quite dusty.

Thursday—19. Came about 19 miles, still warm but good breeze. Tomorrow will reach the Platte.

Friday—20. Got to the Platte bottom and came three miles, camped by a good spring and ranch.

Saturday—21. Camped again. See the first Indians today, of the Pawnee tribe. Weather very fine. Washed and cleaned up on the bank of the Platte. Very tired.

Sunday—22. Laying still today. First rate grass, good cedar wood by crossing the river. Passed the day looking around. Some indians about, of the Pawnee tribe.

Monday—23. Started this morning again. Had a stampeed this morning and a run off, cool day for traveling. Came about 24 miles.

Tuesday—24. Traveled about 18 miles and camped on the Platte bluff. Good grass, no water.

Wednesday—25. Traveled about 21 miles. Camped on bank of Platte. Lots of good water and best of grass. Wood by going across on the island. Cattle doing first rate.

Thursday—26. Traveled about 20 miles. Considerable talk about Indians. Thirty miles to Kearney.

Friday—27. Pleasant. Big tales of Indians ahead but it is getting further away all the time.

Saturday—28. Stopped at noon in sight of Kearney, washed some, pleasant and cool in evening. Fort Kearney is a pleasant little place. 100 soldiers here.

Sunday—29. Just ready to start. Quite a train came through Fort Kearney. Came a few miles and camped.

Monday—30. Fine day, rather dusty, storm of wind in the evening, camped on the banks of river. River very high.

Tuesday—31. Crossed Plum Creek this morning, little toll bridge there about three feet wide. Served medicine, took it in whiskey.

Wednesday, June 1. Another wind storm last night. 26 teams camped together last night. Had to stand guard. Cool this morning.

Thursday—2. Camped over today. One woman in our train had twin babies last night. Cloudy and some rain.

Friday—3. On our way today. Some cloudy. See the first Sioux Indians today. See two jack-rabbits. Traveled about 22 miles. Camped on the bluff.

Saturday—4. Some of our cattle strayed this morning. Three miles to Cottonwood[3] Quite a little place. 200 soldiers here to rob the immigrants.

Sunday—5. Quite pleasant. See a boat on the Platte this morning. Going to travel some today. Camped by the bluff, cool this evening. 16 wagons here this evening, more in sight.

---

[3]The formal name of this locale was Fort McPherson, which was established in the 1860's to protect the Platte River route. The more popular name was Fort Cottonwood. It is in Lincoln Co., Nebraska. Aubrey L. Haines, *Historic Sites Along the Oregon Trail* (Gerald, Missouri, 1981), p. 70.

Monday—6. Crossed Gatens [O'Fallon's?] bluff, lots of Indian huts. Indians in camp begging. Plenty of water, not much grass. Quite sandy.

Tuesday—7. Started before breakfast, came a piece and stopped for breakfast, cool, have to have a shawl on to cook. Drove 24 miles.

Wednesday—8. Quite warm, camped at noon at Lone Tree Ranch.⁴ Ford here. Seen no timber since Sabbath morning. Looks like a storm coming. Raining.

Thursday—9. Hot now, cloudy, looks like rain. Some of the cattle gone again this morning. Finished my stockings. Camped at ford. bad crossing. Lots of folks crossing.

Friday—10. Going on to some other place to cross. Some rain in evening. Some teams try to cross but had to back out, came very near drowning horses.

Saturday—11. Pleasant. Most ready to start. Will get to Jewelsburg [Julesburg, Colorado] today if no bad luck. Met Mormons. Cold enough in evening to snow. No water or wood.

Sunday—12. At Jewelsburg. Rained this morning, blowing very hard. Going to try to cross the river. High wind. Seen Mr. Carroll. Rain in the night.

Monday—13. At Jewelsburg. River still raising. Prospects of having to move to get out of the water. Raised some five or six inches this morning and still raising. Had to leave.

Thursday—14. Same place. Rain storm last night. Pleasant today, waiting for river to fall. Washing etc.

⁴Frank Root describes this stopping place with apt words: "This station was on Nine-mile ridge, 208 miles west of Atchison, in southern Nebraska, between Liberty Farm and Thirty-two-mile Creek. On a lofty elevation, perhaps forty rods distant to the north of the road, there stood a solitary tree. It was a medium-sized tree and it could be seen quite a long distance from nearly every quarter. To parties engaged in freighting across the plains in the early '60's it was a prominent landmark." Frank A. Root and William E. Connelley, *The Overland Stage to California* (Glorieta, N.M.., 1970), p. 202.

Wednesday—15. Still waiting. River on the fall, warm and cloudy. Cattle all going fine, give lots of milk. Tried to cross the river with cattle and failed.

Thursday—16. Still staying here. River still falling. Immigrants coming thick and fast. Boats running all the time.

Friday—17. Jewelsburg. Not much prospect of crossing yet. Should not suspect much if we stay a week yet. Wind.

Saturday—18. Same place. Very hot. Perhaps cross some today. Seen a wind-fall in Platte this evening, a great curiosity.[5]

Sunday—19. Jewelsburg. Crossed part of our wagons today. Very hot. Have stayed here nine days now and expect to stay 2 or 3 more.

Monday—20. Jewelsburg. Crossing as fast as we can. Cattle all on the other side. Got them all across safe but 8 or 10 head.

Tuesday—21. Jewelsburg. Still crossing. Got so windy in afternoon had to quit. Gentle and Pink on the other side yet, river raising. Very hot and windy. Sage roots for wood.

Wednesday—22. Opposite Jewelsburg. Noon. All over safe and ready to start. Crossed Pole Creek[6] and came 7 or 8 miles and camped by a spring on the left of road. Good grass.

Thursday—23. Took census. Half past six, ready to start. Traveled about 26 miles over splendid road. Nice grass and cactus. Flowers in abundance. Warm but fine breeze.

Friday—24. Laid by until noon and traveled about 10 miles. Crossed Pole Creek again and seen timber at a distance. Started across bluffs. No water.

Saturday—25. Sage roots for wood. Noon stopped at the

---

[5] Could she mean "whirlwind"?

[6] Lodgepole Creek, Nebraska.

first ranch house this side of the river at Mud Springs.[7] Very
hot and dusty. Came on to Pumpkin Creek,[8] 20 miles.
Plenty of water above the ford.

Sunday—26. Went on to Court House and Jail Rock.
Traveled on to Chimney Rock. Hot and dusty. On the
Platte again. The bluffs are great curiosity. A great many
people go to see them and carve their names there

Monday—27. Chimney Rock. Camp here. Passed another
ranch. In sight of Scotts Bluffs. Traveled about 20 miles. A
good rain in the evening. Pretty dusty today.

Tuesday—28. Traveled 8 or 10 miles to Scotts Bluffs. The
road between the bluffs just wide enough for a wagon. 400 or
500 feet high. Rocks on each side.

Wednesday—29. Warm, sandy and awful dusty. Came to
Cold Springs[9] and camped for the night. Indians here came
to camp to beg for bread and trade beads for bread.

Thursday—30. Seen about a dozen Indian families moving.
Cool in the morning, hot at noon. Lots of Indians on the
road. Plenty at camp tonight.

Friday—July 1, 1864. Fort Laramie. Wind storm last night.
Came on and crossed river on bridge for three dollars at Fort
Laramie. Cold this morning.

Saturday—2.   8 miles above the fort. Very cold this morning.
Laying still today. Women washing, men setting wagon-tire.
Any amount of immigrants passing by. Currants for supper.

---

[7]This was a stage station near Chimney Rock. Root, *op. cit.*, p. 127.

[8]Pumpkin Creek drains the vicinity of Courthosue Rock. Haines, *op. cit.*, p. 93.
Merrill J. Mattes writes of it vividly: "This is a stream which impresses observant
travelers today as it did a century ago for its pastoral charm and limpid clarity. But like
the Courthouse it is plagued by a variety of names which continue to haunt modern
writers and map-makers. For purposes of convenience, and to preserve the reader's
sanity, it will be referred to here as Pumpkin Creek, since that name (or its variants
'Punkin' or 'Pumpkinseed') had been used for over 100 years." *Platte River Road*
(Lincoln, 1969), p. 341.

[9] According to Root there were two stage stations named "Cold Springs."

Sunday—3. Crossing Black Hills. Road rough. Train about 2 miles long. Now. I expect there is 100 teams stopped here. A little water and no grass. Came across some of the worst roads.

Monday—4. Mr. Parker very sick this morning. Came about 10 miles, stopped for noon on the bank of Horse Shoe Creek. The American flag floats to the breeze. Hot, resting again. Gooseberries here.

Tuesday—5. Very hot this morning. Came 10 or 12 miles across bluffs to Elk Horn and camped. Poor grass, plenty of water and all is well. Sewing some today.

Wednesday—6. Cool wind this morning. Just starting. Cold wind all day. We camped on the Laboute River [LaBonte]. Came down hill all afternoon. Lots of folks camped here now.

Thursday—7. Laboute River. Laid by on account of the sick man being worse. Quite warm. 50 wagons camped here and they say 100 above at the other ford.

Friday—8. Noon; crossed the Red Hills today. Warm and dusty. Traveled 21 miles. Awful dusty in afternoon, grass short. A good spring in bed of a dry creek.

Saturday—9. Cool this morning. Crossed Elder Creek and two other nice streams. Crossed Deer Creek and came on 5 miles. Camped on North Platte.

Sunday—10. Pleasant today. Mr. Parker died this evening about 4 o'clock about 15 miles above Deer Creek on the North Platte River.

Monday—11. Cool this evening. Laying still on account of the death of Mr. Parker. Expect to travel this afternoon. Come 10 miles this afternoon.

Tuesday—12. Crossed North Platte today. Had to pay five dollars a team. Came over some awful roads this afternoon.

Wednesday—13. Left Platte this morning. Turk sick.[10] Lots of folks on the road today. Came to Willow Springs.

Thursday—14. Turk is dead. Died a few minutes ago (noon). He was poisoned. All grass in low places is poison here. Camped on a nice little creek, very little grass.

Friday—15. Fish Creek, 12 miles east of Sweet Water. Camped last night on a nice little stream, passed alkali lakes. Crossed Sweet Water at Independence Rock. Sold Gentle at noon today.

Saturday—16. On Sweet Water River. Camped handy to Devil Gate last night. Traveled about 10 miles. Lots of dead cattle here.

Sunday—17. Cool and windy. Quite sandy today. Cloudy looks like rain. Came about 10 or 12 miles through another gap in the mountains.

Monday—18. Stampeded last night to another camp ground. Warm this morning. Came through a big canyon and crossed the river three times.

Tuesday—19. Came about 4 miles and stopped. Bought six cows this morning for $45. A splendid shower this evening, laid the dust nicely.

Wednesday—20. Sweet Water River. Came about a mile and crossed the river again then came about 18 miles to the river again. Road splendid, raining now and prospects of plenty.

Thursday—21. Crossed Sweet Water early. Come perhaps 5 miles. Ready to cross again. A half an hour and cross again. Noon raining some, thunder. Camped on bank of Sweet Water.

Friday—22. Hilly and rough. Noon: Came to a nice little place at night on Willow Creek, pretty little stream. 5 miles east of South Pass.

---

[10]"Turk" was an ox.

Saturday—23. Came to Sweet Water, here is where the Landers cut-off is.[11] Came about 5 miles, good spring at left of road. In sight of snow on mountains for three days.

Sunday—24. Came across the main range of mountains and came to Sweet Water again and camped. Pretty warm.

Monday—25. Very warm. Crossed river for the last time. 1 mile, crossed willow Run. Noon: Cloudy. Evening on bank of Little Sandy. Very cool.

Tuesday—26. Rough roads. Noon on bank of Big Sandy. See snow yet. Here is where the immigrants and Indians had a fight 6 days ago. One man killed, three wounded and one little girl wounded.

Wednesday—27. Noon. came 8 miles. To left of road found water and grass. Road sandy. Camped here tonight. 12 miles to Green River. Crossed the desert today. 12 miles without water. Sand not very deep.

Thursday—28. Traveled until noon, crossed middle Green River. Very swift current, water over axel-tree. Washed, cleaned wagons etc.

Friday—29. Came about 10 miles and stopped for noon on the West branch of the Green River. Laying still as usual.

Saturday—30. Came over some rough roads. Crossed one creek and came on to one at base of mountain. These are what is called the Bear River chain of mountains.

Sunday—31. Waiting awhile on acount of very sick child. Don't think it will live long. Disease of whooping cough and teething. Come 10 or 11 miles, all the way between two big mountains. A creek runs here.

---

[11] Diary of Martha Missouri Moore, Volume VII above, p. 282, fn. 11. See also Volume VIII, above, fn. 4, p. 20. There is a good treatment of this cutoff in E. Douglas Branch, "Frederick West Lander, Road-Builder," *Mississippi Valley Hist. Rev.*, XVI (Sept., 1929), pp. 172-87.

Monday, August 1—1864. Lots of pine. Buried the child this morning. Ice half inch thick. Had to climb the mountains today. Some to come up and I guess it was some to come down. Came a piece up another canyon and camped. Creek here. Snow on top of the mountains.

Tuesday—2. Laying over today. Poor grass for stock. Another baby born last night. Stamper got his cow. Washed, baked and chored in general.

Wednesday—3. Noon: Got across another range of mountains. Came down canyon and now going up another. It is so narrow there is scarce room for creek and road. Evening: Came across two big ranges of mountains to Canyon Creek. Bad roads. Stamper's hind axel broke.

Thursday—4. 8 o'clock: Axel all right and ready to start. Traveled among the mountains until noon then came to pretty valley at night. Good grass and water. Good creek.

Friday—5. Drove near 15 miles down a beautiful valley, crossed one creek to another at the mouth of a canyon. This is Salt River. Laid over on account of a sick woman.

Saturday—6. Traveled up a canyon. Past Salt Springs. Gathered some. Traveled about 25 miles today. Good camp ground here. Plenty of grass. One ox gone. Very narrow canyon today.

Sunday, August 7. Captain gone back this morning. Laying still as usual. Come about 10 miles and camped by a lake. Beautiful valley, cold spring. Little rain.

Monday—8. Came about 16 miles to Black Foot Creek. Road pretty good but hot and dusty. More Indians here. Crossed and camped on bank of creek.

Tuesday—9. Bully sick. Came about 21 or 22 miles. Pretty roads only dusty. Back on old road again. Camped beside a big mountain. A little spring.

Wednesday—10. Bully better. An awful wind storm this morning, turned off more mild at noon. On a nice stream of water within 10 miles of Snake River.

Thursday—11. Came to Black Foot against noon. Road sandy. Just got across Snake River all safe. A very large stream but low now. Up over axel-trees.

Friday—12. Came down the Snake River a few miles and laid over in the afternoon. Good grass. Cattle doing fine. Boys fishing two miles above the ferry.

Saturday—13. Morning: Mrs. Stamper very sick. Going to go as far as the ferry. Come 14 miles and camped by big spring. Laying still this afternoon.

Sunday, August 14. Laying still all day. Mrs. Stamper had a baby this morning. She is very sick. Baby dead and buried. The rest of the train pulled out. We are opposite Fort Hall.

Monday—15. Laying still today. Mrs. Stamper better in afternoon. Just pulling up to start across the desert. Traveled until midnight over rough roads and lots of sage brush. Roads very bad. Rocks all the way.

Tuesday—16. Sun about an hour high and ready to start. Got some grass for cattle and hauled water for them. Got across desert to a little spring. No water for cattle yet. Got to go 12 miles yet to get water. Resting.

Wednesday—17. One day—Lost River. Got to water last night about 10 o'clock. Going to rest cattle and sick woman today. Noon: Started and axel-tree broke again. Dreadful rock road. Lots of trains passing.

Thursday—18. Morning: 8 o'clock. We will soon be ready to start. Came over 25 or perhaps 30 miles. Got to water about nine o'clock. A big spring at right of road. Very dusty.

Friday—19. Very warm. Not very well this morning. (Disentary) Resting awhile. Going to start pretty soon and go 9 or 10 miles to more water. Stopped at middle of rock. Plenty of good water and grass and wood.

Saturday—20. Came 15 miles today over the roughest road we have had, very rocky. Got along safe and camped on Rattlesnake Creek. Plenty of water and grass. Laying over this afternoon. Very dusty.

Sunday, August 21. Came about 10 or 12 miles to Willow Creek and camped. Very windy and awful dusty. Come nine miles more and camped on Little Wood River. Indians here. Bannocks.

Monday—22. Came about 6 miles and struck Big Wood River. Came about 13 miles and camped by a big spring. Good grass, wood and water in a pretty valley. The prettiest valley we have seen.

Tuesday—23. Come 8 miles to Big Wood River again, crossed, come 4 miles and stopped for noon at a spring there, hitched up and come about 12 miles farther and camped.

Wednesday—24. Stopped at noon in a pretty valley by a spring, plenty of grass, very windy, stopped for night at splendid spring. Good Grass.

Thursday—25. Camas Valley. Come about 12 miles till noon, across a splendid valley. Come about 9 miles. Seen lots of nice hay, only 10 cents a lb. Camped this evening by a spring branch.

Friday—26. Came about 10 miles, another spring run. Looks like rain. Hope it will. Came about 8 miles. Lots of people stopping here putting up hay. Gold and silver mines handy. Rolling.

Saturday—27. They say we have rough roads today. Come two miles and stopped on little Camas Prairie. Here we found Carroll's folks and we lay over. Gold mines here.

Sunday, August 28. Left Carrolls this morning, drove until

noon and stopped. Quite warm but a good breese. Camped by a spring. Plenty of good wood and water.

Monday—29. Traveled about 10 miles over the hilliest road we have had on the road worse than the mountains. A good rain. All well.

Tuesday—30. Still raining. Some milking cattle gone but found at last. Noon: A terrible hail storm and cloud burst. Our wagons washed under, Log chains gone. Shoe and tool box gone.

Wednesday—31. Drying our things out this morning. Had to dig our wagons out. Don't want to see the like again. Traveled about 9 miles. Ranches all along here. Vegetables for sale.

Thursday, September 1, 1864. Come about 20 miles today, no grass or water for cattle. Camped on Boise River about 3 miles above the city. No grass of any account here, looks like civilization.

Friday 2. Stopped at a ranch and bought some onions. Every kind of vegetables at 10 cents in gold or 20 cents in greenbacks. Crossed Boise River and came through the city.

Saturday—3. Morning: 12 head of cattle gone, found 5 head. Hunted all day for the rest but found no cattle. Beautiful valley here and lots of ranches. We are four miles below the city.

Sunday, September 4. No cattle yet. Men all out again. Found them about 10 o'clock but did not travel. Quite windy. lots of teams going along.

Monday—5. Laid over till noon then come about 8 miles to Dry Creek. Plenty of wood and water. Grass pretty scarce. A nice new house built here.

Tuesday—6. Climb to Piatte [Payette] River today. Came down a big hill. Road pretty good. Grass at the bluffs.

Wednesday—7. Came 20 miles down river to the ford and

camped. There are ranches all along from 1 to 3 miles apart.

Thursday—8. *Oregon*. Crossed the Piatte River and came about 7 or 8 miles to Snake River again and crossed in a flat boat for $2 a team. Came 1½ miles and camped.

Friday—9. Quite warm, noon: Come about 12 miles across a sage desert to Snake River again. Dusty and rough. Lots of packers. Come about 7 miles to river and crossed slide.

Saturday—10. Quite cool. Have to climb around side of mountain. 6 miles to Farewell Bend of Snake River. Come 5 miles more to Burnt River.

Sunday, September 11. Traveled along Burnt River about 20 miles. A tolerable rough road. High mountains on each side.

Monday—12. Still on Burnt River. One bad hill this morning. Got lots of black and red haws. Some valley. Camped near the Central House. Ride and Beauty are sick.

Tuesday—13. Left Burnt River this morning. Traveled about 15 miles over a good road. Only a little gravel. A cool wind all day. Mrs. Wilkins still has the ague.

Wednesday—14. Ice this morning. Big frost. Got to Powder River a little after noon then came 6 or 7 miles across the valley. See Blue Mountains.

Thursday—15. Andy Stamper very sick. Quite dusty today in the valley. The Blue Mountains run along the west side of Powder River. River all muddy by the miners digging at Orbeu.[12]

Friday—16. Andy still worse. Started, thinking we might find a doctor but only went about three miles till he died then came 3 miles to water and stopped.

---

[12]This was her rendition of "Ox Bow," a common term for a U-shaped bend in a river. This descriptive term was found in a number of places in Oregon. Lewis A. Mc Arthur, *Oregon Geographic Names* (Portland, Oregon, 1982), p. 567.

Saturday—17. We buried Andy this morning. Mulkins and Stampers went on and we staid here at the ranch. Porter is working on a new house for $2 per day.

Sunday, September 18. Laying still today. Lots of immigrants and packers going by. Feel kind of lonesome all day. Mr. Baker's team laying over here today.

Monday—19. Still here and working on the house. Cattle doing fine. Lots of immigrants going along.

Tuesday—20. Working at the house for J. Newman. More immigrants going along. Some in sight all of the time.

Wednesday—21. Still working here. Cattle doing fine. Cold and cloudy. Threatens rain.

Thursday—22. Quite cold and cloudy this morning, more moderate this afternoon. Dr. Whitson and Fingsbury and Parkers[13] drove in this morning.

Friday—23. Hitched up this morning and come about 14 miles and camped on the Grand Ronde Valley. This is a pretty looking valley.

Saturday—24. Passed through the city of La Grande. A very pretty place. Drive on to Grande Ronde River and camped. Cloudy, looks like rain.

Sunday, September 25. Rained last night. Camped by the Blue Mountains last night at a little place called Oradell [Orodell]. Crossed one range of mountains. Road wet and slippery. Only came seven miles today.

Monday, 26. Raining and some snow today. Considerable snow on top of mountains. Come about 16 miles across the summit. 15 miles yet to valley.

Tuesday—27. Big frost and lots of ice. Rose sick all night but better this morning. Came in sight of valley and camped for night. Beautiful road today.

---

[13]We have so far been unable to identify these travelers from their surnames alone.

Wednesday—28. Traveled about 16 miles in the Umatilla Valley, Indian Reservation here. Quite pleasant after we got off the mountain.

Thursday—29. Little rain last night. Crossed Birch Creek and came about 14 miles and camped by a ranch. Nobody home.

Friday—30. Cold. Traveled till noon. Stopped by a little spring. Came about 16 miles today to Butter Creek. Cold and windy.

Saturday, October 1, 1864. Quite cold this morning. Traveled about 20 miles over a heavy road to a splendid spring and a ranch house.

Sunday—2. Came some 15 miles today to a creek and a ranch. Quite pleasant today. Nothing important transpiring.

Monday—3. Pleasant this morning but cool. 65 miles to The Dalles. Came about 20 miles today and got to Rock Creek a little after dark. Cattle very tired and everybody willing to stop.

Tuesday—4. Came 11 miles to a spring over rough heavy roads. Very warm today. Crossed John Day River.

Wednesday—5. Came over a nice road to Mud Springs. A nice day. A ranch house here just put up. 30 miles to The Dalles.

Thursday—6. Deschutes River. Beautiful morning. Most ready to start. Uncle Hugh[14] met us here today on the Deschutes River. Awful hilly here.

Friday—7. Traveled a short distance. Very warm, dusty roads. Here is the Five Mile House[15] to The Dalles. No grass.

---

[14]Uncle Hugh Lee was a relative of the diarist, whose maiden name had been Elizabeth Lee. He and his family had settled in Linn County, Oregon, not far from Albany. *Historical Atlas Map of Marion & Linn Counties* (San Francisco, 1878), p. 72.

[15]"Fifteen Mile House."

Saturday—8. Came up to town. Baking and fixing to go down the river. Quite a city here. Have to pay $15.00 per wagon and $6.00 for persons over 12 years.

Sunday, October 9. Quite warm. Porter and Taylor gone with cattle down the trail. Uncle Hugh Lee staying with me.

Monday—10. Took boat at nine o'clock to Cascades. Then the cars for 6 miles,[16] then the boat for Portland. Got to landing between sunset and dark.

Tuesday—11. Pleasant. Waiting for cattle to come. A very nice town. Uncle is still with me.

Wednesday—12. Cloudy all day. Nothing of importance transpired, only it rained this evening.

Thursday—13. Pleasant. Evening—no men yet with cattle.

Friday—14. Very pleasant. Still no men. We waited, washed etc. Evening: no cattle yet.

Saturday—15. We are camped near State Prison. See them marched out to work every day and see them shake their blankets this evening.

Sunday, October 16. Cattle, men came in a little while ago (afternoon) safe tired and sore-footed. We hitched up and drove about 4 miles.

Monday—17. Traveled about 13 miles through a timbered country and crossed Willamette River in the evening. Camped at the Dutchmans.[17]

Tuesday—18. Traveled about 15 miles through a pretty country. Plenty of apples. Nice buildings along here. 12 miles to Salem.

---

[16]What she means here by taking "the cars for 6 miles" is that there was a short portage railroad around the Cascades of the Columbia River, at present Bonneville. Frank B. Gill, "Oregon's First Railway," *Oregon Historical Quarterly*, XXV, Sept. 1924, pp. 171-235.

[17]This would be the town of Aurora, which was founded by German settlers.

Wednesday—19. Noon: today fed own stock in the city. A good road. Uncle Hugh went on home this morning. Glad we are so near home.

Thursday—20. Came to Santiam River by noon. Crossed and came to within one mile of Albany.

Friday—21. Came through the city of Albany and got to Uncle Hugh's almost one o'clock and found them all well.

Friday—28. Went to Peoria and got some dishes. Quite a busy little place. It is on the Willamette River. Rained quite a shower.

Tuesday, November 1, 1864. Moved here to McCulley's today.[18] Took possession for one year.

Wednesday—2. Made first rails in Oregon. Made only eighty.

Thursday—3. Made rails for Hugh Lee.

---

[18]This name should be spelled "McIlree." Charles and Walter McIlree were neighbors of Hugh Lee. *Historical Atlas, op. cit.,* p. 72.

A Trip to the Idaho Mines, 1864

⸘ Clarissa Elvira Shipley

INTRODUCTION

The letter in my hand was dated November 29, 1981. It had been sent to me by Mrs. Fay Toal of Tracy, California. It reads as follows:

> Dear Professor Holmes. You were on Radio Station K.G.O. a few nights ago discussing your collection of diaries, letters, etc. of our pioneers. I am the proud possessor of a copy of my great grandmother's diary as they crossed the plains in 1864 to settle in Rocky Bar, Idaho...It is the diary of Mrs. Brice "Elvira" Shipley. I also have a story called "Days of Yore" of early days written by my two aunts — her granddaughters.

The upshot of this letter is that I phoned Mrs. Toal, and we have been telephone friends and partners since that time. She sent me photocopies of the diary, also a typescript with the heading "Reminiscence," written by the daughter of the diarist, Mrs. Arvilla Shipley Paul, and the "Days of Yore," the mimeographed family history written by Eva Paul Leigh and Grace Paul Hendricks.

We do not have the day and the month of Brice Shipley's birth, but the year was 1832, which means that at the time of the 1864 journey he was 32 years old. He and Clarissa Elvira Aldritch were married in Knoxville, Iowa, on December 3, 1857. She was born on July 20, 1840. There were two young daughters with them on the trip to Idaho: Agnes Arvilla, age 11, and Emma Etta, age 9.

The 1860s were golden years for mining in the American West, and the Shipley family was attracted westward to the Idaho country. They had heard that there were fabulous riches to be

mined in the Boise River area of southern Idaho, particularly in
Rocky Bar, some 30 miles east of Boise. They could have gone to
a dozen or so other gold regions (California, Colorado, Oregon,
Montana, northern Idaho, etc.) but they chose Rocky Bar. It
turned out that this locale was a short-lived source of precious
metals. They arrived there on Tuesday, July 5, 1864, midst rain
and snow. This would foretell a cold winter in that high country.
They stayed a few unrewarding years, and in 1869 moved to Boise
City. There the federal census taker recorded their presence on
July 20, 1870, telling of Brice's job: "Works on farm," with $550
worth of personal property. At the time of the next census, the
one in 1880, they were still in Boise City, and Brice was listed as a
farmer.

In 1874 the Shipleys filed on the rich bottom land along the
lower Boise River a mile away from the spot where the town of
Parma would be established. Brice ran a dairy, becoming as a
consequence one of the earliest alfalfa and clover growers in the
rich lower Boise Valley. They also planted orchards. On the side
Brice was able to add to their income by freighting. Elvira started
cooking in a newly established hotel and eventually managed a
hotel of her own. Brice died in Parma in 1895. Elvira lived on
until May 29, 1923. One historian of the city of Parma described
Elvira's impact on that community as follows: "For years
'Grandma Shipley' was practically a community institution."
(Helen Powell and Lucile Peterson, *Our First Hundred Years: A
Biography of Lower Boise Valley, 1814-1914*, Caldwell, Idaho,
1976).

THE DIARY

Knoxville, Iowa 1864

Thursday, April 7   Bade goodbye to Father and Mother,
sisters and friends, and started our weary way acrost the
plains. Camped for the night at Jerry's sawmill, of course did
not have much cooking to do for we had prepared a bountiful
supply before leaving home.

Grandmother Shipley and first hotel in Parma built in 1897
Courtesy, Lucille Peterson

Friday, 8th   Sprinkled a little, but nevertheless we are not daunted by that, and with our breakfast over we start on our journey. Had quite a pleasant day, and stop for the night.

Saturday, 9th   Nothing very exciting to happen — only travel along — stop for lunch at noon, and to rest our teams awhile. Then go on until evening and camp for the night in a nice place to camp.

Sunday, 10th   Traveled part of the day. Arvilla not very well today — has sore throat and some fever.

Monday, 11th   Arvilla no better this morning — traveled part of the day then camped, put a fire in the tent, got it all warmed up, then I gave her a hot soda bath, some fever drops, and other medicine that were in my Drug Store.

Tuesday, 12th   Well, this morning Arvilla is all broken out, and I think she has scarlet fever from her symptoms. Traveled until about 2 O'clock, then stopped for the rest of the day. Heated up the tent, and gave her another soda bath and put her in a warm bed.

Wednesday, 13th   Arvilla well broken out so we fix her warm in bed and drive until the middle of the afternoon. Stopped in a little town called Adel [Dallas Co.]. Called a doctor to see her. He said she had the spotted plague, and he could do nothing for her unless we would stay there a week or ten days. Turned and walked away. We got some more fever drops, and went on, and I continued my own treatment.

Thursday, 14th   Arvilla is some better this morning. I think it looks very much like rain, and so it did part of the day, but we were well prepared to keep dry.

Friday, 15th   After nights rest we are now ready to move on. Arvilla was considerably better this morning — so we traveled, and just our last mile we passed over some boggy ground and mired the wagon. Had it not been for the grit of our horses to pull, we could have been left in a mud hole hub-deep.

Saturday 16th   Our usual work through with we are on our march. No more in our crowd than we left home with, so we jog along, cook, and eat, and try to be merry.

Sunday, 17th   This is Easter. It has rained some, and we have traveled part of the day and are now camped for the remainder of the day and night.

Monday, 18th (10:00 Oclock)   Pulled into the outskirts of Council Bluffs — camped and will stay here the rest of the day and night. The menfolk will get our supply of provisions that we will need on our journey for ourselves and horses. Arvilla is up today, and will be all right in a few days with care. Here we saw our first Indians. They came to our camp while the men were gone. I found out they were friendly ones. That made no difference then, for to be on the safe side of them I had given them plenty of food to eat, and they left us unharmed.

Tuesday, 19th   Today we drive out of Council Bluffs — cross the Missouri River, and drive about 30 miles out to Elkhorn. There we are to camp for 3 or 4 days waiting to make up a train to go on to Denver, but it was such slow progress. So with 5 or 6 teams we pull out and go with some that were going farther west. Some men that were from Africa,[1] but *no* ladies in their outfit — all men. In all 7 teams and 19 people.

Wednesday, 20th   Arvilla has gotten over her sick spell, eats well, and seems to be all right now. So up the road we go not knowing where we will stop and no place in view.

Thursday, 21st   Up and off early in the morning — the country and roads all look alike, although it is pleasant.

Friday, 22nd   Still on the go. Well, I bundle up and lie down in the wagon on a bed I had fixed up in there so I would be comfortable. Do not see much of the country.

Saturday, 23rd   The same old view today, do not see much change only sandy roads.

Sunday, 24th   On and on we go — it rained some today, and of course the wind blew to top it off.

Monday, 25th   Pleasant day today, but we had to pull through considerable sand and are now camped for the night.

Tuesday, May 3rd   Now here comes a vacation of a week. I don't see how I missed this week, but it is gone and cannot think what all had happened, but I expect about the same travel all day and camp for the night — get up next morning, and jog along over the country.

---

[1]She evidently means African-Americans or Blacks.

Monday, May 10th [9th]   Morning, got breakfast, and went down to the water and did a big washing. Sunburnt my arms almost to a blister. Went up to the wagons about two o'clock, and the sand was blowing so that we could hardly see. Everything was full, so we hitched up and went to a cottonwood grove and stayed all night. It makes me think of home, we talk of it too, but it is a nice place to camp. We have plenty of wood, water, and grass.

May 17th   Tuesday morning — up early and breakfast over — off we go. Passed the fort,[2] and bought two bushels of corn for twelve dollars. In the afternoon we came to a good spring, the best water we have had. Camped early tonight. Plenty of pine and cedar wood to burn.

Wednesday, May 18th   Started very early this morning and the same thing. Off we go over the hills and up the mountains. It is very mountainous through here today, and rocks, there is no end to them. The wagon goes hop and jump over them, or we come to one that is about half a mile along and it is so rough that we walk up it. We travel this way all day, and camp for night on top of a high bluff. Pinewood to burn, and the wind blows. We are fixing our things for a hard storm.

Thursday, 19th   Up this morning and everything all right, not much of a storm after all. This morning two indians come along just as we got breakfast ready, so we have to feed them. The roads today are hilly, but good. We are traveling over what is called the Black Hills. Rained on us at noon — so we wait till it quits and then we start out. Night finds us on old Platte again, and a beautiful place to camp, but the water is as muddy looking as a mud hole. It is sand, and will settle some tonight.

Friday, May 20th   Up this morning, but not in much of a

---

[2] Fort Laramie.

hurry for it rained last night. The roads are not very muddy as they are so sandy. We travel over hills and hollows. There were six of the boys went on top of one hill, it was so steep and high that I was afraid they would fall, but if we had been stopped I expect that I would have been one of their number. We camped for noon at the foot of some big hills. Dinner over, and it looked as though we were going to have another storm. Rain and hail, so we hitched up and off we go for we have some hard pulling ahead to do, and if it rains the hills will be hard to climb. We did not go far through the storm till four o'clock we obey the captain and stop On the same old stream, the Platte. It was so muddy that it was almost like cream for coffee. Plenty of wood and grass, and as I have told you before plenty of water — such as it is. It stopped storming soon after we halted.

Saturday, May 21   Morning. We did not start very early for it was wet and bad. The sun shone out very bright this morning, but it soon began to cloud up, and about noon it commenced to rain and rained all afternoon. Through the rain we go again all the afternoon. The roads are getting very bad. Plenty of "reds"[3] in our camp tonight. Some of them dressed up — you had better think, with their strings of silver plate hanging halfway to their feet.

Sunday, May 22   Not a very early start for it rained hard again last night, but it is clear this morning. The sandy roads are very wet and heavy. The reds were in camp again this morning before I was up and stayed till after breakfast. At noon it commenced raining again, it has rained on us every day for ten days. It rained this evening very hard after we stopped and thundered and lightening, but it is clear and pleasant now. On the opposite side of the river right before us we can see plenty of snow on the mountains, and if it were

---

[3]Her term for Indians was "Reds."

not for the river we would have some of it. While I am
writing this Brice is out guarding the horses. He stands till
twelve o'clock. The children are both fast asleep, and all in
camp is abed, but me. There are some seven teams camped
above us tonight. They have been with us all day, and there
are three families with them.

Monday, May 23, 1864   Up early — breakfast and
everything done — so off we go through the sand, till ten
o'clock — then we stop. We are going to stay here and wait
for some more immigrants to come on so we can have a big
train to go through with. There are plenty of reds in camp
here. Still on the Platte — cross over today. I will be glad
when we leave it.

Tuesday, May 24, 1864   Breakfast over and my house all
set in order. Nothing very interesting happens. A great
many reds in camp, squaws begging bread for their papooses.
They would beg all we have if we would give it to them.

Wednesday, May 25   Morning, still camped on old Platte.
Did my ironing today that I washed a week ago, Monday.
Had some antelope and potatoes boiled together for dinner,
and had what is called mountain rabbit fried for supper.

Thursday, May 26   Morning. Breakfast over and about
nine o'clock we roll out. We go to where the others are
camped and try to organize a company to go the cutoff. But
we go the old road, for the farthest way round is the safest
way home.

Friday, May 27   Not up very early this morning, it is cool
and they all slept well. Everything all ready and we leave the
rest. Bid goodbye to Jim[4] for he is going to try the new road,
but much against his will. I thought it was hard to part with

---

4"Jim" was James Aldritch, Clarissa's brother. Another "James" accompanied them:
James Shipley, her husband's brother. She always distinguishes them as "Jim" and
"James."

friends at home, but it is nothing compared to parting with them out here. But at seven o'clock we gave a hearty welcome into our camp again, he had got Sam[5] to come on. Maybe you think we weren't a happy set of folks. The children jumped and ran to meet them.

May 28th   Saturday morning. Started moving early this morning. A nice warm pleasant day and roads good. Saw an antelope that some men ahead of us had killed. Camped for noon and I am now sitting on top of a solid rock about 7 feet high, and pretty steep. Now I go to my dinner, after the horses pick the grass while we roll out. Roads some muddy this afternoon. We cross Sweetwater river, payed $1.50 to cross it, drove five miles and camped within a mile of Devil's gate.

May 29th   Sunday morning. Up this morning and work all done up and the other ladies and myself start out to see the sights. The Devil's gate is where the river runs through the perpendicular rock four hundred feet high. I went in as far as I could for the water is about three quarters of a mile, and we had to walk about four miles to catch up with the wagons. We are now stopped on Sweetwater for dinner, took the horses across the river for grass. We are now ready to roll on. This afternoon three more teams that are going to West Bannock [Idaho], joined us. The mountains here are on solid rock. There are some on the opposite side of the river from where we are camped tonight. We have to travel on Sweetwater for 4 or 5 days yet. There is considerable alkali on it — so we have to watch our horses very closely. We saw five dead horses along the road this afternoon. Our wood is dry sage roots — we have used them for three days. Brice went out since supper and got a sack of buffalo chips to get our

---

[5]Samuel Gray was a neighbor of the Shipleys back in Knoxville, Iowa. He, too, was drawn to the west by the lure of gold.

breakfast with. He has to stand guard tonight again. We guard our horses day and night.

Monday, May 30   Up early and everything ready — off we go again. Just as we get ready to start there comes along a California train of eleven teams, and when they went to drive around our teams one of them tipped over and spilled everything and broke their wagon bows all to pieces. I thought that could do them, but they soon went around all of them. The roads have been sandy today all along the river, but when we were off the river they were good. At noon we stop for dinner, I went up on top of the mountain — about 200 feet. It rained this evening hard for a little while, thundered and lightening, and scared the horses. We are camped on the Sweetwater again tonight. Buffalo chips are our fuel.

Tuesday, May 31   Off early. Cool misty and rainy all day. Roads are some sandy. Passed a soldier fort about noon.[6] Saw more antelope today. Six of the men went after them, but as usual did not get one. Camped for the night on the side of a hill. Have good wood tonight, wild sage, it is very large and dry and makes a splendid fire. We have burned some as large as any tree.

Wednesday, June 1, 1864   Up early, but it was so cold we did not get an early start. You should have seen us hunting up our winter coats. It was raining, and the wind was blowing. It rained all forenoon, we are stopping for dinner, and it is snowing as hard as it can. I can look out of the wagon and see a snow bank. We are now camped for the night on Sweetwater again. It snowed about two hours, it had rained all the afternoon since it stopped snowing, and is raining now

---

[6]This was evidently the Three Crossings Military Station. In the 1860s there was a telegraph and stage station there, near the mouth of Sage Hen Creek. Aubrey L. Haines, *Historic Sites Along the Oregon Trail* (Gerald Missouri, 1981), p. 219.

at ten o'clock. We have dry willow for fuel tonight. We have had good roads today. Passed some rock and saw several names that were written there, but in '59. We thought it quite a curiosity to gather snow from a snow bank, but more of one when it began to snow. I have snow now at my side as I sit here.

Thursday, June 2   Up early this morning before it was light for we had no grass for the horses — so we started out before breakfast to hunt some. It is not raining this morning, but cold. Saw two antelopes, the men shot at them 2 or 3 times, but didn't hit. Passed lots of snow today. It is now about three o'clock, and we are stopped, grazing our horses. Now we hitch again and go about five miles and camp for the night. Met a train of Mormons and some soldiers. Saw three men that were from West Bannock. It rained and blew tonight and threatened us with a big storm.

June 3   Did not start very early this morning for the grass was thin, and we had to give the horses time to eat, for they were tied last night on acount of the storm. We have poor grass for them today noon. Rained while we were eating dinner and hailed on us this afternoon so we had to stop and turn the horses around for they would not face the storm. Crossed Little Sandy and camped about two miles this side of it.

June 4th — Saturday   We had good grass last night, so we were up early this morning, and off at six o'clock. We have had the best of roads for the last two or three days. Two horses could take our load on such roads as these. We have just eaten our dinner, and it is beginning to rain. Good grass for the horses today noon. Crossed Big Sandy this forenoon, camped for the night. It has rained all afternoon, and hailed again so we again had to turn around and back the storm. It is not raining now, but looks very much as though it would.

June 5, Sunday   Not up very early this morning for it is
raining. I have not been out of the wagon this morning yet
— it is so wet and bad. Brice got breakfast and fetched mine
and the children's to us. We had crackers and tea for our
wood does not burn very well, it is wet sage. Brice and
another man was on guard last night, and it was so dark they
had to stay out all night. They are fetching the horses in now
and we will soon be ready to roll to find a better place for
camping if we can. Crossed Green River about ten o'clock
today, paid six dollars a team to be ferried across. Camped on
Green River tonight. Plenty of wood and water and grass.
Rained and hailed again this afternoon, and we had to back
the storm again. It was the hardest hail storm we have been in
yet.

June 6, Monday   The guard shot off their revolvers and
woke the camp this morning early, so we started a little after
six o'clock. We have had bad roads yesterday and today. It is
some warmer today than it has been. We are now camped
with plenty of snow in front of us on a big bluff or mountain.
Everything is called mountains in this country. We are now
camped where the river and little streams run to the west. To
look at them it seems as though they were running the wrong
way.

June 7, Tuesday   Up early this morning and are all ready
to start. It is very pleasant and warm this morning. We
crossed a little stream yesterday and it was so straight down
into it that the front of the wagon had come down on the
tongue and split it. The men are fixing it now. We stopped
at nine o'clock at the beautiful stream of water and a good
spring. We all did some washing there, and left about three
o'clock. Went about five miles on some mountains. They
were covered with stone and plenty of snow, yet there is good
grass.

June 8th, Wednesday   Off early this morning. Roads very bad, over hills, mountains and across sloughs, some that were very bad until noon. We camped on a stream called Ham['s Fork]. Dinner over and we cross it, and strike for the mountains — the highest we have been on yet. It was covered with rock and you had better think it was rough. We called it the "Devil's Backbone." We were on snow today, and the way we made the snowballs fly was a funny thing. We have a beautiful place to camp tonight. Plenty of grass and wood and water from a good cold spring right out of the bank and snow all round it.

June 9th, Thursday   Camp stirs by daylight this morning so we get an early start. We came only about one and a half miles when down went one of the fore wheels to our wagon.[7] Every spoke broken out but one so we are trying now to fix it. We take the stick we have for a spreader and our neckyoke and Jim's and Mr. Smart's spreaders and make 8 spokes and make four more out of spruce and pine. It is ten o'clock we have our wagon fixed and are now ready to start over some big mountains this afternoon. The worst ones we have had to climb. Up and down, rock from top to bottom. No more bad luck to us. There were 4 men going through in a small wagon, and they broke down a wheel.

June 10th, Friday   Off early again this morning. Good roads and we get over them pretty fast. Stay on Bear River for noon, good grass here. We are camped for the night, camped early for we have some mountains to go over again, and they say it is 8 miles over them, and we could not make it this afternoon — so we stop and try it in the morning. We have paid three dollars and a half for ferrying today. It looks like a storm tonight.

---

[7]The making and repair of wheels is well discussed in Eric Sloan's classic book: *A Museum of American Tools* (N.Y., 1974) pp. 96-97 and *passim*.

June 11, Saturday   Another beautiful morning and we are off for the mountains. We had some speckled trout for breakfast. After we left the mountains we had good roads, and the mountain road was not bad as we have come over. We are now camped by a Mormon Town,[8] saw some sheep and chickens. Good roads this afternoon, passed another Mormon settlement, saw corn, peas, beans, onions, and sorgham growing. It is in Bear River Valley.

June 12   Another Sabbath morning dawns on us, it is cold, we look out upon the mountains and behold they are white with snow. It rained last night. The roads today have been middling good. Saw great many curiosities. Passed Soda Springs [Idaho]. We are camped by some of them. They boil up out of the ground all the while. Some of the men made bread out of it tonight. It looks very nice.

June 13, Monday   Monday morning finds us all up at an early hour for some of us want to go and see the wondrous sight, the Steamboat[9] Springs. Some went to see them last night. It boils all of the time and every little bit it puffs up like a steam boat. It used to puff up and out of the ground, but the Indians have thrown rocks in the hole and steamed it up. Just a few steps from this is a rock in the shape of a big kettle. It will hold two barrels of water. Etta says it looks like a tub.

June 14th, Tuesday   Morning finds us all well. Everything ready, breakfast over and all for an early start. All the country that we traveled over yesterday was a curiosity. Pools of soda water walled in with solid rock, and the rocks laying all piled in every shape, they have been blown up. We

---

[8]This could have been Montpelier or Bennington, both founded by Mormons in 1864. Lalia Boone, *Idaho Place Names* (Moscow, Idaho, 1988) pp. 26 and 259. This is a major new geographic history source that has just been published.

[9]This was a spouting spring in the bank of Bear River, part of the Soda Springs complex; now covered by Soda Point Reservoir. Boone, *op. cit.*, pp. 359-60.

are camped tonight not far from them. We have reds in camp with their ponies.

June 15th, Wednesday   Off early this morning, roads good all but some sand that makes the wagons run very heavy, but we took the wrong road and that made it worse. We crossed Snake River about 1 o'clock on a ferry. Paid six dollars for passage again. Drove 7 miles after we crossed the river then stopped and got supper and at six o'clock hitched up and drove 9 miles after night for we have thirty miles to drive before we can get water for our horses.

June 16th, Thursday   Off this morning by five o'clock to try our long day drive! Oh! but the roads are rocky. Bill and Pall[10] came pretty near going out, but we had our keg full of water. We stopped about 3 o'clock and gave them a gallon of water and a pint and a half of flour apiece. At 6 o'clock we stopped for awhile for we thought we had come to a spring, for one of our men had traveled the road before. We could not find it, so we hitched up again for we have ten miles to make it to water, if the horses can get there. Some of them I think will not get farther.

June 17th, Friday   Did not start very early this morning for our horses are all tired. We came about a mile and a half last night, and then we found a spring. The horses and mules were almost crazy, they number some 50. We do not think of going far today. Ten miles to Skunk Creek. It is a beautiful stream of water and we have a nice place to camp. I busy myself boiling some beans and dried apples and peaches. Also washed the children's bonnets and baked some bread as we can get an early start in the morning.

June 18th, Saturday   Off this morning by half past five o'clock for we have 20 miles to make today with out water again, and the roads are so very rough. Saw six or seven

---

[10] Horses.

prospectors and packers. They tell us we are within 150 miles of our stopping place, but one day we are 150 and the next 250. We make our calculations to get there by the 4th of July. We have had some of the roughest roads today that were ever traveled. Over rocks by the bushel, they look as though they were burnt. Everything has the appearance of a great volcano.

June 19th, Sunday   Another beautiful day has dawned on us here among the mountains. Another day without water for 20 miles, and another day of rough roads and climbing over the mountains. We have traveled at the foot of them for 2 days. It is a curiosity to see the rocks here, they are piled every way and shape, some on the top of others, in some places they are rolled up and look like plowed ground.

June 20th, Monday   6 o'clock finds us ready to go, so I start ahead of the teams to take a walk. We have some mountains to go over today, but not so bad. The roads are some better, but they are rough enough. Plenty of water today. We cross [Big] Wood River, it was in such shape that we had to go through six different streams before we were on the other side. We camped last night in Spring Valley, and tonight we are camped on a little stream.

June 21st, Tuesday   At the usual hour we are ready to leave camp. It is quite cool this morning, and has remained so all day. Looks some like rain. The roads continue to get better. We had one very bad hill to come down today. Crossed Wood River again, and it is as much of a curiosity as it was yesterday, for we had to cross it 8 times in succession. Camped tonight on the outskirts of Camas Prairie,[11] by a spring. Dry willow for fuel.

June 22nd, Wednesday   This is a pleasant morning and we

---

[11] Camas root was a major Indian food. There are numerous camas creeks and valleys. This is in Camas and Elmore counties in Idaho. Boone, *op. cit.*, p. 351.

are all in a stir and off. We travel till 8 o'clock when we cross Soldier Creek,[12] and where we find some campers that had not been with us and had gone on ahead. They had found pretty good prospects for gold, so we stopped with them. Six of our number started out, it is 12 miles over the mountains. Mr. Downing, Mr. Smart, Henry Warren, Jim, Harvey Jones, and Sam — leaving 6 with the wagon train. If it pays we will stay here.

June 23rd, Thursday Not up very early this morning. There was a heavy frost last night. We are close to snow for the mountains are not more than 12 miles. 6 more teams drove in and camped below us last night, they are going to stay a day or two among us. Brice found an old acquaintance. George's wife's brother, he left in Ohio in February. He is a miner and has been in California 7 years, and is on his way to Bannock or Boise Basin. I have done a big washing today. Our crowd numbers 12 men to we women. Mrs. Jamison, myself, no children except my two.

June 24th, Friday Morning finds us not up very early, for we are all on a rest and we want to improve the time. Ironed some today, and at 11 o'clock our boys came in and not much of a show, at least they did not find much. We did not stay any longer there, after dinner we drove out. Some 10 or 11 miles today and camped about a quarter of a mile from a little creek. We have plenty of dry willows wood, grass and water. Brice went fishing today, but didn't catch anything.

June 25th, Saturday We are all up early for we want to get an early start. Last night we sold three pounds of sugar for $1.75 in hard money to some prospectors. Saw 6 or 8 more packers again today. At noon the children went up on a big rock that was close by. We hitched up and drove till 4 o'clock

[12]Several localities in south Idaho are called Soldier Creek. This is probably the one in Camas County. Boone, *op. cit.*, pp. 62-63.

when we called a halt for there were more gold miners and silver miners through here and we are going to stay and see what can be done. We passed a ranch today, they were just hauling their blocks for a house, it was a lonely looking place to stay. It is for a stage station, the daily mail route is laid out through here. It commences to run some time soon.

June 26th, Sunday   Another Sabbath morning dawns on us here, with mountains on all sides of us. I have my work all done up so I pass the day reading in the Testament and the Hymn Book and Evangelist till an hour of sun down. In the cool of the evening, Mrs. Jameson and I take a walk up on top of one of the mountains, about a mile and a half in height. It has been very warm today. James and two of the other boys have gone over to the town of Rocky Bar.[13] They will not be back for 3 days. Two more teams drove into our camp today.

June 27th, Monday   Up early for one of the boys is going out prospecting. This has been another warm day and I have knitted some and read some to pass the time. I would like to find a place to stop and make a home. I am getting tired of traveling, although we have had a pleasant trip, indeed.

June 28th, Tuesday   Not up very early for we have nothing to do. The boys that went out yesterday came in about 11 o'clock today, and it is all of a hoax again. Nothing worth staying for   James comes in this evening just as we are eating supper. The two other boys stayed back in Rocky Bar. In the morning we start for that place. He says it is rough road, but we are used to that.

---

[13]Rocky Bar was their destination in the Idaho mining area. It was a typical rough and ready mining town. It was laid out in 1864 after gold was discovered there. It had a relatively short life span. Most of the gold was gone by the end of the decade of the 60s. There are two classic sources for the Idaho gold rush: William J. Trimble, *The Mining Advance into the Inland Empire*, reprint (New York, 1972), and Merle W. Wells, *Gold Camps & Silver Cities*, Idaho Bureau of Mines & Geology, Bulletin 22, (Moscow, Idaho, 1964).

June 29th, Wednesday   Out this morning by nine, so as to get ready to try our rough road. James leaves us and starts to Boise City with two packers that came in with him last night from Junction Basin.[14] He thinks he can get a hundred dollars a month from them. He will be back Sunday or Monday, if he goes on farther than the city.

June 30th, Thursday   We camped on Boise River last night, by the side of a ranch. We had hard road yesterday. While we were camped for dinner the reds caught a big salmon that weighed 20 pounds. We traded them some bread for enough for supper, and, Father, that was the best fish I ever ate. I wished for you to have some. I told them I would willingly do without myself if you could only have it for your supper. Another day of rough roads, but not so bad as yesterday. We crossed Boise River too, today, and just before we crossed it the last time our wagon broke down again. Every one of the spokes broke out of our hind wheels and let us down again.

July 1, 1864, Friday   Some of the boys went over to Rocky Bar and some went over to Happy Camp[15] today, but Brice and Jim went back after our wagon and things. Took Jim's wagon to fetch our things in and bring the wagon up on a pole. We will take it to town that way, and sell the old frame. We are camped on Boise River in the timber. The timber is principally all large pine trees. I have a good spring to get water from today.

July 2, Saturday   Brice and Jim and one of the other boys are going up to town today to see the big rocks that are in the streets, and see what they can do. Sam is not very well, so he

---

[14]This was so-named because it was at the junction of the Bannock Road from the east and the Mormon Road from Salt Lake City, Boone, *op. cit.*, p. 203.

[15]This was so-named for the joy in the hearts of miners who took part in the first gold rush in the area in 1864. Boone, *op. cit.*, p. 170.

stayed in camp with me. I baked bread, boiled some beans, and cooked some dryed apples and peaches, so as to have supper by the time they got back.

July 3, Sunday   This is another beautiful morning that has dawned on us, and I have my house all in order. I pass the time off reading and writing letters to dear ones at home and wishing I had a letter from them to read. Where we are now we are surrounded by mountains.

July 4th, Monday, 1864   This is the 4th of July the day of our Independence, and I have spent the day in getting our things into packs so we can go up to town tomorrow, and talk about where we spent the 4th last year. Billy and Dock, two of our horses, have the mountain fever. Dock is past danger, but I do not know whether Billy will get well or not.

July 5th, Tuesday   We are up early so we can get an early start, it rained yesterday and this morning. It is cloudy now. We hired a packer and his ponies to pack our things through for us. I got one of his ponies to ride. Brice rode Billy and took the children one behind and one before. I got on the cayuse pony and off we go for a ten mile ride over the mountains along the pack trail. It began to rain about the time we were half way, and rained and snowed the rest of the day.

July 6th, Wednesday   Spent the day drying the things that got wet yesterday.

Seven Months on
the Oregon Trail, 1864

∮ Mary Louisa Black

EDITOR'S PREFACE

> From my research and interviews with people who remembered
> her, I think she was a very strong, determined woman. It was her
> idea to emigrate to Oregon as it was her people who had come
> earlier, and were already settled here.

These words appeared in a letter written from Jacksonville,
Oregon, to the editor of this set of books. The writer was
Marguerite W. Black, whose husband, John M. Black, is the
grandson of Mary Louisa Black, the writer of the following diary.

Mrs. Black had heard about this publishing project as a listener
to the all-night talk show on Radio Station KGO, San Francisco.
Her letter was written on January 19, 1980. I telephoned her
immediately after receiving an initial letter from her. She told me
that she was a kind of family historian, how the family papers were
destroyed in a fire in the home of one of the daughters in the
1930s, but that the diary and family Bible had been loaned to her
and thus were saved.

I have asked Mrs. Black to write an introduction and epilogue
for the diary for publication, telling of the family relationships as
revealed in the diary.

INTRODUCTION BY MARGUERITE W. BLACK

The writer of the following diary of the day to day life in a
wagon bound for Oregon in 1865 was Mary Louisa (McRoberts)

Black. She wrote in a 3½ by 5¾ inch leather covered note book in which she had been keeping household notes and farm accounts for several years. She was the wife of John Maupin Black, and they lived on a farm near Mexico, Audrain County, Missouri, at the time they decided to emigrate to Oregon.

A brief background of her life reveals that she was the eldest of eight children born to John McRoberts and Sarah Stevenson (Caldwell) McRoberts. She was born on a farm in Champaign County, Ohio, July 15, 1835. Some time between 1850 and 1854 the McRoberts family moved to Audrain County, Missouri, where the last of the eight children was born. As the eldest in such a large family, Mary Louisa learned responsibility early in life. She had a good common school education, and was skilled in all the household tasks common to rural pioneer life. She helped with the farm animals and poultry. She also was familiar with the use of a few basic drugs and home remedies for the common illnesses of the time.

Her husband, John Maupin Black, was the sixth of the ten children of Isaac and Sarah Maupin Black, born December 5, 1830, in Callaway County, Missouri. His parents were born in Kentucky in the 1820s, bringing with them several slaves, as was common in the South. John Maupin grew up on his parents' farm, and it may be assumed that the Black family and the McRoberts family were well acquainted, for they all lived in Audrain County in the 1850s.

It is recorded in the family Bible that Mary Louisa McRoberts and John Maupin Black were married on June 16, 1856, in the town of Mexico, Missouri, by the Rev. N.L. Fish. John Black was twenty-six years old, and his bride was twenty-two. They made their first home on his father's farm. It appears that they lived there nine years, and during this time four children were born to them. The first, a daughter was stillborn in 1857. The second, another daughter, Sally, was born in 1859. A third daughter, named Myrtilla, was born in 1861, and a son, Isaac Clifton, was born January 21, 1865.

John's father, Isaac, died in September 1864. His will mentions his wife, Sarah, and provides for her care. The rest of his estate was divided among his five living daughters and three sons. John received "the land upon which he resides, and a negro girl named Jane." A change in their lives was about to take place.

Stories about the wonderful land of Oregon were widely circulated in the midwestern states during these years. Many families sold out and joined the migration to the west. Among these were relatives of Mary Louisa Black. Mary (Caldwell) Hanna, and her husband, Josiah, with their adult children, Joseph and Jemima, had made the journey to Oregon in 1862, settling in the Upper Rogue River area in Jackson County.

Josiah Hannah had been trained in the potter's craft in a pottery owned by his wife's people, Robert and Thomas Caldwell, near Fulton, Missouri. He carried his potter's wheel with him to Jackson County, Oregon, and set about establishing a pottery. Suitable clay was found in the area, a kiln was built, and the Hannas were soon making jugs, crocks and other items for the pioneer housewives.

Mary Hannah wrote to her niece, Mary Louisa Black, about the possibilities of land being available adjoining theirs and offered help in getting settled if the Blacks would make the journey to Oregon. This was evidently an encouragement to John and Mary Louisa Black, so they began making preparations for the overland journey in the spring of 1865. The farm was sold and everything not needed on the journey was also sold or given away. The slaves were given their freedom.

Among the supplies that Mary Louisa carried with her was a collection of drugs from a list given to her by their family doctor, complete with instructions for their use. In the diary she frequently mentions taking these drugs for various illnesses experienced by members of the overland party. This list is here published at the end of the epilogue.

They started out with two wagons and two teams of work horses, several extra horses and some cattle. The second wagon was driven by a man called "Wat." When he left them at the California cutoff, Mary Louisa drove it the rest of the way. The baby, Clifton, was a little over five months old. Myrtilla nicknamed "Tilla") was three, and Sally was five years old.

The Blacks were to join a wagon train being organized by James T. Kirk and his brother, of Kirksville, Missouri. With James Kirk were his wife, Virginia, and their four year-old son, Crockett. The train was to leave Council Bluffs about the first of May. To reach this place the Blacks drove north on what is now "State Route 15," through the towns of Paris and Shelbina. On the way they met with an unexpected and tragic delay. Somewhere between Paris and Shelbina near the end of April they were camped near a train of freight wagons, which had a chuck wagon and a camp cook. After a visit to this camp little Sally was stricken with food poisoning and died within hours. It was believed that she mistakenly ate some spoiled food. The only written word of this tragic accident is the following listing in the family Bible: "Sally Black, daughter of J.M. and M.L. Black, died May 1, 1865, age 5 yrs, 8 mo, and 24 days." Despite this terrible blow, there was no turning back.

The diary begins with the listing of the town of Shelbina on May 5; St. Joseph on May 8; and Council Bluffs on May 11. The next day, May 12, the Kirk train, made up of 109 wagons, pulled out for Oregon. The train was organized into "wings," each traveling some miles from the others. These wings took turns leading the way. Mary Louisa mentions this arrangement several times in her diary.

When the Kirk train arrived in the Willamette Valley in early October, they scattered in all directions. The Kirk family settled near Junction City, north of Eugene. Others went east, around Heppner, and some settled on the coast. Little is known of some of the families who traveled so close to the Blacks and are mentioned in the diary so often. As far as we know, the Blacks were the only ones headed south to Jackson County.

The long months of constant travel, the sickness and other troubles finally brought them to a halt at a place Mary Louisa calls "Mr. Knight's." Efforts to find out where this was have not been successful. Some time between September 29 and October 22 they stopped there to rest and recuperate.

A message was sent with some south bound travelers to Josiah Hannah as to their location. The Hannahs set out with team and wagon and a load of supplies to rescue them.

As Mary Louisa notes in the diary, they arrived at Hannahs on November 17, 1865, after "seven months on the Oregon Trail."

On the inside cover of the diary note book is the following Bible verse:

PSALM CXXVI

5.   They that sow in tears shall reap in joy.
6.   He that goeth forth and weepeth, bearing precious seed, shall doubtless come again with rejoicing, bring his sheaves with him.

THE DIARY

Shelbina [Missouri]   May   5
St. Joseph   May   6
Council Bluffs   May   11
Plattsmouth   May   12
Salt Creek   May   20
Ft. Kearney   May   30

June 2   Plum Creek

June 5th   Cottonwood   Rain

June   Passed Through Julesburg

June 16   Left right wing   Rain

June 18   no grass near the road   Cold

June 19   Mountains in sight. Come to scatering timber. We will camp near plenty of wood tonight & rest tomorrow (Not much)

June 20   We camped last night near a spring but not much grass. We traveled about 8 mile before breakfast. came to grass &water and some wood by carrying some distance.

June 21   Crossed the Platt by fording at Fremonts Orchard.[1]

---

[1]Fremont's Orchard was a stopping place for the overland stage in Colorado. Frank A. Root and W.E. Connelly, *The Overland Stage to California* (Glorietta, N.M., 1970) pp. 102, 224.

June 22   Traveled most of the time today through grass knee high.

June 23   Last night the cattle were stamping from 10 Oclock till day. We encamped togather. [In margin:] Saw some wigwams   Kirk corelled to fight

June 24   We passed the Ferry this morning. they were crossing 2 wagons at a time & charging $7 for a four horse team & besides having to work the roaps themselves. Numbers were going above the ford. nooned on the Chackle pod.[2] in a nice shady place near a ranch. the cattle mowed their grass for them   John browned coffee [In margin:] Corelled separate. No stampeed. plenty of prarie dogs along the road

June 25   Sunday morn. we camped last night near the Cashlapoo. about ½ mile from the main company. I hear some talk of staying here till noon, & have preeching. The grass is short. They said yesterday, where we stoped to noon, that there was a ranch about every 4 mile. Most of them deserted. We have plenty of wood so far, on this stream Willow & cotton wood. The ranches occupy the best grass. I hear the order to gear up. One weeks time has made quite a difference in the looks of the mountains. we can desern timber on the black hills.

June 26   The Arapahoos, about 20 came into camp yesterday evening. Exhibiting all the characteristicks of natives, excepting they had long hair filled with ornaments. That is 3 of the number. I suposed 2 to be chiefs & one of their squaws—

Nooned 26 at the foot of the black hills. We passed kirks train stoped to rest & water. They have passed us about half and halted. They are passing on I think from their whooping

---

[2]She spells *Cache la Poudre* three different ways, all wrong, on two pages. Merrill J. Mattes tells us that next to "Robudoux" this French name was mis-spelled more often than any other. The English translation would be "Powder Cache." J. Frank Dawson, *Place Names in Colorado* (Denver, Co., 1954), p. 12; Merrill J. Mattes, *Platte River Road Narratives* (Urbana, Ill., 1988), p. 595.

they are crossing Cashly poo, which seams to merge from the Black hills to the left. Evning camp. we travailed up the canyann till camping time. Passed a saw mill and several nice cabins. I saw 3 hens quietly picking in front of one of the cabins, first I have seen since we left Salt creek. The Canyan is about ¼ of a mile wide. The grass is grazed almost too close. I climed one of the second rate hills, & had a fine view of the camp and the valey we are going up, but could see nothing of Kirks encampment.

27   Morning—I rested well last night. They are in a rush to get started. no alarms during the night. We nooned near the top of the hills. Some of the teams belonging to coopers Train stampeed, runing against the hindmost wagon of our train, smashing one wheel. They took back a wheel, and brought up the wagon & divided the load. we came up some very steep long rocky hills. Day fell on a large rock three times.

28   About 10 o'clock A.M. Every one is busy. John is having his horses shod, while a great many are helping to repair the broken wagon. I was quite sick this morning with diareah. I took a full dose of Laudanum this morning, and some quinine about 8   I feel some better. I have just finished cutting out a pair of drawrs for myself. The women have finished their washing. we camped near the junction of the two mountain roads. Dodson lies about 2 mile ahead   when we camped we passed the place Kirk camped about 11 A.M. The left wing leads this afternoon. A horseman came forward just now to halt the train. Another stampee. some of the mule teamsters would not lock coming down a long hill. they ran by some ox teams, causing them to stampee. thats the first report. Wat mounted the black mule and has accompanied the man to the rear. a cold mountain wind is facing us   The stampee commenced before they came to the hill. & they ran

down running against the hind wheel of a hack occupying a place near the front of the right wing. It was accasioned by a matrass falling from the hind hounds of a wagon. it was an abandoned one laying by the road side, and the man picked it up.

29th   We camped in the mountains again. I am still sick this morning, had a rundown just at daylight, some mint, resembling Peppermint & tasted like penoroyl.[3] John gathered the first evening we encamped in the mountains, was a great relief to my stomach. The hills on this side are grey colored rocks, with pines scatered over them. The stage passed this mo   Nooned on the road side. made a fire under a large pine to boil some tea. soon after we halted a soldier came riding up for the Dr of our train to go back to the next station, to take an arrow out of a mans back. he lives at the station & has been hunting for them for a number of years. it was done rite in the rear of our train, by some Arappahoos, who shook hands with him, pretending friendly, and when he turned to leave they shot him, the arrow passed through his lung, the Dr says, the same that visited our camp Sunday eve are the authors of the mishcief. As near as we can learn. The hunter new them.

30 June.   Noon. we have travailed over a tolerable level road to-day. Stoped about 10 Oclock on accont of finding good grass & water. Silas Davis lost an ox last night, he has never been well since we crossed the Platt, Evening encampment. We have just crossed the Laramese river on a bridge, for 50 cts a wagon. not much grass in sight. The musquetoes are so bad on the stock. our horses took the river just below the camp. The young sorrel could not swim, but they all got acros and clambered up an almost perpendicular

---

[3]Pennyroyal is a plant of the mint family, also the oily juice of that plant.

bank on the other side   Mr Kellys mule tied head & foot
attempted to follow, and was drowned.

1 July   I was very sick all day at the stomach. Took a dose
of Calomel & laudanum at noon. John is sick too—

2 July. I feel nearly clear of sick stomach this morning & my
bowels are more quiet than they have been. I ate some
brownd rice boiled for my supper & rested tolerable well
during the night. I have used Paregoric & Tannin freely &
some spirit to strengthen my stomach. Calomel was the first
thing that settled my stomach. We have been travailing over
the roughest rockeyest road I ever saw   We nooned near a
ranch. which had beem vammoosed this morning for we met
them. They reported 100 Indians seen in this vicinity & that
they had kill 2 Emigrants. There was a large bank of snow in
a ravine to the left of the road, in sight of our noon
camp   nearly all of the train got some   Leut Davis gave us
some & Wat broght some to the wagon. We are encamped
tonight, on a nice mountain stream at a respectful distance
from Kirk, Cooper & Dodson. Indians is the chat.[4] John has
gone to the other camp—Tolerable grass.

3d of July. Noon. Kirks train corelled to gather once more.
Just passed the remains of a burned ranch. Lately done.
passed a calf lying near the road with its legs cut off, showing
the Indians had taken a hasty feed from it   the stage
corralled with us. It is about 25 mile to Ft. Halock.[5] It is near
the place we are corelled that a large train has had a fight
lately with indians. a shield with a fresh scalp tied to it was

---

[4]Evidently she means here that the conversation was about Indians.

[5]Fort Halleck, Carbon County, Wyoming, was a short-lived Civil War fort (1862-
1866). It was a strategic post on the Overland Stage route. It was built by the Eleventh
Ohio Volunteer Cavalry. *Wyoming, A Guide to Its History, Highways and People* (New
York, 1952), p. 237; Mae Urbanek, *Wyoming Place Names* (Missoula, Mont., 1988), p.
70.

found near the place, and a chiefs head dress. and some of the trinkets they wear round their neck. Some of Coopers Train found them. The shield consist of raw hide taken from the face of a buffalo stretched over a hoop about the size of the top of a large woden bucket. There is considerable excitement in camp. we met 2 stages with heavy guard this morning moving every thing from the stations—

4th of July. No alarms during the night. John is still complaining. all hands endeavoring to get an early start. A halt. we passed the remains of a wagon that had been plundered and burned. part of one wheel was left & some of the cooking vessels and a good many small pine boxes. coming on a short distance was some clotes and feathers scatered over the ground, apparently the contense of a feather bed. We have been halting for about an hour. we are in the rear of all the trains. and those that have come back say there is a very bad hill to go down— We are over the bad place—

July 5. We camped last night within 3 mile of Hallack. Where we are now halted in the place. aranging as I thought to pay tole but I think I was mistaken, all ranches are deserted ecepting those at the tole bridges, where they always keep a guard to collect. Sure enough, we had to pay 50 cts for crossing little tole bridge. The travelers give the soldiers here a bad name. a great many of then have Indian wives. The stage that correlled with us night before last lost their team last night. The station near which we have camped say the Indians tried to run off their stock today. They think they are in a large body in the mountains near here. It is the opinion of som that they are trying to moove south. It is reported at the Ft that the Indians killed one of the Sheren boys & scalped him. he is buried at the Ft. Those that went in the P.O. say there was an ox team load of eastern mail at Hallack.

July 5th   After candle light. Today been a busy day. Mrs McClure gave birth two twins. one lived till 12 Ocl A.M. The other but a few minutes. They were buried at the ranch.

July 6th. We came to the ferry across North Platt over a very rough mountain road. had to go out 4 mile to get grass for the cattle.

July 8th   washed this fore noon. Kirks train ferried this fore noon we will endeavor to cross this evening. The boys left us the 6th. Silas and family occupy their place. we have had a busy day. The right wing of our correll is nearly over. The soldiers at this place showed us about 30 steel pointed arrows that had bin shot at them yesterday, while ther horses to graze. one did serious damage to one of their horse. They hardly think he will recover   About 4 Oclock P.M. All the wagons are acros but 4. They cross 2 wagons at a time & swim the cattle & horses. John has come. Reports all right. We will travail to grass to night.

July 9 P.M. we are encamped in a barrain mountain country ¾ of a mile to grass. no water fit to drink. a great deal of dissatisfaction through camp. some want to go on.

10th   Nooned near a ranch plenty of wood and water but *short grass*

11th of July. From the length of the shadow I would take it to be near 12 Oclock. We are halted on a high mountain, a wagon haveing broken down, and they are removing the load. We must be very near the summit. There was snow near the road yesterday, but the water we camped last night on was flowing east. Emaline had a very high fever all day yesterday, she thinks she is some better today. I am so much pushed with work I have no time to write. Tilla has the flux too & requires a good deal of attention   We came about 2 mile from where the wagon broke down, and correlled on the hill side among sage brush and rocks. There is some nice grass in a small valey, surrounded by high hills excepting the side next the camp, which gives us a fair view of it. There is a nice stream running between the correll and grass, & a spring comes out. I tried to fish some but having no success. I washed some of the babes clothes. The train is going separate in order to accommodate each other on account of the scarcity of grass. We remain with the main portion.

12th of July   The rigt wing moved forward and when we halted to noon it kept on with the exception of 2 families   Mr Farris & Mr May's. Mr Farris' wagon broke down in both the hind wheels. the train cannot move on untill they are repaired   Mrs Davis is some better. We have been traveling down the western slope since yesterday morning.

13th of July   We travailed till after night last night, & had to stop in a place where we had no grass for the stock, nooned today on a desert place, without water & I cannot tell the prospect for grass. the stage passes us nearly every day. Camped to night at the watering place. had to go of with the stock to get grass. traveling through a barrain country

14th   Our road to day has been very rough & dusty, no grass near the [trail?]   got some by going about a mile & half from the road. but we hauled water for cooking, no wood but sage brush. but that is as good as chips. We had some rain at noon, which made our travail this evening more pleasant.

15th   To day our road has not been quite so hilly, and the day has been cloudy occasionally thundering. the earth & streams show there has been rain quite recently. The hill have assumed a striped appearance. some say we are now within 100 miles of Bridger. The train keeps grass hunters a head. which they have succeeded in finding so far within 2 miles from the road. we camp near the road, and detail hands to take the stock & keep them all night

16th Sunday. I rose this morning with the sun as John went out last night with the horses. I gethered sage brush & made out my yeast biscuit & put them on to cook, & Emaline finished the balance. It is now ready. Silas is on the sick list this morning—

17th We are geared up ready to start. Went about 4 mile to grass, and not very good at that. encamped near a branch tolerable good water. We are now traveling down Bitter creek. We moved on till about 1 Oclock. we came near the creek & camped near Rock station the houses have been built of rock for some time. I am not well atal I think it is the water that physics me.

18th They took the stock out to hunt grass but failed to get any for the cattle, which they brought back and correlled. John & Silas found grass for the horses, but it was very hard to get at. the most of the horsemen came in with the cattle, which made me feel quite uneasy. Tilla fretted with the ear ache nearly all night. which was very cold and windy and drizzling—

19th They took the stock to grass with the expectation of staying all night but came in directly after dark.

21d. I have been too sick to write any for 2 days. I have the flux now, but I do not feel as badly as when I was first taken. we have been travailing through a rough barrain country, can get cedar and pine wood to burn, no good water yet. but we will soon get to snow water. Where we have encamped there is a range of level toped hills off to the left along Bitter creek. to the right is a rocky range with some scatering dwarf cedars and pines, & some tolerable grass — last night we had to feed our horses grain we had been saving for an emergency. they correlled the cattle and we had to tie some of the horses to our wagon, and they tore the curtain badly, and kept me awake nearly all night.

22nd   We are at Green river, we have got dinner, and drove down to the landing and watering the horses, we will soon commence crossing. the right wing leads today, and our wagon is 4th   It is about 3 Oclock P.M. nearly all the train is acros   have crossed since 12 Oclock. 1 wagon at a time. There is a train on this side, and it does appear that they must be making wages to day. $1.50 per wagon with 4 head of stock, a large freight train crossed this A.M. Reeds wagons of Mexico [Missouri] are with them & one of the Gilberts of Long-branch. We have corelled facing a strong cool wind. I am some better to day. but was very sick last night Green River *will do* to drink. John reports another train coming in sight on the other side. he is hitching up—.

23rd Sunday. They found good grazing for the horses but most too short for cattle, about 1½ miles from camp. I got out yesterday evening and helped about supper. still had flux at night and up once through the night. took a dose of salts this morning & some Jamaca ginger, which I think has been of benefit or getting to better water. I cooked some peaches and fried some pies for John to take out with him we have stayed all day at this place. they had to go down some steep places to get to grass, and some very narrow side mountain road, just room for the horses to go single file. we are drinking Green river water, which looks green—

24th   The flux is not so frequent but when I have actions I am puped out.

24th   Now we have passed the station which was said to be 14 mile from where we camped yesterday. we are near the creek. I wish we could get out of the mountains. I would judge from my feelings it is about 1 Oclock. I feel little able to cook. Geared up and made a short drive came to good grass about ¼ mile from the road. we are correlled once more in a grassy place, plenty of mountain currants   I have never used them

25   Encamped for the night on Blacks fork of Green river, about 30 miles from Bridger. The road we have been traveling has lead us across Hams fork 3 times   we have come in sight of the snow mountains again but our road today has been very good. we nooned on Hams fork just at the ford, on good grass. I am getting able to do a good part of the cooking. John & Silas killed 1 rabbit & 3 sage chickens   the[y] ate well.

26th   We found out this morning that we had left the Bridger road last evening so Uncle Billy Davis decided he would leave the train before he would miss going by Salt lake, which he did & Silas still remains with us much against his mothers wishes. We are traveling the direct Origon rout.

27th   This morning John had to get breakfast. Emaline is still sick & I had a return of f[l]ux last evening. Took a dose of salts and intend to diet from this time out. I have been eating fresh meat. we had good grass & water by traveling till sun down. camped again on Blacks fork   Nooned near Blacks fork. Silas has gone to the hills for Cedar to cook with which is a mile distant to the left. Some talk of sending to the Ft for letters. The Levi & John Faris geared the buggy and started for the Ft   They all washed this afternoon. I was not able

28th   We crossed Blacks fork soon after we struck the Bridger road. We are nooning on good grass, no water but what we hauled, but we watered the teams when we crossed the creek. I must help get dinner — After dinner, wrote a line to leave for Thompson who waited at the Ft for us, and had gone back to the next station. The Whites said expecting to meet us. but we came to the sight of the Ft. on a much leveler road.

29th   We have just crossed a very bad ford on a small creek a tributary of Green river & while halting for the rest of the train to get over (as our wing leads today) two Indians came

riding down the hill to the right. There must be more of
them from the amount of dust we saw in that direction. This
morning we just decided it to be another train. but I expect it
was a gang of Indians. The 2 are painted red.

30th   We are geared up ready to start, but have had a
detainme[nt] on account of the cattle having strayed up the
branch. we are encamped on a grassy place and plenty of
water. Sold our old feather bed for a sack of flower   Nooned
near a spring plenty of grass. Silas' babe is sick & I have all
the cooking to do & glad that I am able to cook too   This
afternoon our road resembled a walk through a flower garden
we traveled till late before we could get to water   passed
plenty of grass.

31st   Old Mr Enna a consumptive going to the mountains
for his health, died last nigt, and was buried about 9 Oclock
this morning. we will stay here till we eat dinner. The babe is
not much better.

August 1st   We walked all day yesterday on account of Old
Mrs Turpin being too sick to be moved. we are travailing in
Wasach or Bear mountains over a very rough hilly road. I am
writing during a halt in the train caused in the rear as we are
forward this morning and Mrs Turpin is near the rear of the
other wing   I fear she is worse, is the cause of stops. They
caused a stop to wait for the train to close up after crossing a
bad ford in a small creek. We are nooning on Bear river, a
fine looking stream.

Aug 2d   Last night ice froze ⅛ of an inch in the grass. The
snake indians come in to barter fish & antelope hides for
bread, coffee

3d   Mrs Turpin is very feeble. We are halting till noon on
her account. I see they [are] fixing the cariage. I expect we
will move out after dinner   John bought a Elk hide of an
indian for a small camp kettle. After 12 Oclock. I have just

awoke from a short nap after dinner. John made a hair line yesterday and caught some fine fish. the largest was about 15 inches long speckled and had very small scales and the meat had a yellowish red cast.

4th   We are geared up ready to start. The left wing leads to day in order to get Mrs Turpin out of the dust. We paid 2 $ tole today   came a new road down the river bottom   came to a vilage, got some onions lettice & butter. we are near the line between Idaho & Utah. irrigated from the mountains off to the right. They are mormons.

5th   We are geared up ready to start   they say 30 mile to Soda springs. About camping time, late too, we met some packers who told us it was 10 mile to wood and water, but we took a road turning towards the river, had to travail till 2 hours after night & I then had to get supper. Their is flax growing in these bottoms but not much in a place. very scatering.

6th   Sunday morning   I feel quite well this morning with the exception of a soarness in my face caused by some decay in teeth I have. John got breakfast this morning, as I canot stand the cold mountain air before sun up. the nights are pinching cold. Nooning at Soda springs. I have to brown coffee so I must get at it. I have browned and ground my coffee. The Indians come round begging & picking up the scraps. we have detained too long in this place. We came a few mile and encamped near the river. as they say here we have a long drive before we get to water again. The next waters we strike is of the Columbia.

7th   Nooning on a nice stream in a valey in the mountains, so the statement about the waters of the Columbia was not so.

8th. Morning. We came to this place in good time last evening. a regular camping place. a stream with willow and grass. Lewis buried an infant here yesterday   still born.

They moved out this morning while we were at breakfast
There is several sick in our train. I saw the full moon rise
from behind the mountain last evening.—

9th Noon. After dinner. being the first leasure I have had
when the wagon was still. we have come over a rough road to
day, in one place just room for the road between high
mountains. some think we have come over the summit. This
has been the dusty's road we have had. This evening, not
much grass either.

10th   Nooned without grass. passed a station. The country
is very barrain and dusty   We are encamped near a fine
stream, with plenty of grass—

11th   All of them raised their wagon beds but us. we raised
our load. we have to ford the stream and it is full. We
travailed till after night. We passed good camping places, but
too early to camp.

12th   We are laying by to-day in consequence of our
tiresome travail yesterday. I sided up my wagon, swaped a
large tin of peaches for as many beans and cooked half of
them for dinner, and washed some in the evening.

13 Sunday. Mrs Turpin Complained terably last night. I sat
up from 10 till about 1 Oclock but she got no ease. We are
detaining again on her account. There is several sick in the
train. we are using spring waters   John killed 3 chick   I
cooked them for dinner. gave 2 to the sick   It is about ½
mile to the River, which is suposed to be the head waters of
the Columbia.

14th   We passed the falls that have been in hearing of our
camp for 2 days soon this morning. some thought it fell near
40 feet. all the streams have falls. we nooned near another
Cascade in the river, but quite small. I could not see the
principle one till after we passed by. it looked like snow. it
was so white. We travailed till night before we came to the

river bottom. There is the only place where there is any grass. it was very near eaten out here. the road has lain over steep mountains mostly all evening.

15th   We are nooning on a small branch with plenty of grass near what seems to have been a station, but [?] less as have been 2 others we passed yesterday. Tilla is complaining. We travailed till late, and then had very indifferent grass & no water. went to bed without supper.

16th   Started by day light without breakfast. Travailed till after 10 before we came to water. I was quite sick during the night with diareah. it looked like I would give quite out before I could get something to eat. the sun shone but our road has been very steep and rocky, and very dusty, almost insufferable. We nooned about 3 hours in order to give the cattle time to graze—

17th 18th   I have had the diahria for two days this morning is the first time I have felt able to write since I wrote the last. I feel clear of misery but am very weak We are encamped near the river. The hills here are composed of large round dark colored rock that is the hills we have to travail over about like a rocky creek ford. Nooning on a branch road this fore noon.

19th   We encamp within a few mile of a ranch, on a place that has lately been mown. It rained last night and the sun is shining as brigt as I have always been used to seeing it do after a storm. and I hear some tiny notes of birds among the willows on the branch. It lightened and thundered about like it does in Mo— We halted on the same branch and as it is 25 mile to grass, they stay here till morning.

20th   started early. came to a ranch about 10 and stoped long enough to water the teams. They say 17 mile to grass. We came to the ferry about noon. got our dinner and was soon crossing the Snake river in a row boat. We had to come down a very steep side mountain road. The wagon I was in came very near run off. I had to get out and walk about a quarter down hill. we had good grass for the stock.

21st   The right wing came over last evening. The wind was against the progress of the boat. This morning is still and the[y] are making rapid progress. The wagons & horses are over & they are swimming the cattle. There is a river coming out of the right bank forming several falls before reaches the bottom. it makes quite a noise. The bluffs here are almost perpendicular, there hight is beyond my estimation. 10 Oclk A.M. The order is to get dinner and start a few cattle are on the other side the[y] could not make [them] swim the river. they are going to bring them on foot. The cattle crowded up on the boat and sunk it and came near drownding some of the men. They had their boots and clothing on. They all went to the other bank. They were late night getting them over.

22d   The train is trying to get in motion, her mooving now resembles a stern wheel boat at a low stage of the Mo R going up stream — Noon camp. The hill we had to come up to get out of the river bottom was about the worst we have had. The bottom was sandy. The midle portion side mountain, and the top pure rocks in steps about 2 foot high, and on a turn — watered at a spring and had a little grass too. the road is deep sand   heavy pulling — Travailed till about 10 Oclock before we came to water. They say there is grass near but it is too dark to hunt it as the horses are tied to the wagons. Morning light did not find much grass for the stock. The word is another long drive to supplies of grass & water

23d   We stoped at noon long enough to rest the stock & let them pick from scanty fare afforded. We came to grass & water, *nice* place to camp   Dean is stopping a short distance above & Easton went up there to rest his sick family   his oldest child is not expected to live   hiself & wife both sick—

24th   Considerable trouble with the stock. they scattered considerable. Old Sorel to the other correll. Puss lost hiself in the willows. McMurrain, McClure & us came on about 5 mile to the next station, in the night

25   Came to water at about 5 mile. we watered the teams, and drove till noon. had some dry bunch grass. 10 miles to good grass & water   twelve Ocklock is ecceptionely hot. evenings & mornings cool. we drove till after night last night   We came to good grass and water, several acres of blew grass. looked nice but the stock would not eat it. There was plenty of rye. Old Sorrel is very poor in flesh and spirits.

27th   We got up early this morn   got to a ranch where there is indifferent water and some grass. we fed the last shelled oats to Old Sorrel. a heavy rain fell last night, and it was very hot. I did not rest well. We camped tonight site close to a small stream coming down from the mount north of us. Tolerable grass. Lewis and Cravan camped near—

27th   We watered our teams at a ranch said to be 10 miles from where we camped last night. Whites came on in the night. camped just behind us. I am trying to write home but I have so little time I make slow progress   I have bread cooked for dinner. I will employ all the leasure that gives me. we are encamped in a place that has been mown long for the grass to start which makes it good grazing.

28th   Started early this morning after having good grass and spring water but the long drives are bringing down our stock. morning after a five mile drive, at a place where they raised some vegetables by irrigation   I bought 2 lbs of potatoes for 31 cts and cooked them for dinner. They were small & I think had been dug some time. They looked wilted some of them   got good grazing by going 1 mile up the mountains—

29th Tues   We camped last evening on a hill. Craven is

encamped on the valey. We came 5 mile farther than White & Lewises.

30 Weds. Came over some very rocky dusty hilly roads. stoped and hired pasture at 25 cts per head, within a short distance of Boise City. sold the shot gun for 14 oz of gold dust valued at $20   Sold Old Sorrel for $25.

31st   We passed through Boise yesterday, considerable place. bought sack of oats there. Then met a man hauling in a load and traded the elk hide for another sack $11   came about 5 mile fed on oats. Camped at a camp   we came on with some mule teams from Mo going to Oregon. McClure wanted to fall in with White again. McMurrain is not going as far as we are. I am writing during a halt to fill the water kegs—

1st Sept. We camped last night where we stoped at noon. The wind blew so hard we could not go on. Today is cold   we have come down a steep hill. the most of the road has been hilly very hilly. The M come on in the evening very happy about our going ahead. We are traveling down Piett [Payette] river. nooned on a branch grass looked green and nice but was salty. Durham is the name of the Old gentleman we are traveling with son in law Brown & family   2 married sons and families & Mrs Bell his sons wifes mother [unreadable word] going to Oregon   very clever folks. Just about camping time a heavy storm set in and we were compeled to halt, and it soon commenced pouring   The hail in balls a size larger than buck shot. The horses showed every sign of there intentions to beat a hasty retreat, and the men had to unharness during the thickest of the shower.

2d   This morning is cold and drizling rain. We made a poor nooning came on to the Piatt and crossed it., then drove till late and camped in the snake bottom & grazed the stock on an island in the river.

3   We had a good road this forenoon   encamped on a small stream called the Weazen [Weiser]. drove constant this afternoon. reached the camping place about Sundown ranches all along

4th   There is a large pack train encamped at this place. About 10 Oclock. We have crossed the Snake again & waiting for the balance of the wagons to come over. They make quick trips and drive the wagons with 4 horses on at time. we brought all over at one load, except our le[a]d mare [unreadable word] Tilla is very sick with diahrea & the road today has been rough   we are now in Oregon—We encamped on Burnt river. passed some packers that had lost some of their stock. Old Mr. Durham is very uneasy   John went out with the stock to stay all night

5th   Tilla was very sick in the night. I gave her a dose of worm medicine. when it operated she vomited and was very sick. We are nooning in a place almost destitute of grass. John fed his horses some oats. The roads have been side mountain mostly & hilly. Our drive this afternoon has been as rough as well could be. we camped near Burnt river and got good bunch grass by going a mile up the Mt.

6th   Late in the evening   we halted today on account of Mr Durhams little son's being very sick. I have been washing all day. I never saw nicer water for the purpose. the bed of the creek are composed of bare rock which stand up out of the water and one can walk in on them and dip up the water without soiling it. John started early this morning to make breaks to both his wagons   he has finished the one on this wagon.—

7 & 8th   Today & yesterday have both been cold   we halted today about 3 Oclock on acount of the cold wind. it is as cold weather as we have the first of Nov in Mo. it rained last night and we have come facing a cold west wind to-day & yesterday.

9th   So cold this morning I can hardly write, heavy frost, &
ice. We meet large pack trains. Met 11 yesterday. we are in
Powder river valey, camped in hearing of a quartz mill

10th   We passed by Ringo yesterday evening   came 8 mile
to this camp. got supper after night. it is raining this morning.
we are in the valey skirted by snow crested pine covered
mountains. we are noonin on the summit of the Blue
moun[tains]   we have been coming up all the forenoon. the
horses are very.tired. drizzling all the time too   we travailed
till late through a cold rain. stoped close to a deserted store
house   I cooked supper in it. Tilla is very sick.

11th   Late in the evening. Encamped again in the Blue Mt.
rained all day. The road has been hills all the time. They say
we will have better roads from here to the Landing. we have
good grass for the cattle.

12   They are stopping to trade for some beef. The roads
have been fine since we left the Daily ranch at the foot of the
Mt. some men at the quartz mill gave John a fine hound that
some emigrants had left at the house just before we came to
this   a fox hunter had a mate for him, and offered John a
sack of flour 50 lbs for him   worth here $6.50. John sold it
to Mr Durham for $5. intends taking it in horse feed. it
looks almost like a miracle.

13th 14th 15th   Morning we laid bye here yesterday, at the
junction of Daily and Grand Rond road on account of Liza
Durhams being to sick to travail. Jackson, Ringo, & some of
our friends of Kirks Train we had not seen since we left are
camped with us. Thompson passed bye yesterday morning.
The name of the creek is Birch creek. Tilla has been very
sick for several days, which has gave me such a press of
work   I have not had time to write

16th   During a halt at a ranch I avail myself of an
opportunity to write. It looks more like living than any thing

I have seen. plenty of grain stacks, pigs in a pen near where we are stoped and fatning hogs and hens singing around and plenty of little chicks, all black with white toping. we have had some steep hills to climb this morning. Emaline is complaining.

17th Sunday Morning. We are going to make a short drive this fore noon & rest the balance of the day, at a large spring, those say that are acquainted with the road.

18 Monday noon. I finished a letter home yesterday which occupied all the leasure I could get   we came to the spring about 1 Oclock & stayed till this morning. John was quite sick when we stoped. Took Opium & slept all evening Emaline and 2 of her children on the sick list   I have my hands full with sickness & stubbornness. I am almost at a loss to know what to do but resolve to do my duty.

19th   This morning Silas says Bell is sick. I doctor myself & children & feel conserned about Bell but he has neither asked for medicine nor my advise. I would not have even known it if it were not for my own observations. There is a good physician in the train. That is enough — we are encamped close to a willow branch I do not know the name   Gresham is just below us. Ringo above. To judge from the down hill we came in on—

20th 21st   We are stoped to noon. Silas called the Dr this morning for Bell, & said he must stop at the John Day river till he could come up to see her, so we came on as our team is weak, and needs to be on grass. The mules & rone [roan] can stand it better than our other poor mares since we left them. it has been up hill all the way. They will be apt to be late getting in. The Dr has an ox team. They passed just as we were getting ready to bring in the horses

22d   We took the Mt. road this morning. 2 of Mr Durhams sons and families Mr Fort and Gresham of our train went to the landing to ship. Cooper, Ringo, Old Mr Durhams family, Brown, Rosenberger & our selves are encamped convenient to the first water we came to. that is about that we came to-day Emaline is very complaining, & Bell is very low & they gave Cora a dose of blue mass to-day.

23d   Evening camp. we arrived at the camping place about 2 O'clock. Bell is low   Emaline not able to tend her, I took her in my wagon and tended her till we got here. her recovery is very doubtful—

24th 25th 26th   Silas family have been so sick and Tilla sick too. I have not had any time to write. Bell is better. I carried her yesterday in my wagon & tended her & Tilla. she is so low she cannot raise her head. Emaline is down & will not take a bit of attention from my hands. I make her diet for her & get Mrs Brown to take it to her. she is some better I think   all the train have tried to prevail on Silas to stop with his sick family. but he still insists on crossing the Mt. we tarried yesterday till about 3 Oclock. we could get good pasture at 10 cts per head by making a short drive, and we were paying 25 cts. I washed and baked light bread. The women near where we were camped brought some delicacies to the sick   we had desperate roads. Cross De shoots river [Deschutes] on a tole bridge $2.00

27th Morning. We made the drive by sun down. camped within The Enclosure & they could just unharness the teams & let them go on fine grass, and nice running water near us. Mrs Durham's little girls have taken up with the children, & Tilla is enjoying herself finely. We came to a very steep side Mt road & all the teams had made a start up but our Old wagon   when they went back to help Silas up he told them he believed he would go back & stop as Emaline was worse, so they had to stop there untill Mr Black & Will Rounberger took him back. We gave them $10 leaving us but 16. While they were taking him back to house where they left him as comfortable as could be expected, as those that were left tried to get the wagons up with the assistance of some men travailing in a light 2 horse vehicle. The third drive our wagon got nearly to the top of a short steep turn in the road and stoped. The wagon commenced running back. I called to the inexperienced foreigner to hold the wheel but he kept beating the horses untill they became ungovernable and the wagon turned off the road   he then tried to hold it by grabing the fore wheel   The man that was driving behind jumped down from his seat Hallowing for those within to get out, and just got to the hind wheel in time to save the wagon. I made all the haste I could to get the children out. it then took all hands to get the wagon back on the road.

28th   Nooning at the entrance into the Mt. called Barlow's gate   they talk of making a short drive into the Mt. I am not well.

29th   In the Mt. detained to mend the hind axle of Mr Browns wagon, which has just broken down after a steep short drive & a late start. The sun is shining brightly when we came to the camping place late yesterday evening. we found Mr Brown & Rosenberger there long enough to have good fires. Rosenberger had made his fire against a very tall pine which stood near his wagons about 10 Oclock   Will raised the alarm that the tree was windshaken and rapidly burning down. They all went to work and backed the wagons up hill on sideling ground and then cut the tree down to make all things safe, which fell square across the road, which had to be cut off and drawn to one side by oxen this morning which detained us considerable.

Oct. 22. At Mr. Knights, where we stoped because was not able to travail. I am now able to walk about & all the rest are sick. Sent for the Dr for Mr Black, as he was worse than ever last night.

Nov. 3   Left Knights—Landed at Uncle Josiah Hannah

17th [Dec.]   December 1st Isaac arrived at Uncle Jo's

2nd [Jan.]   It snowed last night in the valley. This morning is rapidly melting

10th   Raining. Rogue river out of its banks. Still at Uncle Joes

1866   January 10th   Moved home to a little cabin about one and half miles above Uncle Joes close to the river.

Jan 19th   Heavy snow fell last night & it has been raining all day and had a nice time getting a bucket of water.

EPILOGUE

Mary Louisa and John Black, with the two children, stayed at Hannah's eight weeks, and they paid them $10, according to a later entry in the notebook. John bought land as soon as possible, and they lived in a cabin already in existence on it until a large hewed log house was built. In the yard near the road Louisa planted five shell bark hickory nuts which she had brought with her from Missouri. Two of them grew, and one is still alive as of this writing. The trunk is about 14 inches in diameter, and the tree has wide-spreading branches because the top has been cut to avoid contact with a power line directly over it. A crop of very hard hickory nuts is produced every year on this lone shell bark tree. The old log house was still intact until the early 1920s. Some time during those years a new owner took it down and replaced it with a different type of log house, which still stands today.

Isaac Black, John's older brother, arrived in December 1865. He stayed with them from time to time, but he did not take up land. He became a miner. Records show that he had a mining claim with two other men on Jumpoff Joe Creek in Josephine County, Oregon, in 1867. He was living with the Blacks in Jackson County when the census was taken in 1870. He returned to Missouri about 1875.

Over the years the Hannahs and the Blacks worked together to develop and farm their land on opposite sides of the Rogue River. Within a year or two Josiah Hannah built a ferry boat and operated it between their two properties. Soon other settlers were crossing on it, so Josiah Hannah applied to Jackson County for a license to run a toll ferry. The license was granted in June 1869, and by 1872 the county had surveyed and opened a public road to Hannah's ferry, which gave better access to the Upper Rogue country and to Fort Klamath. Hannah's ferry operated until 1874, when a new road and another ferry came into use.

Tragedy struck Mary Louisa and John Black again in 1867 when baby Clifton died in a diphtheria epidemic. They buried him at the edge of a field below the house. There is no trace of the little grave today, as the fields have been inundated by floods several times over the years.

Two years later on October 14, 1869, a son, Lee, was born, and four years later, in 1873, another daughter, Martha, saw the light of day. Mary Louisa taught her children to read and write in her own home, as there was no public school close by until 1890. They were as competent as any of their peers. Before she was twenty, Tilla took the teacher's examination, and she taught a few terms.

As the family grew, they all helped to make a living. The girls tanned deer skin, made gloves and sold them. They also raised turkeys and chickens and sold eggs. Lee worked as a logger in the woods and also in the hay fields in Klamath County. He and his father killed deer and sold the fresh meat to the miners around Jacksonville. In 1891 John M. Black won the bid to operate the county ferry across Rogue River about three miles north of their farm. His salary was $25 per month, and he carried out his contract faithfully for four years.

Martha was the first of the Black children to marry. She married Peter E. Betz in 1904, and they lived on an adjoining farm for over fifty years. They had no children, but they were devoted to their nieces and nephews. Next to marry was Lee. In November 1905, he married a local school teacher, Helen Holtan, and brought her home to live with Mary Louisa and John. Two daughters were born to them while they lived there: Olena Martha, b. September 1906, and Lottie Myrtills, b. February 1908.

John Maupin Black died on February 20, 1907. He was buried in Central Point Cemetery, near Central Point, Oregon. The property was divided up among the three children. After the estate was settled, Lee sold his share, and he and Helen started looking for a farm of their own. They found one on Forest Creek about ten miles from Jacksonville in the Applegate River valley. It consisted of 268 acres of land mostly timbered, with about 45 acres under cultivation. There was a small house, log barn and other buildings, on the site of an old saw mill. Lee and Helen, with their two small daughters, moved to this ranch in June 1908.

After the death of her husband in 1907, Mary Louisa made her home with Tilla. Two years later Tilla married bachelor neighbor, Chris Bergman, and he built a simple board and batten house for them. They farmed his land as well as hers for many years. In 1910 Mary Louisa's health began to fail, and she passed away on June 20, 1911. Over on Forest Creek just six days earlier, on June 14, 1911, her grandson John Maupin Black II, was born to Lee and Helen Black. She probably never got to see him, but we hope she knew about him before she died.

Lee and Helen Black had two more children, a daughter, Ruth, born 1915, who died in infancy; and another daughter, Helen Isabelle, born April 26, 1918. Lee and Helen Black lived out their lives on this ranch. She died in 1928, and he lived until 1945. They are buried in Logtown Cemetery, near Ruch, Jackson County. John M. Black II inherited the ranch, and with his wife, Marguerite, still lives there.

MARGUERITE W. BLACK

LIST OF MEDICINES

This was evidently provided by the Black family's doctor for use on the long overland journey. It is among the Black family papers.

Feb 13, 1865

Dear Friend,

I give you below a bit of medicines for your trip across the plains. Such as are in powder form you must get the druggist to give you a sample of the dose to enable you to administer it.

Laudanum	4 ounces
	dose 25 drops
Turpentine	16 ounces
	dose 1½ teaspoonful
Castor oil	1 bottle ½ pt
	dose ½ tablespoonful
McLeans pills	3 boxes
Calomel	½ drachm
Blue Mass	½ drachm
Quinine	4 drachms
Sugar of Lead	4 drachms
Coal oil	1 pint

Eye Water made of 2 grains of Sulpt of Zinc to one ounce water. Get two ounces made up.

Paregoric — 8 ounces and mix one ounce of Tannin with it — for bowel complaint of children — dose your oldest child ½ teaspoon — for the infant give ten drops — for Tillie ¼ teaspoonful.

Ipecac	2 drachms — dose 20 grains, 5 grains every 15 minutes
Epsom Salt	¼ pound
	dose heaping tablespoonful
Mustard Seed	½ pint or 1 box ground mustard
Blister Plaster	2 ounces

One thumb lancet and tooth forceps for the company. One will do the crowd.

Blue Stone	2 drachms
Hartshorn	½ ounce

You are likely to take no other diseases on the route besides common Diarhoea, Dysentery, and Mountain Fever.

For Diarhoea give the paregoric and tannin — for an adult, 1 tablespoon is a dose. Or take a dose of tannin with 25 drops of Laudanum and repeat every 3, 4, or 6 hours. Sometimes a dose of the Blue Mass at first is best, then begin on the other.

If you take dysentery or flux (all the same) be sure and not keep the bowels locked up over 12 hours at a time. You must begin on Salts — full dose, after they act two or three times (which you will know by a change in the stools to a more natural character) then quiet the bowels with a full dose of Laudanum and repeat it in six hours. Then at the same time, on the next day that you gave the Salts, you give another dose and give Salts every day at the same time of day, repeat dose in six hours if the first dose not act — then follow it with Laudanum as before. Nearly all of the deaths from flux are from keeping the bowels too much closed.

Mountain Fever — This is the easiest thing treated in the world. You first give a very active purgative, nearly a double dose of McLean's Pills or Blue Mass and Calomel combined, then 40 drops of Laudanum, and sponge the body often with tepid water — repeat the Laudanum from 25 to 40 drops so as to keep the patient under the influence of it 48 hours. Then if there be any fever left, repeat the purgative (a common dose now) followed by the Laudanum.

Colic — give a double dose of Castor oil with ½ teaspoonful of turpentine — repeat every three hours. As soon as it acts your colic is gone.

Cholera Morbus — give oil and Laudanum with mustard over the whole bowels.

To California by the Mormon Trail, 1865

§ Ruth Shackleford

INTRODUCTION

Was it by accident or was it written in the cards that my wife, Inez, and I should meet James and Gladys Howerton while both couples registered in a motel in Santa Barbara, California, on that December 17, 1979? The Howertons live in Lincoln, Nebraska; and the Holmeses live in Monmouth, Oregon. In Santa Barbara we four visited back and forth and went for walks on the beach together over several days following.

It was Jim who asked me, "What are you doing here in Santa Barbara?" I answered that I was visiting the University of California Library searching for records of women on the overland trails. Mrs. Howerton spoke up, "We have one. We'll send it to you when we get home."

Sure enough, not long after we returned to Oregon, there came in the mail a package from Lincoln, Nebraska, containing not one but two diaries written by Ruth Shackleford, a distant relative of James Howerton:

DIARY I, 1865 — Clark County, Missouri, to San Bernardino, California.

DIARY II, 1868 — San Bernardino, California, to Sherman, Grayson County, Texas. This diary will be published in proper time sequence later in this volume.

Probably the best way to get to know the Shackleford family members is to look at the 1860 United States Census of Missouri, available on microfilm from the National Archives. Their residence at this time was Shelbyville, Shelby County. They were interviewed by the census taker on August 25:

Shackleford, W.F.,	age 27,	a carpenter,	b. Virginia.
Shackleford, Ruth	age 25		b. Missouri.
Shackleford, Sarah	age 3		b. Missouri.
Shackleford, Mary	age 2		b. Missouri.
Shackleford, Debbie	age 1		b. Missouri.

These dates, when applied to the overland journey of 1865, would convert to the following ages: W.F., 32; Ruth, 30; Sarah (Sallie), 8; Mary, 7; Debbie, 6 years old.

The family descendants today remember the names of other children of William Frank and Ruth Shackleford, but their knowledge of key dates and what happened to them is sketchy: Frank, Charles, Maggie, Addie. The father, William Frank Shackleford, is always referred to as "Frank" by Ruth, the diarist. One interesting entry in the diary is that of July 31. She writes, "my birth day," which tells us she was born on that day, 1835.

There was one other Shackleford who accompanied them on the overland journey: That was Anna (also referred to as Ann), who was the wife of Atwell B. Gatewood. Ruth refers to Atwell many times, calling him either "At" or "Att." He was thirty-six years old at the time of the journey; Ann was thirty-eight. They traveled with several small children. Their home was Union City, Missouri, the locale of Ruth's first entry in her diary.

Another name that crops up several times in the Shackleford diary is that of Kirkland. Members of the family remember today that a close family friend of theirs was Abraham K. Kirkland, who's wife and children traveled with the wagon train. He was a blacksmith. One member of the family has a souvenir, a hatchet, given to one of the boys by Mr. Kirkland.

Ruth Shackleford also writes several times of the "misses Rhyne." We thought for a while that she meant two sisters, Mary and Susan. As a matter of fact she meant three misses Rhyne, the third one being Maggie. The Rhynes were a family from Virginia who had spent the last ten years in Missouri. Their father, Isaac

N. Rhyne, was a widower whose wife, Eliza Nesbitt Rhyne, had died in 1850. These people became permanent settlers in southern California. He was well-known as a general farmer whose land was on the banks of the San Gabriel River near Downey.[1] Mary became the wife of Asa Todd of Los Angeles, and Susan married T.J. Wood of Riverside. The third daughter, Maggie, never married, but she kept house for her father.

There were other travelers with this wagon train. Some joined it for a short time, others stayed longer. Ruth Shackleford, as was the case with most of our diarists, mentioned family members by their given name and non-family members only by their surname, making it very difficult to identify them.

The most tragic aspect of the western journey of the Shacklefords was the number of deaths of members of their party. The first was Nellie Kerfoot on August 13. Ruth Shackleford has a difficult time with Nellie's surname and renders it several different ways in the rest of the diary. Nellie was buried on the banks of Green River in Wyoming. Frank Shackleford, the carpenter, made her a coffin. We have not been able to identify her or her family.

Ruth and Frank Shackleford's daughter, Mary, a 7-year-old, died on August 17th. Ruth says, "Frank made her a right nice coffin, lined inside; the top was covered; couldn't get anything to cover the sides. She was dressed in solid green merino, a white collar and gloves, black belt and net. They said she looked very natural." The body was buried on the banks of Bear River.

On September 18 Ann Gatewood, the sister of Frank Shackleford, and the wife of Atwell Gatewood, died in Fillmore, Millard County, Utah. She was buried in the town cemetery. A local doctor said she died of mountain fever.

On October 14 Ruth wrote, "Att came to our wagon and told Frank to drive out to one side of the road for Jeffie [Gatewood] to die." Then she added, "Mrs. Kirkland dressed and laid him out.

---

[1]There is a short biography of Isaac N. Rhyne in *An Illustrated History of Los Angeles County* (Chicago, 1889), pp. 612-13.

Frank made a coffin for him and we put him in the coffin at 11
o'clock at night." They buried him on the banks of the Muddy
River on October 18th.

Att Gatewood would experience the death of one more child
when "little Annie" died on November 2 on the banks of the
Mohave River in California. Ruth wrote in her diary, "Little
Annie died this morning just before daylight. She died very hard.
She was teething and had diarrhea." They washed and dressed the
body and kept it in a wagon for burial in San Bernardino. The
burial took place on November 5th in the town graveyard.

One more aspect of the Shackleford's journey west is the route
they followed to southern California. The first part of their
journey involved the crossing of the Missouri River at Plattes-
mouth, Nebraska. Thence they took the Great Platte Road
overland to Salt Lake City. From the Mormon capital they
traveled what Ruth Shackleford calls the "California Road,"
which is what is usually called the "Mormon Corridor."[2] This
route stretched to the southwest from below the Great Salt Lake
to San Bernardino, California. After leaving Utah, the route
crossed a tiny corner of Arizona and a portion of southern Nevada,
then made the precarious crossing of the Mojave Desert, and on
through Cajon Pass to San Bernardino. There were a number of
small towns on the Utah portion of the trail, which made travel
fairly easy. Ruth Shackleford's diary describes them in fair detail.
This route approximates today's U.S. Interstate Highway 15.

We have already published the Sarah Pratt diary of 1852, which
followed the same basic route in somewhat less detail.[3]

---

[2] An excellent summary of this route is found in Milton R. Hunter, "The Mormon
Corridor," *Pacific Historical Review,* VIII, no. 2 (June 1939), pp. 179-200.

[3] *Covered Wagon Women,* vol. IV, pp. 169-207. A new approach to trails in Utah is
covered in William B. Smart, *Old Utah Trails, Utah Geographic Series* (Salt Lake City,
1988), no. 5, *passim.*

THE 1865 DIARY

CLARK COUNTY, MISSOURI, Monday Morning, May 1, 1865. This morning we started from Clark in company with two other families, those of Mr. Gatewoods and Mr. Rhynes. I feel very sad and low spirited on account of Frankie being sick and seeing them part with their friends. It makes me think of parting with you all. We travelled today over very rough, muddy roads. The children and I rode in At's horse wagon, the cattle being unruly and it raining. Frank's team stalled twice; had to pry the wagon out with fence rails. We are camped tonight two miles west of Fairmont at a Mr. Miller's. It being a very cold evening, we were politely invited into the house to warm. We made coffee on her stove and ate supper in the wagon. Ann and I slept in the house with our sick children. Frank and the other children slept in the wagon.

Tuesday, May 2—We made coffee on the lady's stove and ate in the wagon. We had a big time getting the unruly cattle yoked. It is still cloudy and the roads are awful muddy. Every now and then the women and children have to get out and walk through a mud hole. We are camped tonight by a house in a lot; turned the cattle in the lot and fed them. The wind being very high, we liked never to get supper, it being the first time we have cooked out of doors.

May 3—A beautiful morning. We all slept in our wagons. Frankie was sick all night with a pain in his side. I feel very uneasy about him. After breakfast they yoked up and started through the mud, and every now and then we were in a mud hole up to the hubs. We passed through Memphis [Missouri], a very pretty little town. We stopped there while Frank got two iron rods made to put in his wagon; paid $1 for them. Circuit court was in session. The girls went all over the town to look at it. This evening another family caught up with us, a Mr. Mays, his wife and young Mays. We are camped tonight in a lane. The family which lives here have the measles and we all have to keep our children close.

May 4—Last night was a very cold night, though we all slept comfortable in our wagons. We all started again through the prairie, up hill and down, through the mud, though they all seem in good spirits except Mr. Rhyne. One of his cattle is sick. He seems to be a little discouraged. We came on within three miles of the Iowa line. He bought another yoke and paid $125 for them. We crossed the line this evening. Just after we crossed we met a man coming in full speed with a flag on his horse. He told us the rebels were cutting up thunder on ahead. We came on through the mud, though not so bad as it has been. We camped for the night, turned the stock out, fed them, got supper over and to bed.

May 5—A very warm morning, with appearance of rain. Mr. Rhyne's ox is better. We started again today. We have got along very well, though it is very muddy. We passed some very nice houses and some very hornery [ornery] ones. Women were out making garden. We are camped tonight in a bottom near a big well. The house is on a big hill. They turned the cattle in a lot, had to carry feed a long way for them. We made a fire and got supper. The children are running up and down the road hallowing and playing. Mrs. Mays is sitting under a big tree writing to her father. The girls are washing their faces and combing their hair. Ann is nursing her baby. I am sitting on the wagon tongue with Frankie. Mr. Mays let his bucket fall in the well and could not get it. They all sit around and talk until they get tired and then go to bed.

May 6—We made a fire, got breakfast, fed the cattle and started. The man charged them for damages. They refused to pay but he followed them till they paid him. He told us we could not get a bit of feed for 50 miles. We had one very steep hill to pull up. Frank has to walk all the time. This evening we passed through a Union town. We are camped tonight on Soap Creek bottom, near a bridge. We stopped about two o'clock and are going to do some washing. They have turned the cattle out on the bottom. After we got through washing we got supper and then sat around the fire and had a sing. The people that live here heard us and came to our camp. They said those who camped here before made the woods ring with oaths. We sung until ten o'clock and then went to bed.

Sunday, May 7—We got up about sunrise; got breakfast over. Ann and I cooked some bacon and beans, stewed some apples, fried some pies for dinner. This evening Mrs. Mays and I baked light bread on the lady's stove. Miss Rhynes and Mary walked around through the woods hunting flowers. The lady that lives here showed us about 20 likenesses. She is the ugliest woman I ever saw, yet had twelve of her own. I suppose she thought she was good looking to her company. They all came to camp tonight to hear the singing. They sang till ten and then to bed.

May 8   We all got ready to start. The man charged us $4 for the cattle running on the bottom. Our cattle being rested, we got along fine. Frankie is almost well. He can get out of the wagon at night when we camp. The roads today have been tolerable good, except hills. Iowa is full of them. We passed some nice houses and some shabby ones. Everything in the shape of a house had a lightning rod on it. We passed through two little towns. We camped tonight on the prairie. After supper they all sat around the fire talking and laughing until bed time.

May 9   We came twenty miles over very rough roads. We came through Chariton, a little town in Lucas county, Iowa. As we passed the graveyard they were burying someone. We

girls stopped awhile. We stopped in town. Miss Rhynes and
Mary went all through town hunting some shoe strings. At
last they found some at 5¢ a pair. This evening the wind rose
and turned very cold. They stopped and bought feed for the
stock. We are camped tonight on the high prairie; turned the
stock out, got supper and went to bed.

May 10   It is so cold we cannot get breakfast. The wind
almost took our breath. We gathered up and came three
miles, then got breakfast. We set our table on a big stump. We
travelled all day through the prairie and liked to froze. Here
and there is a house that looks desolate, everything shivering
with cold. We are camped tonight near a big slough, not far
from Osceola. Some of the girls are writing home.

May 11   Nothing of interest has occurred today. We
travelled over some very rough roads. We are camped on the
bank of a creek. There are some wagons in a camp on the
other side. After supper, Mrs. Mays and the girls went over
to see them. They came from Nebraska. Ann and I are baking
bread for tomorrow.

May 12   Got up by daybreak and went to get wood for the
breakfast fire; got stuck in the mud and had to come back
without any. We did not get a very early start this morning.
The horses are gone and they are hunting them. They have
come in with them, found them four miles from the camp.
We came over very rough roads. The woods were so thick we
couldn't see ten steps. We had to come down one awful hill
on the Chariton river. Just as we got to the top the bow came
off Frank's big ox. He couldn't stop them and we came down
with a rush. I thought we would have a smash-up. They run
At's wagon over a stump. Mr. Rhyne couldn't stop his team
to lock and we all came down in a harraugh to the bridge.
There are five wagons camped here. Their horses are all
gone. The men have been hunting them nine days. After we

crossed the bridge, we came out on the prairie. It was so cold we had to keep the wagons closed. I did not get to see much until we got to Afton, Union county, Iowa, a nice little town. We came down Main Street. They have a cannon sitting by the flag, all ready to fire. We are camped tonight a mile from town on the river. We made a fire by a big log to get supper. The wind is very high. We had an awful time getting supper. Ann got the handles melted off all her tin cups.

May 13   We travelled all day over prairie. Not a house did we see, except one that had just been put up. We stopped this evening about three o'clock on the Little Platte to stay until Monday. It began to rain about the time we had supper ready—the first rain we have had since we left home. We all kept dry in our wagons.

Sunday, May 14   Still cloudy and misting. We all sat around reading and sleeping until 2 o'clock when it cleared off. The girls walked up and down the river hunting flowers. We all got supper over and went to bed.

May 15   Still raining and the roads are all very slippery. We have travelled farther today than we have any day since we left home. We passed through a little town in Union county, Iowa, called French Colony, an awful looking place. All the houses were built of round poles, covered with plank, about six feet square. The tavern had three rooms built of poles. A poll in front had a bell on it. Just before we got to town we passed a stable a quarter of a mile long, covered with straw. I counted 33 young calves in the lot. As we came out of town they had another stable for their horses and hogs. We then came down a long hill, crossed a bridge, and up hill into Queen City, which looks a little better. The houses were frame and painted white. We came on then to Quincy, the county seat of Adams county, a hilly looking place. There are two or three nice houses there. We are camped tonight on the banks of the Ottawa river, two miles from Quincy. After supper the girls and boys went fishing. About dark the blackest cloud rose, bringing thunder, lightning, wind and rain. We all thought we were going to have a hard storm. Our wagons leaked some.

May 16   This morning At bought a rifle for Frank; paid $20 for it. We only came 8 miles to the Big Ottawa and stopped to do our washing here. We came in company with five other wagons, some of At's acquaintances. We were glad to see them.

May 17   We all started together. There were six other wagons camped just below us. They caught up with us and we had a considerable train out on the high, desolate prairie. We had not gone far until Frank's hard-headed cattle ran off down a branch and liked to upset the wagon. At run in before them and stopped them till the children and I could get out. We passed through a town called Frankforde [Frankfort]. All it has was the name and flag. We then came on to Red Oak, the county seat of Montgomery county. About a quarter of a mile from town we came to Middle river. The bridge had fallen in. They had a flat boat to take teams across   It worked by ropes. They charged us $3.50 for five wagons. They could only take one yoke of cattle and one wagon at a time. The wagon and children all got out of the wagons and stood on the boat. We are camped tonight on the same river. There was a terrible accident happened in a company behind us this evening. Mr. John Milburn was shot. He and Mr. Ralman were fixing to shoot some prairie chickens. Mr. Ralman's gun went off and killed him. All he said was, "Raise me up." They buried him in Frankforde [Iowa].

May 18   We travelled today through some very pretty country, but came over some very bad roads. We are camped tonight in a bottom on a big creek. It looks like everybody has camped here. Just on the other side is a town called White Cloud. They have a mill going here all the time. Ann, Sue Rhyne and I rolled a big log up, made a fire and got supper. After supper the girls and boys went fishing. Frank went over in a tow boat and bought me a paper of needles.

May 19   Mr. Rhyne was sick. He went to the mill to sleep. The man there gave him some fresh fish which he brought to camp and gave Ann and I some for breakfast. We passed through town and on this side is the prettiest cottonwood grove. The trees are all set in rows a quarter of a mile long with a plank fence all around them. We travelled a few miles over nice prairie roads and then into the hills. They are very rough, being cut up with the wagons while muddy. One long hill I never will forget. Frank got out to drive his mean cattle. In spite of all he could do they ran the wagon into a deep rut between two logs. Frankie fell out head foremost close to the fore wheel. I began to scream and got out some way. I thought I could hear the wheels crushing him between the logs but he had crawled out of the way. His little fingers on his left hand were bruised. He said the wheel done it. I was so frightened they had to lift me into the wagon. The crowd gathered around and had lifted him up before I saw him. This evening we had some awful hills to come down. I was afraid some of us would get killed, with the unruly oxen. We came down one long hill, with a high bluff on one side and a big slough on the other; just room for the wagon and driver in the road. It took Frank and At both to drive our team down. We then came out on the river bottom. The roads are awfully cut up. We came through a little town called Glenwood. We stopped and bought flour at the mill. We are camped tonight in flea town, one mile from the river. I have sick headache so bad from my fright I can hardly sit up. Frank made tea and we had tea and crackers for supper.

May 20   A very warm morning. We have to stay here today.
The men have all gone to the river to see when we can cross.
The whole bottom is white with wagons. This is a terrible
town, with five or six punchen houses and a steam saw mill.
The people that live here look half Indians.

Sunday, May 21   We all got our breakfast and then got in
our wagons to write home. Frank and At went up in the
bottom to see the cattle. They saw some families from Clark.
At's acquaintances. They came back, bundled up and went to
where they were. After we got here we all went to see Mrs.
Kerfoot. We saw Miss Milburn, sister of the man that was
killed a few days ago. She was the most distressed looking
person I ever saw. She sold her team and will start back home
Monday.

May 22   A very warm day. I am not very well. The men
have all gone to the river to see when we can cross. I have
been writing to George Shackleford; Ann and Mary have
been writing. Frank and At got us a stove apiece and Frank
bought him and Frankie each a hat.

Tuesday, May 23   We started early to get to the river. The
whole bottom is covered with wagons. It being a very warm
day we all got very tired standing in the sun and sand. Frank,
Mary and Miss Rhynes went over to town and stayed until
the boat came back. We saw two boats land while we were
waiting and one after we crossed. Our time came about noon.
The women and children went on and went upstairs to a nice
little room. Little Mary was almost wild to think she was in a
house. It took me and Miss Rhynes to keep them from
running overboard. There was hardly a place on the boat as
big as my hand but what there was a name. They drove on
eight wagons and teams. The cattle were frightened; I
thought some of them would get hurt. The men sat on the
railing while they were crossing. We came across fine and had
a very steep hill to pull up as we came out. They charged us

$1.50 a wagon to cross. We drove into town [Plattsmouth, NE] and stopped at a tinner's shop. This is a nice town with all kinds of business going on. They have some of the prettiest storehouses I ever saw. They all went around to the stores and left me at the tin shop to watch the children and the cattle so I did not get to see much. Frank's cattle run against a post and would have broken the wagon if some man hadn't unhitched them from the wagon. While I was standing at the shop waiting for them I was looking up the street and who should I see coming from the hotel but Mr. Hillias. I was so glad to see him. They got ready to start about 4 o'clock. We came two miles and camped. We passed one of the best springs I ever saw, with water as cold as ice. We passed three or four houses that were just sticking on the bank and looked like a hard wind would blow them over. We are camped on a creek called Four Mile Creek. We got supper on our new stoves and had the first good bread we have had since we ate up what we baked before we left home.

May 24   Cloudy and misting rain. Frank is going back to town to get some salt and horse hobbles. I have a big washing to do. Mr. Hillias came to camp with Frank and stayed all night.

May 25   Clear and warm. Ann and Miss Rhynes are going to do their washing. We are waiting for Mr. Morrison and Harden.

May 26   We all started together. We passed two or three nice farm houses and corn fields and could see the green corn in rows across the field. This evening Frank's black ox got sick; had to take him out of the yoke and drive him along. We are camped tonight on the prairie about a mile from water, but when we got it was the best kind of spring water. We had to cook with weeds. Ann and I gathered a big load of weeds, then Mary Rhyne and I went to the spring after water to get supper with. It was after dark when we ate supper. We couldn't have done any cooking if we hadn't had stoves. Mrs. Kirklin's little boy is very sick. I don't think he can get well.

May 27   We came ten miles, as far as Salt Creek and had an awful hill to come down. At the creek the women and children had to get out and walk down to the water, then get in. They had to lock both wheels and then some of the men stood on the wheels as they came down. They have a mill on each side of the creek and a town but I didn't hear the name of it. They were washing sheep in the creek when we crossed. We are camped on the banks of the creek. It is a right nice stream with plenty of fish. The water is too salty to use. There is a spring here from which we got water for cooking. There are some of the roughest-looking people camped here I ever did see—women with short dresses and barefooted. Here was the first dirt house I ever saw.

May 28   A very warm, disagreeable day. Some of the women are washing. The boys got in the canoe and went fishing so we had what fish we could catch.

May 29   A very pleasant morning. We all started again. We stopped in town awhile for more of the company to get some black smithing done. Frank bought three yards of cotton. We stopped and took dinner out on the plains. We are camped tonight near a ranch. They have a big dance in a corral just above us. They said it was not worth while to ask any of our crowd for they were all Missourians and would not dance.

May 30   A nice day for travelling; cool and pleasant this evening. In a company behind us some women were in a buggy when the horses took fright and ran off, throwing them out. Some of them had their arms broken and some were hurt other ways. We are camped tonight near a ranch in an awful looking place. There are two women living here. They say their husbands are freighters. Frank is on guard tonight.

May 31   We got up early. It began to rain about the time we got breakfast half ready and rained for an hoiur and a half. We had a wet time. It stopped about ten and then we had a beautiful day. The roads have been very good, only slippery.

Thursday, June 1   We did not get a very early start as they had wagons to fix. We took dinner on Clear Creek, a beautiful stream. The water was as clear as crystal. We got across very well. Some had a big time pulling up the steep sand bank on this side. We are camped tonight on the Platte river bottom in a low, swampy place. There is a ranch here with one of the oddest looking houses I ever did see. It is built of round logs divided into 2 rooms and a very large cellar underneath divided into two rooms. There is no one living here. The family was run off by the Indians. We suppose it was built for the accomodation of travellers and have no doubt but many a one has been murdered there and buried in that dismal cellar for their money. Smith's company have a dance upstairs here tonight. No kind of timber here but cedar.

June 2   We travelled all day along the side of the Platte, a muddy stream that looks like it was running on top of the ground. We passed several ranches that the Indians have burned down. We are camped on the Platte.

June 3   We came ten miles and camped to stay until Monday. It is a very pretty place, but plenty of alkali. We dug a well and the water made some of us sick. The children and I were right sick for awhile. We drank plenty of vinegar and soon got over it. Ann and I done our washing. Frank had to wade the river for wood. It is about 50 yards wide and waist deep in places. We passed two ranches that have been burned by the Indians.

Sunday, June 4   A very pleasant day. We spent the day in reading and talking. This evening the men had an election to elect their captain. They elected Mr. Hardingbrook.

June 5   The bugle awakened us this morning. We all started in company together. We came through some very deep sand. Mr. Kerry stopped at a ranch and bought a bottle of whiskey. He gave us all a dram. We came ten miles and camped close to a ranch. The Indians had run the men off that lived here. We enjoyed ourselves till ten o'clock and then went to bed.

June 6   We had a fright last night. About midnight a man came to camp and reported that Indians had fired into their camp. At awakened Frank to go with him after his horses. It began to thunder and lightning with the appearance of a hard storm. The men all got out and chained the wagons down to keep them from blowing over. I had to get up and tack the sheet down on the wagon. I thought the wind would blow me off. Frank got back about daybreak and saw no Indians. We travelled up the Platte, passed two or three mud houses. We camped early and got our work done up before dark.

June 7   Cool and cloudy. We all started again. We stopped for dinner in front of a ranch where one man lived and kept groceries. They turned the cattle out. It began to rain very hard and some of the cattle ran off. We had to stay three or four hours until they found them. We came three miles, roads very slippery. Camped for the night.

June 8   Cool and clear. Nothing worth relating has occurred today. We all got along very well. We camped for the night, got supper and sat around as usual, the men all in a huddle, talking and whittling with their knives.

June 9   We stopped about noon to stay until morning. We heard they would not let us pass through Carney [Kearney] with less than a hundred men.

June 10   They stayed here until ten o'clock talking about what they would do and started. We passed below the town. They would not let us go through. I saw two long houses. I suppose it is their fort. Plenty of soldiers there. We passed through a village called Dogtown.[1] We then came through another town called Doby. I sent a letter to the office by the Captain for Bettie. He brought me three letters. The girls are all at Mrs. Mays' wagon to hear her play the guitar.

June 11   We travelled today the first Sunday since we left home. It does not appear much like Sunday. We passed several sod houses. Some have been torn down by the Indians. We women walked a long way this evening. It is cool and pleasant. The girls are gathering flowers to make bouquets for the boys. We are camped on the Platte and here are the ruins of another house the savages have burned. The stage just passed with a large escort of soldiers with it. The girls and those who can sing are enjoying themselves singing. We all went to bed expecting at any time to hear the Indians yell.

June 12   A cloudy morning, misting rain. Just after we started we met a man coming back in full speed, who told us a company on ahead was surrounded by the Indians. Our captain ordered all to drive up close and be in readiness and not to be frightened. Every man had his revolver buckled on and his gun on his shoulder. His ox whip was in his hand. We marched with our eyes stretched but when we got there they had crossed the river below where we had camped the night before. The roads have been very rough. We passed the graves of eleven men this evening that were killed by the Indians last year. They were all in one grave close by a telegraph post. We passed a large fort on Plum Creek. They say the Indians are dreadful bad and from the appearance of things it is true. Soldiers think they have a telegraph office here. They had a little straw bridge to cross. They said they would charge the company three dollars for crossing on it. We are camped not far from the river. About sundown we had a shower of rain.

---

[1]This town was called both Dogtown and Georgetown. It was later changed to Glenville. Lilian L. Fitzpatrick, *Nebraska Place Names* (Lincoln, 1960), pp. 42-43.

June 13   Nothing of importance happened today. We all got along very well. We are camped on the Platte by a ranch.

June 14   We all started out as usual. Everything looks alike. We are camped on the muddy Platte on the other side; ragged bluffs; in some places tall cedars.

June 15   A very warm day. We passed the graves of several that have died on the road. It is very windy though not dusty. This evening the boys started up a jack rabbit and ran it to the bluffs, Van with them. We never saw him any more. Frank went back to look for him as far as it was safe for him to go. We are camped tonight between the river and the high bluffs. Just as we got supper ready the blackest cloud rose. The captain ordered the men to corral the cattle. They all started and before they got half way to them the wind was blowing, it was thundering and lightning and the rain came down in torrents. The cattle stampeded and ran into the bluffs. I never was so badly scared in my life. We all had the wagons chained down but expected they would blow over. The storm lasted an hour and a half. I got wringing wet trying to keep the sheet up in the wagon door. I was so glad when I heard Frank speak. The storm was over when they got in. Frank has to stand guard tonight. He said it made him think of the thunders of Mount Sinai.

June 16   We travelled till noon and stopped to stay until tomorrow to dry our wagons and to do some washing. We passed through Cottonwood. It is a very pretty little town; nice hewn log houses. The soldiers were re-covering their houses with sod. Frank put a letter in the office for George. We put our things out to dry. In an hour a black cloud rose. We thought we were going to have another storm but it was only a gentle shower.

June 17   A very warm day. Some of our cattle are gone. They are hunting them. The girls have gone up on the mountains to look for flowers. After dinner, Ann, Mary, Mrs. Kerry and I took a walk up on the mountains; Frank was up there getting wood. Mrs. Kirklin [Kirkland] stayed at the wagon with her little boy. He is not well yet. I never expected to see such sights in my life. We went up on one about 200 feet high and looked down on the tall cedars in the valley. Mary and I started up to a cedar tree on the top of one but the wind blew so hard we could not climb. We got wood to last some time. I was so tired when we got down I thought I could not get to camp. We met Frank coming after us. He thought the Indians had taken us. We got to camp about sun down. They had just got in with the cattle.

Sunday, June 18   We started early and drove five miles, then stopped and got breakfast. I have a sick headache and cannot sit up. We stayed until the cattle got their fill of grass. We passed the grave of a young man who shot himself last week. He was laid close by the roadside. We passed the junction house,[2] the finest and largest house we have seen since we left. It was built of cedar. We had a shower of rain about noon. We are camped alone by a ranch. I still have a sick headache. The captain's wife made me a cup of soup but I was too sick to eat it. Mrs. Walker has it also. The doctor has given her some medicine. The girls are singing to pass away the time.

June 19th   We started early and it being cool and pleasant we got along fine. We passed the grave of a lady, Mrs. Rachel Drain, who died May 19, age 40 years. It makes me feel so sad to see a lone grave here in this doleful looking country and kneel at the head to read the name. I can't keep from crying, thinking how I would hate to be left on this road. We

---

[2]Near the confluence of the North and South forks of the Platte was a famous ranch named Junction House. It was thought of as being half way between Omaha and Denver. Merrill Mattes is glowing in his description of the owner of the ranch, Jack Morrow. *The Great Platte River Road* (Lincoln, 1969), pp. 276-277.

are camped tonight on the banks of the Platte. About sundown the prairie dogs raised such a fuss. The girls and boys went out to see them but they all ran into their dens and they didn't get to see any. They then came back and enjoyed themselves in singing as usual.

June 20   A very pleasant morning. the women all walked a long way to see what they could. We are camped on the banks of the Platte where there is not a stick of timber to be seen. Nothing but the bluffs on one side and the bare plain on the other. There is plenty of alkali. Just as soon as they unhitch the cattle from the wagon they run them to good water and then they don't drink the alkali. We have none sick yet. Where it is bad we counted as many as 25 lying around. The young folks are fiddling and singing.

June 21   We travelled on till noon and stopped on the banks of the river for dinner. The girls are gathering water grass and plating it for employment. We are camped on the river.

June 22   An awful warm day. The women all walked as long as they could stand the sun. We passed two graves on the side of the road with no names on them. We travelled along the banks of the river in about ten feet of water. The girls walked along the bank throwing clods in the river for a dog to jump in after. They seem to enjoy the trip fine. We are camped tonight eight miles from Julesburg, [Colorado]. The men tried a shot at an antelope but it bounded away.

June 23   We started on the march again. We came over some very bad hills and sand and passed one grave on the roadside. We met about sixty soldiers with some Indian prisoners they had taken in a fight near Laramie and were taking them to Carney. There were some squaws and papooses. The squaws were on horseback with a pole, one end of which was tied to their shoulder, the other end on the ground. The papooses were tied on the pole. We stopped on a dry sandy place for dinner. There is a grave here, a Mr. Kingman, who shot himself. They drove the cattle across the river to get grass. It was a half mile across and very deep in places. We stood on the banks and watched them cross. Some of the men waded in water up to their necks. They had a big time getting them back. We passed a place where the Indians and whites had had a fight. One grave had 17 men in it. We passed a ranch and some of the company said they saw two dead Indians in it. We then came to Julesburg. It was not what I expected to see—a few sod houses and plenty of soldiers. They would not let us have any water to put in our kegs. They had a beat made between the road and ranch with a soldier with gun and bayonet stationed there. He would not let anyone cross his beat. They were just starting a company of soldiers out to fight the Indians. We are camped tonight not far from Julesburg.

June 24   We started very early. Soon after we started it began to rain and hail, though it lasted only a few minutes. Just behind us was the worst hail storm we ever saw. Some of the hail measured 13 inches around. It knocked a man down twice and liked to have killed some of their horses. The women had to get under the wagons. It tore the sheets full of holes. This evening is cool. The girls are walking, having a fine time running lizards. I never saw the like of grasshoppers in my life. The ground is covered with them. The men have shot a jack rabbit. They have never killed any anteloupes yet. The ground is covered with prickly pears. We passed the ruins of an old fort which the Indians have destroyed. They attacked a train of wagons, which ran into the fort. The Indians then burned the fort and 25 wagons. The people fled for their lives. It occurred last winter. We are camped tonight where there has been a very large ranch burned by the Indians.

Sunday, June 25   A very pleasant morning. Most of the women are washing. After breakfast I watched the children and then wrote a letter to Mrs. Sours. Frank went up on the bluffs to gather buffalo chips to get supper with. At three o'clock this evening two Methodist preachers came up from a camp below us. One of them preached for us from Revelation, third chapter and 20th verse.[3] After the preaching we all got supper. I had batter cakes, molasses and coffee for supper.

June 26   The captain called us before day to get ready to start. Everything looks as usual, dry and dusty, with sand about a foot deep. I have been patching my old dress. We stopped for dinner. Ann and I washed while we were there. We are camped tonight in a low, swampy bottom, with the appearance of a storm. Frank is on guard. They have to corral the cattle.

June 27   A very pleasant morning. We travelled through very deep sand. We stopped for dinner in the bottom. It is very warm. Frank is noon herder and the children are enjoying themselves fine. Ann is quite sick. The bugle blows for them to bring the cattle in. It began to thunder in the west, with the appearance of a hard storm. We travelled on until night, corraled the cattle, got supper and to bed.

June 28   Ann is better. We got our breakfst and started. Frank has a very bad headache. I tried to drive the team but have no whip stock and they won't mind me. We came over one sand hill with the sand almost to the hubs. Most of the wagons had to double team. Part of the road was very narrow, just room to pass between the high bluffs and the river. We stopped for dinner. I made Frank a cup of tea and he layed down and took a nap. His headache is much better. Ann's baby is very sick and she had to have the doctor. About 60

---

[3] "Behold, I stand at the door and knock: if any man hear my voice, and open the door, I will come in to him, and will sup with him, and he with me."

soldiers passed the camp just now. The bugle blows for the cattle and we start. Of all the windy evenings I ever saw this is the worst. We camped for the night but the wind was so high we could not get supper. The girls had to sit still. The men seemed to enjoy it fine, to see the ladies' dresses blow. We have crackers and water for supper. Ann's baby is no better. The doctor came to see her again.

June 29   Calm but cloudy. Frank is still complaining. I had to get out of the wagon and walk to get warm. I have been gathering flowers to send back home. The girls are out walking with their beaus. We came over some very rough, sandy road. We had to cross a very ugly slough. Our wagons came near turning over. Frank had to jump out in the water to turn the oxen. We passed a ranch where we had to pay 50¢ a wagon for toll. We stopped and began to corral for dinner. A soldier came running up and would not let us stop. They wanted the grass for their horses. We drove on a mile or two further and stopped. We all sat around talking until the bugle blows for the cattle. One of Mr. Morrison's oxen got poisoned. They gave him some vinegar and lard and he soon got over it. We are camped tonight in a beautiful bottom, with grass knee high. As soon as we stopped I got out and milked the cow, which is the first thing I always do after we stop. I then went and gathered a load of wood to get supper with. Frank went to the river after water. After supper we cooked some bacon and beans, stewed some apples, baked bread for tomorrow. The girls and boys are sitting around the fire laughing and talking, some singing and some playing guitars and fiddles. Frank and I sat by the fire till half past ten and then went to bed.

June 30   This morning was as clear as crystal. We are in view of the Rocky Mountains. Our captain says we are 150 miles from them. They seem to be covered with snow. Frank is so hoarse he can hardly speak. The roads are very dusty. We camped for dinner and part of the company take other roads, some to Denver and some to Oregon. Frank gave a young man 1$ [2 unreadable words] to help him drive the team. His name is George Mays. We ate our dinner   are started. It is very warm and the roads are very sandy and dusty. Mr. Harden's team ran off with the wagon and came very near running into the river. Att and Mr. Sheridan caught them. They both hurt their ankles in the race. We came by two very nice looking ranches this evening. Frank stopped to get some ink but they had none. We camped for the night. I milked the cow and Frank gathered buffalo chips. Ann's baby is worse and they had to have the doctor again. After supper the captain came around and told us we must start before breakfast in the morning. We fix up everything and go to bed.

Saturday, July 1   Our captain called us up before daybreak. We came six miles through sand and came down one sand hill about 50 feet long to the river, where we cross at Freement's orchard.[4] We got breakfast and after we ate went up on the bluffs about 50 feet to watch the wagons crossing. After we got tired looking at them we took a look at the snow covered mountains and then went down. I went to washing while they were ferrying the wagons. We had to take everything out and put them on the floor to keep them dry. About 11 o'clock they get ready to cross. I gathered up my clothes and put them in the tub. Frank tied his wagon and Mr. Rhynes together and put eight yoke of cattle to them. The children and I and Miss Rhynes got in our wagon and started into the river. It was a mile wide and swift as could be. Where we started the water was over the wagon bed and when we got half way across the water was over the oxens' backs. We all got

---

[4]See the "Table of Distances" for the stage line in *Covered Wagon Women*, vol. VIII, pp. 11-12.

across safe and had a very steep hill to pull up on this side. As soon as we got across I went to washing. Frank and the boys took the oxen back after Att's two wagons and brought them across. The wagons were crossing all day and some crossed after dark. Ann and I and Miss Rhynes done our washing this evening. After I got through Frank and I reloaded our wagon, then got supper. Frank went out to milk the cow. They came for Frank to stand guard but he is not well enough and they let him off. We are camped tonight with the Platte on our left, close to the river. There are about 200 wagons here and stock out of all reason.

Sunday, July 2   This morning is calm and cloudy. I got up about sunrise and got breakfast. We will stay here until Monday. Frank went to look for the cow. Some of the cattle are gone. Frank is better. Most of the women are washing. I have never washed on Sunday yet. After breakfast, Frank gathered me a load of buffalo chips to get dinner. I cooked some bacon beans, and light rolls and baked a great big molasses cake. After dinner Frank took a nap. I baked light bread and toasted coffee. Ann and the Miss Rhynes are baking light bread. Att has been asleep all day. Of all the whooping and hallooing, I never heard the like. Some of the men went hunting and killed three anteloupes. Mrs. Hazelwood gave me enough for breakfast. This has turned out to be a very warm day. There is preaching in another camp close by. Frank, Mary and Miss Rhynes have gone. Ann and I stayed with the children. Frank says he heard a good Baptist sermon, text: "I am not ashamed of the Gospel of Christ." [Romans 1:16]

July 3   A very pleasant morning, cool and clear. The bugle awakened before daybreak. I got up and got breakfast. Frank went to look for the cattle. I had some anteloupe steak for breakfast, the best meat I ever ate. While we were at breakfast a Missourian gave me a bucket of milk, which was very acceptable. We are in plainer view of the snow covered mountains. We have all hurried to get ready to start this morning. At last we are all ready and there are about 200 wagons starting. There are two large corrals on the other side that will start today. We came over awful sandy, dusty roads today. I have seen nothing new except some trees which is a right smart sight to us. We came up one sand hill and the most of the company had to double team to get up. We stopped for dinner and turned the cattle on a very nice bottom to feed. Att went hunting and killed two anteloupes. Frank has just got through cleaning. Matt has laid down under the wagon to sleep. Ann is in the wagon patching a shirt. My children are all under our wagon in the shade. Mr. Morrison is shoeing oxen. Ann and I took our kegs and went a quarter of a mile to get some water. They then yoked up and started, with the sun shining as hot as it ever did in old Missouri. We only came six miles this evening—over awful roads with sand about two feet deep and up hill at that. The women all had to get out and walk. Ann has to drive the horse team through as Att had gone hunting. We went down the river to get out of the hot sun but the buffalo gnats soon made us get away from there. I was almost given out when we got through. We passed one ranch but no one was living there. One of the men said he saw three Indians there when he came up but none of our company saw them. We are camped tonight in a beautiful bottom with grass waist high to the men. They feel uneasy on account of the Indians as it is a good place for them. There are about 100 wagons here, with the river on our left and the bluffs on the right. Frank unyoked the cattle and I milked the cow. Att has not come from hunting yet and Ann is very uneasy about him. We got supper. I have biscuits, coffee and anteloupe soup for supper and Ann has the same. I cleaned up the children and put them to bed. The boys came in with one anteloupe. Ann got Att's supper and we all sat down in the grass and talked until bed time.

July 4 A beautiful morning, but very warm. After breakfast, we started and the sand was still deep. We passed one corral that had laid over to celebrate the Fourth and to celebrate a young one that came to camp the night before. The sand was so deep we only came six miles and stopped for the cattle to rest. I walked a long way and gathered some roots to cook with. We came down one sand hill almost straight up and down. We stopped right on the river bank, unyoked the cattle and drove them over the river on an island to get feed. I washed some clothes and cooked some bacon and beans and stewed some apples. Ann scoured her buckets and the girls made a swing and enjoyed themselves for awhile. It is the worst day we have had since we left home. The boys all went in swimming. We all got ready to start again and found the roads rough but not sandy. Att had a chill and is very sick. I have been doing some patching. We are camped on the prettiest bottom we have been camped in yet, with a pretty cottonwood grove on the river, a sight we are not used to seeing. We got our supper. It has turned very cool and is misting rain. After supper Frank greased the wagons, then he and I took our keg and went for water and wood for morning. The children have a play home by the wagon and are playing like they did at home. Sue Rhyne is sitting under the wagon writing in her journal. The other girls have gone to take a walk and gather flowers. Ann is nursing her babe.

July 5 A very pleasant morning, cool and cloudy. Att is better. I have a headache and don't feel well. We got our breakfast and started. The roads have been tolerable good. We got along fine. Some of the men have gone hunting. We passed two nice hewn log houses but no one was living in them. We then came to a house full of Indians. Some of the

girls went to see them and they said they looked clean and nice
and had some furniture. They wanted nothing but a large
looking glass. They said they were good Soo Indians. We
stopped for dinner on a dry, sandy place and it don't look like
the stove can get anything to heat. I feel very bad. Frank
made me a cup of coffee and I feel some better. Sue and I took
a walk to the river and the prickly pears were so thick we
could hardly walk. The children all have to stay in the
wagons to keep them from getting their feet stuck. Frank
took a nap and I have been writing. The bugle blows for the
cattle and they yoke up and start. The wind is blowing very
hard. A very black cloud is rising and it has the appearance of
a storm. While we were at dinner ten or twelve men rode by.
They said they were on their way from California after their
families. We passed the ferry this evening where they have to
pay five dollars a wagon to cross. We are camped tonight in a
very ugly place and scarcely enough grass for the stock. Just
as I had supper ready it began to rain and the blackest I ever
saw came up. We were afraid we were going to have a bad storm
but it is clearing off now.

July 6   Cool and cloudy with some rain last night. We all got
ready to start. We leave the Platte and are travelling up Castor
Pool [Cache la Poudre], a very pretty stream, with plenty fish
in it. The roads are good and we travel fast. We have stopped
for dinner in a dry looking place. We passed two ranches but
no one was living in them. We are in sight of the Black Hills.
Our captain says we will get there tomorrow. Frank is shoeing
his black ox. We started again. I just finished making Frankie
a blue cotton waist, then took a nap, after which I drove the
team so Frank could sleep. We passed three ranches this
evening. I can't tell how they make a living in this doleful
looking country. We are camped tonight in a beautiful place
with a nice bottom for stock to run on. A big patch of wheat in
the bottom is just heading out. We are near the Black Hills

and saw it rain in torrents this evening with thunder and lightning but it only sprinkled where we were. We had fish, caught out of Castor Pool, for supper tonight. Frank is on guard tonight.

July 7 A pleasant morning cool and cloudy. We all got ready and started over the prettiest place I ever saw, up Castor Pool. There are ranches all along the banks, with nice wheat fields. Mary, Sue Rhyne and I got out and went down to the banks. The prettiest trees are growing here and the sweetest perfumes. Some said it came from Balm of Gilead.[5] About 5 feet under the bank we saw the clearest water running out from under the rocks but it was not good. The ground is covered with prairie dog hills and they come out and bark at us and dart in again. Just before we stopped for dinner we passed through a place where the grass was very high. We had to cross a very small stream and just as we got across four Indian squaws stuck their heads up out of the grass. Some of the women went and shook hands with them. We stopped for dinner on a creek. The water is clear but no good. It is sweet and greasy. After dinner Ann went to a ranch to trade off their lame cow. I look in the wagon for the bullets Frank lost. They yoked up to start. Frank and I took a look through the spyglass at the snow-covered mountains. The snow looks like it had just fallen. We have nice roads and passed one ranch where the stars and stripes were floating over it. Mr. Kirkland killed a prairie dog and we all had to take a look at it. They look more like a squirrel than a dog. We passed three Indian camps with many Indians in them. Women got out and went to see them but for my part I can see enough of them from the wagon. They said they were frying fish. We are camped tonight at the foot of the Black Hills and what sights! Frank and Att had gone back after some of their

---

[5]The black cottonwood tree.

cattle the boys left behind. George got me some nice pine wood to get a supper with. Frank has come back and is now shoeing his cow. Her feet are worn out so he cannot work her. The girls have gone up on the hills to see what they can. I am sitting on the wagon tongue thinking about the folks in old Missouri.

July 8   I got up early and the moon looked like it was lying on top of the hill. I feel very bad. We got breakfast over and Ann, Mary and the Miss Rhynes went up on the hills. I stayed at the wagons with the children. We started out through the hills and passed some houses, wheat fields and one saw mill. They have ditches dug to water the fields. The girls have come back. Ann says she wouldn't have missed the sights she saw for anything. She saw corn fields, nice gardens and houses. The hills seem miles high and are covered with cedar and rocks as large as houses, some of them almost square and look like someone had taken particular pains in placing them there. The soil and roads look like they have been burned. It makes me think of the crucufixon, when the rocks rent. Just before we stopped for dinner we passed a little grave on the roadside. A nice rock was laid on each side, with the edges together, one at the head and one at the foot, with the name and age cut on it: "T.T. Thail, age one year." We stopped for dinner in a small valley with hills on each side and no water for the stock. I feel very bad and can hardly sit up. The roads today have been awfully hilly and rocky. Frank's cattle being unruly, we would come down hill a teaming. I thought we would smash up. We stopped awhile to rest the cattle. We passed some of the prettiest hills this evening. You can't imagine how they looked. I counted four in the shape of houses, all in a row. The largest one with a smaller one at one end, looked like a church with a cupola. Some are round and very high with steps all around them. We counted five different colored rocks, which were placed so nice they looked almost like hewn logs. We are camped tonight in a pretty little valley with plenty of grass and water, the water running down from the mountains as clear as crystal. While I was getting supper a group of soldiers came bearing down out of the mountains on their way to Fort Halleck.[6] After supper Frank and I went a quarter of a mile from camp to get wood. We got some dry cedar and walked over rocks that were like walking over a house flu. I still feel sick. We sat around the wagon talking until bed time.

Sunday, July 9   A beautiful morning. We are going to stay here until Monday. After breakfast Frank and I went for water. We found a spring running from under a big rock with water as clear as any snow water. After dinner the girls and boys took a walk up on the mountains. They could hardly walk   they said they never expected to see such giants. They could hardly climb up for the rock. The boys had to pull them up. One of the boys found a mountain sheep's horn. That beat all the horns you ever heard of. It weighed ten pounds. It was carried all around the corral for a show. This evening Frank and Att took a yoke of cattle and went for wood to take with us.

July 10   The bugle awakened us before day. We fixed up and started over the hilliest, rockiest roads you ever saw. We passed a grave on the side of the road. I got out of the wagon to see the name: "John Thomas, died, 63". We stopped for dinner in a dry looking valley. After dinner we started out again with the roads rockier than ever. Although I have a very bad headache I had to get out and walk to look at the pretty rocks and fine trees. I gathered some fine burrs for the children. We passed another grave this evening. I went to see the name but it was so dim I could not read it. I think it was

---

[6]Fort Halleck, Carbon Co., Wyoming, was a post stop of the overland stage established in 1862. It was abandoned in 1866. Mae Urbanek, *Wyoming Place Names* (Missoula, MT, 1988), p. 70

T. Wibbler. Tonight we camped in an ugly place with high mountains all around us. I am too sick to sit up. I cannot get out of the wagon. I can see one rock in front of our wagon in the shape of a sugar loaf, about 100 feet high. Just before we passed a ranch and post-office, with soldiers stationed there.

July 11   Cool and cloudy. I am still sick and not able to sit up. I have been taking medicine from the doctor. The company was right smartly frightened last night. The horses stampeded and ran. They thought the Indians were coming. We travelled over hills and rocks this morning until I thought my head would burst. I would sit up in the wagon and hold my head with both hands. We stopped for dinner in a valley where we have plenty of water for the cattle. After dinner we left the hills and are now on the Laramie plain. The roads have been good, except some hills. We passed one ranch and just as we got to it we had a big hill to come down. Frank's cattle ran off down hill as hard as they could go. We came near having a smash-up with Att's horse wagon. I don't know where they would have gone to if some man had not run in before them. We are camped tonight in a very pretty place between a big alkali pond and a nice running stream with a spring close by, water as cold as in one of the mountain streams. A loose cow drank at this pond and died in about 15 minutes. I am still very sick. Mary Rhyne made up my bread for supper.

July 12   I feel some better and am able to get out of the wagon. We all started again and got along very well with nothing out of the ordinary. About 11 o'clock we crossed the Big Laramie ar.d are camped on it now to stay until morning on account of there being no water and grass that we could get to. This is a nice river and runs very swift; the water is clean as can be. They had a bridge to take the teams across and charged $2.50 a wagon. We thought it cheaper to ford. The water was nearly to the wagon beds. Ann and the Miss Rhynes are washing. I am not well enough to wash. Frank put a letter in the post-office for cousin. Frank was on guard tonight and liked to have been ate up by the mosquitoes.

July 13   The bugle awakened us before daybreak and we got breakfast by moonlight. It is cold enough to wear a shawl. This morning we passed a big alkali pond, about 20 feet wide and 50 feet long and looks like ice. The snow covered mountains are on one side of us and the bare plains on the other. We have stopped for dinner in a dry looking place with not a drop of water for man or beast. We have travelled today over very rocky roads. About three o'clock this evening we passed a ranch where they had fresh meat for sale. Mr. Hazelwood got out of his wagon to get some, giving the lines to his little girl to hold. The horses got scared and run off, with his sick wife in the wagon. The wagon was broke and we have to stay here until they get it fixed. We are camped on the Little Laramie, in the Indian country. The guards said they saw 10 or 12 last night.

July 14   Our company is left here alone, waiting for Mr. Hazelwood to get his wagon fixed. He got it done about 11 o'clock. They yoked up to start and just as we were ready to start his little girl ran under the oxen after her pet crow. The ox kicked her on the forehead and cut a gash about two inches long. The doctor wanted to sew it up but her mother said she could not bear to hear her cry. We started and it began to rain. We stopped to stay until morning. The roads today have been very rocky. They call this the Laramie plain, but I think the right name would be Rocky plain. We are camped in sight of a very large lake. I never heard the name of it. I am still sick and feel very bad.

July 15   Still raining. They drove in the cattle to start and about half of them are sick. They all got better and they are

now yoking up ready to start. Mrs. Kirkland is very sick and
the doctor has been to see her. We came eight miles and
camped for the night. We crossed two branches with the
clearest water from the mountains. The roads have been
awfully rocky, almost jolts us out of the wagon. We passed
one grave but there was no name on it. There is a ranch on the
branch. We are camped in a valley between the mountains
with but little grass for the stock but plenty of alkali. The
women who were well enough went to cooking. Ann cooked
some bacon and beans, stewed some apples and baked light
bread. I have the same except the beans. I have apple
dumplings. My children, Mrs. Kirkland's and Mrs. Mortin-
sen's are having a supper in front of our wagon on an ox yoke.
I have been making Mary a bonnet and am now going down
to see Mrs. Kirkland, who is still sick. Frank has gone to
milk. Some of the cattle are sick yet.

Sunday, July 16   They awakened us before daybreak and we
got breakfast. The captain told us he would only make a short
drive and stop for the day but we travelled until one o'clock
before we stopped for dinner. We all got dinner and they are
yoking up to start again. We travelled through some pretty
country today, with mountains on each side. On one side they
are covered with tall pine trees, on the other nothing but
weeds and rocks. The roads have been too rocky to talk
about. I had to get out of the wagon, sick as I am, and walk to
keep from getting my breath knocked out. We crossed Rock
Creek and it has the right name. I never saw the like of rocks
in my life. They have a bridge at the ranch and charged 75¢
a wagon to cross. It was up to the hubs and awful rocky. Att
had to jump out in the water to turn Frank's mean cattle. We
came on two miles and stopped for dinner. We passed one
corral in which I counted 50 children from Maggie's size
down. It is called the Pilgrim Train. I had some gooseberries

and snow. Mary Rhyne and I went down to the branch to see the snow water running from the mountains. There is plenty of wood on the branch. We came six miles this evening over tolerable good roads, except two or three big rocky hills. We are camped tonight where there is no water for the cattle. This evening we saw where the Indians had burned one wagon loaded with wheat, corn, beans and so on.

July 17   This morning we saw where Indians had burned two ranches and some wagons. Today it has been raining so we could not travel. Tonight is so cold we are almost frozen. The men are wrapped up in their overcoats and comforts.

July 18   We started this morning before breakfast and came over some places that looked like it would be impossible to go with the wagons, but we all got along safely. We travelled till ten o'clock and stopped for the day. We are camped on a creek where there is no grass. We have to drive the cattle to the canyons in the mountains to get grass. Frank is on guard. Most of the women have gone to the creek to wash. Some are gathering gooseberries. We have a big log fire to keep us warm. We suffer as much with cold as we did last winter. We could get plenty snow if we wished to tonight. It is cold and raining and very disagreeable and I am sick and feel very bad.

July 19   We travelled over rough, rocky roads until we got to Hallock. After we passed there they were very good except two or three bad places with one very bad place. The women and children had to get out and wait. Fort Hallock is on a little branch. There are eight Indian tents and three or four cabins for the soldiers. They have a postoffice and a store, with a large pen, like the one around the courthouse, which is their fort, I suppose. They had a few round poles across a drain and charged us 50¢ a wagon to cross on them. We came through the most dolefull looking country—down a valley between the mountains—this side of Hallock you ever did see. We met a train of Californians going back. They gave the country an awful name. We are camped tonight on a bottom and have to drive the cattle across the creek to feed. I am too sick to get supper.

July 20   Cold and cloudy. I have been sick in bed all day and have not seen much. We haven't been travelling in the mountains and the roads were nice and level until within a few miles of where we are camped, when we came into the mountains again. It rained very hard this evening. We are camped tonight on the north Platte with mountains on each side, solid rock hundreds of feet high. I am too sick to get out of the wagon and Frank has all the work to do. They have to drive the cattle four miles from camp to get grass and they took 25 men from camp to guard them.

July 21   Still cold and it rained all night. We crossed the river and stopped for the day. The soldiers had a flat boat there and could only take one wagon and one yoke of cattle on at a time. They charged $4 a wagon so our company, except five wagons, all forded. We propped up our wagon beds about six inches and came across very well. The women are all washing and Ann is washing for me. I am too sick to sit up. They have driven the cattle two miles from camp to feed. This is an awful place to camp in. There are four corrals here besides ours. We have 46 wagons in our train.

July 22   It rained all night and is very cold and windy yet we came over such rocky roads I thought it would kill me. We crossed Sage Creek this evening and it was an awful crossing. The wagons would pitch off a log into the water and mud up to the hubs. Att's horse wagon got stuck and had to be pulled out with oxen. One man fell out as he came in but happened not to hurt himself. We are camped tonight at the foot of a mountain, where there is nothing but sage brush. We have to corral the cattle and have nothing for them to eat. It is

Frank's night to stand guard but he could not leave me. It is thundering and raining. Att took his horses and went to the mountains with them to get something to eat. Some of the men got snow and melted it to cook with.

Sunday, July 23   This morning is cold and clear. We started before breakfast, came six miles and stopped for the day. We are camped in the valley and drove the cattle over the mountains to feed. We are camped where the Indians ran 80 head of stock off last week. Two more wagons came into our train today.

July 24   Clear and pleasant. We came over the roughest roads you ever heard of. About 4 o'clock we crossed the top of the Rocky Mountains and are now going down. I am still sick in bed all the time and can't see much. I could not begin to describe how they look on the left and they are beautiful on the right. They are covered with rock and look like they have been placed by a quarrier. We crossed a creek where we had an awful hill to pull up. Frank's oxen came very near upsetting the wagon. We passed Mr. Niel's house and there is not another house within twelve miles of him. The house was built of round poles, two rooms. They have a blacksmith shop and stage and seem to have plenty of work to do. There are five hacks standing there. They have another round pole bridge and charge 50¢ a wagon to cross on it, with 200 wagons crossing there today. We camped about 2 o'clock to stay until morning. We turned the stock out on grass. They had not been there long when the captain of the ranch came up and ordered them to be taken off. They drove them in the corral about dark.

July 25   Clear and cold. It rained last night. There were some loose horses in the corral. They scared the cattle and they stampeded and broke out, breaking one wagon wheel all to smash. We started and came three miles and stopped again for the cattle to eat. We crossed one creek and had a very steep hill to pull up. Att's horse team stalled and had to be pulled up with oxen. Frank pulled up three wagons besides his with his big cattle. The girls and boys went up on the mountains and I crawled to the wagon door to see them, the first time I have been up for eight days. The girls looked like they were about two feet tall, they were so high up. I saw one man standing on top with his gun in his hand and I thought he would fall head foremost. He came down in a hurry. We came 8 miles and camped for the night. We are camped on Mud Creek, near a ranch. They turned the cattle on the bottom to feed. This creek has the right name, as the water is as muddy as can be.

July 26   Clear and pleasant. They are yoking up to start again. We passed a stone house and they have a stone wall all around the lot to keep their horses in. They have stopped now to fill the kegs and to water the cattle. Soldiers are stationed here. We will not get any more water now for 20 miles. We came through the awfulest looking country you ever did see, with not a sprig of grass, just a few sage bushes. We passed another stone house, with soldiers living here. They say this is a God-forsaken country. We are camped tonight in a nasty, dusty place and the dust is four inches deep. The wind blew the dust in our faces all evening and it is half soda. When we wash our hands they feel like we are washing them in soda water. They have to dip water out of a spring with buckets to water two hundred and forty head of cattle and it is three miles to grass.

July 27   The captain says we had better go in small companies on account of grass and water. They talked and studied about it until four o'clock, then twenty-five wagons pulled out and started. We came over the roughest roads and the dust was so thick we could not see ten feet. It is like going through an ash bank. We passed another stone house with the soldiers sitting in front of the door. They looked lonely here in the mountains. Their house and stable are built together on account of the Indians. They have to haul their water six miles. We passed two rocks that were in the shape of a cuppalo. They looked to be about 50 feet high from where we were. One looks like it had two doors in it. On the other side of the road is a mound of dirt in the shape of a hay stack. There is not a drop of water nor a sprig of grass and they corraled the cattle.

July 28   The cattle were so hungry they broke out past the guards. The men had to jump up and run after them. They had not had anything to eat for a day and a night. We started about day-break and came six miles, where we found plenty of grass. They got breakfast and will start at one o'clock this evening. Today is the first time I have been up for days and I am so weak I cannot stand alone. The mountains are almost gone and I am so glad for I am so tired of tumbling down hill in the wagon. Att is sick and Frank has to take his horses out to the herd. We came through the most doleful looking country this evening you ever heard of. The dust is about six inches thick and our faces look like we have been wallowing in ashes. You would laugh to see Fank. We crossed Bitter Creek, a nasty looking stream. The water looks green and is poison. They say one of the loose cattle got mired in the creek and had to be pulled out with ropes. There is a stone house just this side with three rooms and a porch and a stone wall around the lot. I saw one very nice looking lady here. We came over one place this evening where there was just room for the wagon to pass between high bluffs, with nothing growing but sage brush. That is what they have to cook with. It is the best kind of stove wood. We have plenty of good spring water. They have to water all their stock at the spring.

They talk of staying until Monday on account of sickness. I can sit up some. They have to drive the stock three miles to get grass. Our old captain is camped a few yards below us.

July 29   Clear and cold, with ice on the water in buckets. Some of the women are washing and some cooking. I am not able to do anything. Just now a terrible accident happened to Miss Rhyne. She had set some salt raising [bread] and just as it began to raise one of the horses turned it over. Ann divided ours with her and we all had a nice pone of light bread. This evening is very warm. Frank has to go on guard at three o'clock and will be on till seven in the morning.

Sunday, July 30   They have driven in the cattle and are going to start. The sick are some better. Frank says he had a fine time last night. They killed a jack rabbit and cooked it. We came through the awfulest looking country, the whole earth looks like it had been burned. The road which we are travelling in is like ashes and the wind blows all the time. Our faces and hands feel like lime was on them. Our old captain passed us this morning before we started. We caught up with them and travelled on together as we have done before until they stopped for dinner. We drove on. We passed a stage station. The house was built of rock and the windows they have in their houses are about eight inches square, I suppose on account of the Indians, but by the goodness of God we haven't had any trouble with them yet. The stage runs now without guards but awhile back there was an escort of 20 to 50 soldiers with it. Then we felt more afraid. Our captain wouldn't let us have a light in our wagons at night. We are camped tonight on Bitter Creek. The water is clear but very bad, though it is all we have. Oh! how I do wish for a drink out of our old well in Shelbyville. There is nothing growing here but sagebrush. We are thankful for that although they have to drive the stock two miles to grass.

July 31   My birthday. I was very sick all night but I feel some better this morning. We started out again through this dreadful looking country. Ten wagons are all we have together now, all that were bound for Oregon, six families in all. We passed another station and I can't tell how they content themselves to stay in this country with nothing to interest one at all. You can't imagine how the bare mountains look, covered with rock and in the valleys sage brush. They say we have to drive the cattle two or three miles over the mountains where they get plenty of bunch grass. We passed a company of packers with their ponies packed down. We stopped for dinner and to water and the cattle, with not a mouthful for them to eat. Frank is shoeing one of Att's oxen. I am very sick. We passed another company of packers from the mines. We are camped on Bitter Creek and the water is just running. The banks are about 20 feet straight down and there are only two places the stock can get down to water. One of Att's horses got mired in the quick sand and had to be pulled out with ropes. They say there is a bitter weed growing on the creek that is very poisonous.

Tuesday, Aug. 1   Windy and cold enough to sit by a big fire. They have driven in the cattle and had to take two or three down at a time to water. One of Mr. Hazelwood's horses got mired in the quicksand and Frank had to pull it out with his big oxen. We passed a very nice looking ranch with a large stone stable on one side of the road and the house on the other. We saw one lady there. We have stopped to fill our kegs out of the sulphur spring. They all brag on the water being so good but as for me I can hardly drink it. We caught up with another train and I thought the dust would choke us. Sometimes the dust was so think we could not see any of the cattle but the wheel cattle. These are the roughest roads we have come over since we left the Black Hills. We crossed

Bitter Creek again and it was an awful crossing. The wagons were almost straight up and down. We are camped tonight with Bitter Creek on our left. They drove the cattle two miles over the mountains to get grass. They say they can get plenty but to look at them it don't look like there was a sprig of anything growing on them. The cattle all look well though. This evening just before we camped a white man and an Indian squaw passed us going to Virginia City on pack horses. They had two horses packed with their provisions and clothing. She was riding like a man with a little one in her lap.

August 2   Clear and cold. I was very sick all night and haven't been up since Sunday. The mountain fever is a mean, low, lingering fever. We passed a grave on the side of the road. I could not go to see the name. It is a doleful place to be left in. We passed a ranch. We have been travelling up a valley today about 50 feet wide, with the high, ragged mountains on each side. We are camped tonight at a ranch by a spring, 30 miles from the Sulphur Springs. The water is so bad and I am worse and can't sit up at all. There is another lone grave a piece from where we are camped. They drove the cattle two miles over the mountains to feed. There are two wagons here. Their mules are all gone and they are left.

Aug. 3   Clear and cold, with ice on the water. My fever is rising. I am lying in bed writing. Frank has all the cooking to do. They drove the cattle but did not find grass until this morning. We will have a very late start. They have concluded to stay here today on account of sickness. This evening Att went to hunt grass. He found a spring about five miles from where we are camped. He yoked up and we went there. As soon as they stopped Frank went and got me some water and I drank as much as they would let me have. I then got to perspiring and went to sleep. Just as I had got to sleep Ann came to the wagon and said: "Ruth, did you hear that terrible accident that happened just now?" That scared me into a chill. I thought some of our company had been killed. There were three wagons started after us. They were about two miles behind us and two of the men had a fuss before they started. Frasier got his hatchet out to knock his wagon tire on and the other man thought he got his revolver out to shoot him and shot him three times and then went back to the ranch. One of the men came for some of our men but none of them went. They put him in a wagon and brought him to where we are. They drove the wagon with the dead man in it right in front of our wagon and I could not look out without seeing him.

Aug. 4   About ten o'clock they layed him out on some ox yokes, straightened him, brushed off his clothes, covered him with a white sheet and he lay there until 3 o'clock. It rained very hard. They wrapped him in a brown blanket and buried him. Frank cut his name on a rock to put at his head. He had a little boy with him and left a wife and six children at home. The doctor caught up with us this evening and he seemed to be surprised to find his patients worse. He gave me more quinine.

Aug. 5   They are waiting for the sick to get better. Nothing of importance happened. I have been very sick all day.

Sunday, Aug. 6   Clear and pleasant. I am no better. Frank has his hands full with all the cooking to do and me and the children to wait on.

Aug. 7   We came as far as Green River, a nice stream, with water as clear as can be and running very swift. They had to raise the wagon beds to cross.

Aug. 8   I am still sick and feel very sad. The doctor told Frank he would have to stop travelling with me or I could not stand it many days longer. Ann and the Miss Rhynes are washing. Mary Rhyne washed some for me. Frank cut my hair off short and thinned it out as best he could.

Aug. 9   I have more fever and feel worse. They are all sitting around and look very much discouraged.

Aug 10   I feel a little better. The wagons are passing us all the time, going on.

Aug. 11   I still feel a little better. Nothing of interest has occurred today, only they have been feasting on currant tarts all the time.

Aug. 12   I feel better though very weak. Frank lifted me out on the wagon and put me on a bed in the shade. The mountains look worse than ever.

Sunday, Aug. 13   I have no fever, though I am very weak. About 12 o'clock today Nellie Kerford died. Frank is making her a coffin.

Aug. 14   A very warm day. Nellie was buried about 11 o'clock on the banks of Green River, close to a ranch.

Aug. 15   Mary Gatewood is sick. Att got some medicine for her. We all started this morning and left our old captain on the campground with his wife's brother and little girl. He is expecting his wife to die every hour. We travelled today over very rough roads in the valley, with high mountains on each side. We are camped tonight on Black Fork, a very nice bottom.

Aug. 16   I am very weak. Mary is no better. We came over rough roads and passed a ranch where they had butter to sell at $1.25 a pound. We crossed Ham's Fork   took the wrong road and camped on Black Fork.

Aug. 17   The roads today have been tolerable good, with some rock. It rained very hard this evening. We are camped on Black Fork, 12 miles from Fort Bridger. Dr. Howard came up and gave Mary and me some medicine. Mary is no better. He charged Frank five dollars for a little quinine and morphine.

Aug. 18   We came over very rough, rocky roads with mountains on each side. We crossed several creeks but I never heard the names of them. We came through Bridger, a pretty place with a great many nice houses. Frank met with Mr. Carter here, the man he built a house for in Boone. All the town, nearly belongs to him. Frank got more medicine here. They charged ten dollars for what little he got. He got a letter from Nettie and put one in the office. We came on and crossed the creek two or three times. We are camped tonight five miles from Bridger, where there is no wood, water or grass.

Aug. 19   We started and came ten miles and stopped for breakfast, then came on till we came to a ranch, where we are camped to day until Monday. They found plenty of grass for the cattle up in the canyons.

Sunday, Aug. 20   A beautiful day. Mary is no better. She talks out of her head all the time.

Aug. 21   They drove in the cattle to start but when they got them all up Mary was dying. She died about 12 o'clock without a struggle. About two hours before she died, Mrs. Kirkland took Annie to her and said "Mary here is Annie." She said: "Annie, kiss me," and smiled. That was all she said. Frank made her a right nice coffin, lined inside; the top was covered; couldn't get anything to cover the sides. She was dressed in solid green merino, a white collar and gloves, black belt and net. They said she looked very natural. I never saw her after she was taken sick. Mrs. Kirkland, Sue and Mary Rhyne dressed her.

Aug. 22   They will take her to Bear River to bury her. Ann cannot bear the thought of leaving here where there was no other grave. She was buried by the side of a child of Mr. Richardson's grave. There is a station and several families living here and plenty of Indians, all friendly. We started on across Bear river, with very rocky roads. We are camped tonight in the valley.

Aug. 23   The roads today have been tolerably good. Frank is complaining very much like he was taking mountain fever, though he had to tend to his teams and has the cooking to do. We are camped tonight in the valley and have to drive the cattle to the canyons to get grass.

Aug. 24   This morning we met one of our old company going back. He had sold his freight in Salt Lake City and was going home. We then travelled through Echo Canyon, which is 30 miles long. The roads were very bad part of the way. We then came up to Weber, a nice settlement. They are cutting their wheat. We got potatoes and onions at 2 a bushel. We camped for the night on the banks of the Weber.

Aug. 25   We traveled up the Weber. About three o'clock we met Mr. Lockwood [?] going back. He went back about a mile with us and camped for the night at the mouth of a canyon. They had to drive the cattle over the mountains to feed.

Aug. 26   Frank is no better. We travelled through the canyon until we came to the park. Here they were building a fine stone house to cost 13,000.00. Frank could get five dollars a day here. We came on through the park and camped at the mouth of a canyon to stay until Monday evening. The mountains are covered with tall pine trees.

Sunday, Aug. 27   Cold and cloudy. Frank is a little better and I am able to get out of the wagon. After dinner we started and came six miles, so we can get to Salt Lake City Monday. We are camped in the valley with hardly room for the wagons to stand straight. They drove the stock up in the canyon for grass.

Aug. 28   Frank is right sick and has been taking medicine today. It is cold and misting rain and the roads are very bad rough and rocky and so narrow in places it looks impossible to pass. We passed through a little town and then over the little mountain. Sick as Frank was he had to walk to drive his mean cattle. When we got to the foot they had to lock both hind wheels to go down and then sometimes the wagons would run sideways. When we got to the foot there was a jumping off place of about three feet. We came on, with the roads very bad. We came to a mud hole in the lane and Frank's mean cattle thought they could not go through and ran through the fence. Frank, sick as he was, had to jump out and turn them. They then ran up the fence on the other side. Att ran in and stopped them. They had to unhitch the leaders from the wagon and go across with one yoke. We passed through another little town and came on with roads very bad and it was just raining enough to make them slippery. We got into Salt Lake City about night. It is a beautiful place. The town is all laid out in squares with nice shade trees all over the town. We drove in a large corral, planked in, with the fence about ten feet high. We have to buy feed for the stock.

Aug. 29   Still cold and raining. It rained all night. Frank is very weak. He walked up to the city to put a letter in the postoffice for Cum and to get some medicine. He bought some calico at 25¢ a yard. We have as many peaches as we can eat. The men are coming around the wagons and all have something to sell. Peaches are $8 a bushel and apples $6. About three o'clock we started and came through the town. The houses are all built of adobe made in the shape of brick and dried by the sun. Some of them are plastered on the outside and painted white with nice porches in front. When we left town we took the California road,[7] came six miles and camped in a lane; turned the stock in a pasture and had to pay 25¢ a head. Frank is complaining very much.

---

[7]The "California Road" is the "Mormon Corridor" referred to in the Introduction to

Aug. 30   We travelled all day and the roads have been very good. We came to the hot springs. Mig was driving our team and Frank was in bed. The hard-headed oxen ran the wagon in one of the springs and the hind wheel and part of the bed was clear under the water. Our big Bible and some other books got wet through. We had to unload the wagon to get it out. Att lifted me out and sat me on the ground. I had to sit there until someone helped me up. We are camped here and will stay until Friday. There is a very good bottom for the stock to run on.

Aug. 31   We stayed over for the women to wash. The water is hot enough to wash with. One of the springs is almost boiling. Mrs. Kirkland done my washing for me. Two of Ann's children are sick. Frank is some better. Att traded his three milk cows for a horse and 200 pounds of flower. Flower is worth $8 a hundred. They bought some beans and onions.

Friday, Sept. 1   We travelled all day over tolerably good roads, passed several houses and came through one little town but I never heard the name. The houses are all built of sod. We are camped in a pasture and have to pay a bit a head for the stock. Frank is better.

Sept. 2   Cold and cloudy. The mountains have snow on them. We started and came over very good roads and went through a town called Provo. We stopped in town while Frank tried to get me a pasteboard but they have none. We are camped in a bottom on the east of Utah lake. We are in sight of it and it is seven miles across. The people say they hauled wood across it last winter on the ice.

Sunday, Sept. 3   A very pleasant day. We will stay here until

the diary. It was a shorter route to Southern California by the way of the Mojave Desert and Cajon Pass. There were, and are, towns all the way. U.S. Interstate #15 follows it almost mile by mile today. William B. Smart, *Old Utah Trails* (Salt Lake City, 1988), *passim*, especially map on page 94.

Monday. Frank is better and I am not able to get out of the wagon.

Sept 4   The men are trading or trying to trade their cattle for horses. Mr. Kirkland traded his cattle for horses after dinner. We started and came 12 miles over very rough roads. We came through a town called Springville and passed several houses on the road. Just before we camped nine Indians passed us going to the mountains. We are camped by a big field where there is no water. The cattle were taken three miles to grass.

Sept. 5   We started out again with the roads rough and rocky   We came through a town called Salem. Mr. Kerfoot had to leave one of his horses on the roadside to die. We are camped tonight at a ranch and there are several teams camped here. Frank bought some milk at 50¢ a gallon. They have their churn in the spring house to go by water.

Sept. 6   Mr. Kirkland has his wagon to fix. We will not get a very early start. Just as we were ready to start four Indians came up begging for something to eat. We passed several settlements. The roads are very good. We came through a town where Brigham Young was preaching. Everybody is going to hear him. They have had an election and the Gentiles[8] came near carrying the day. He has come down to see about it. We are camped at Neffey [Nephi] on Coon Creek. Some of the boys went up to town to hear Mr. Young preach. We have a good time getting wood and they drove the cattle to the mountains to get grass but found none. They drove them back but as it was then too late to hunt grass they let them go.

Sept. 7   They found the cattle three miles from camp. Frank bought a bushel of the finest potatoes I ever saw at $1.50 a bushel. Att traded our mean cattle for a pony. I was so

---

[8]"Gentiles" was a name for the non-Mormon population.

glad for they are the meanest yoke that ever walked on the earth. This has been the awfulest windy day we have had since we left home: blowing all the time right in our wagons and almost puts our eyes out with the red dust. Sometimes we could not see the cattle to the wagon. We are camped near Chicken Creek at one of the largest springs you ever heard of. It is about 40 feet wide, 50 feet long. It has been measured 115 feet and never found bottom. It looks scary standing open without a fence around it. They have plenty grass for the stock.

Sept. 8   They have concluded to stay here until Monday. It rained all night and is snowing this morning. They have had a big fire all day. It snowed for a few minutes this evening as hard as ever I saw it snow in old Missouri. A man came to camp and told the men he had a good pasture they could turn the stock in and it wouldn't cost them anything.

Sept. 9   Cold and raining. Frank had a bad time getting breakfast. I am not able to do anything yet. All I do is sit in the wagon and cry. They had to keep a big fire of sage brush all day.

Sunday, Sept. 10   The mountains are covered with snow. Two of Att's horses were gone and they found them in a canyon. Today has been clear and cold.

Sept. 11   Clear and cold. We started and came over some very good roads and some very rocky ones. We crossed a creek called Sevier and had a bridge to cross on. The man where we camped told us the Indians were very bad on the Sevier. We stopped and watered the stock and ate our dinner but saw no signs of Indians, though it is a good place for them to hide. We travelled through the mountains all evening until three o'clock, when we got in Round Canyon. They bought two bushels of potatoes here. They have a ditch dug to get water from the mountains. It is seven miles long. We are camped right on it. They have to dig ditches to get water for the ground.

Sept. 12   We started out through the mountains, with just room enough for the wagons to pass between them and the roughest roads. I have a headache all the time and I thought the jolting of the wagon would kill me. The mountains are covered with cedar and scrubby oak. We only came ten miles and camped. We are camped in a valley where we have plenty of wood, water and grass and cedar trees as thick as they can stand. Just before we camped our cattle ran off across the branch down the canyon. I don't know where they would have gone if Frank hadn't got them turned when he did. Att is sick.

Sept. 13   Ann is no better. Frank has all the work to do. We travelled through the canyon all day. The roads have been tolerable good. About three o'clock we came to Fillmore.[9] They have the largest brick kill [kiln] I ever saw. The state house is here and the houses are all built of brick. Ann is worse. Frank has all the cooking to do and his team to tend to besides.

Sept. 14   The doctor says Ann has the mountain fever. He says he can cure her in a few days. We will stay until she gets better. Frank is fixing his wagon for horses.

Sept. 15   Ann is a little better. Frank and Mr. Kirkland are fixing their wagons.

Sept. 16   A very warm day. Ann is still right sick. After Frank got breakfast over he went and bought some peaches and we had a cobbler for dinner. He is not done fixing his wagon yet.

---

[9] Fillmore is the county seat of Millard Co., Utah. Both of these place names come from the name of President Millard Fillmore, who signed the act creating the Territory of Utah in 1850. Fillmore was the new territory's first capital. The capitol building still stands as an historical museum and park. Rufus Wood Leigh, *Five Hundred Utah Place Names* (Salt Lake City, 1961), p. 24.

Sunday, Sept. 17   A very warm morning. Frank went to church to hear a Mormon preach; this evening Mrs. Kirkland has gone down to hear him. Ann got out of the wagon and sat up awhile. Att cleaned up this evening and we all thought we were going to have a hard storm but it blew away. Mrs. Kirkland got her feet very badly scalded by turning a pot of boiling water over on them.

Sept. 18   Clear and cool. Frank is at work on the wagons. Some of the other men have gone to see the stock. They are five miles from camp. Ann got out of the wagon and sat up this morning. In the evening it clouded up and turned very cold and about two o'clock she took a small chill and died about eight at night.[10] She suffered very much for two hours after her chill. She had but little fever and about an hour before she died she rested easy but never spoke so they could understand her, only she called my name three times like she was going to sleep.

Sept. 19   A calm, warm morning. The sun shines very warm but everything appears so lonely. Frank is making Ann's coffin. He made her a plain, neat coffin, lined inside. He could not get anything to cover it up with. At four o'clock they started with her to her last resting place. They all went except Mrs. Kirkland and Mary Rhyne and as I was not able to go I stayed and took care of her little baby. Mrs. Kirkland and Mary got dinner for the others while they were gone.

Sept. 20   Calm and clear. The men are all trading their cattle for horses. Att traded a wagon for a horse. Frank is fixing the wagons for horses and carving some beef they bought.

Sept. 21   A very windy morning. Frank had to go down to the blacksmith shop to get some work done. I tried to get

---

[10]This was Ann Eliza Gatewood, wife of Atwell M. Gatewood. He is referred to as At or Att in the diary.

dinner for the first time for a long time but gave out before it was done.

Sept. 22   Frank has made a wind-up of fixing wagons and harnesses.

Sept. 23   Frank and Att took the tomb stone down to put on Ann's grave. She was buried a mile and a half from Fillmore at the grave yard. The other men have gone after the stock. They came in with them about two o'clock. We started, came ten miles and camped in a valley where there is no water. We had to get supper after dark.

Sunday, Sept. 24   We started before breakfast, came several miles and camped on Dry Creek to stay until Monday. Just as we got breakfast over the Indians came around the wagons begging for tobacco or something to eat. This evening after they got through with their work they all gathered around our wagon and enjoyed themselves singing. Att traded one yoke of his cattle for a Shanghai pony.[11]

Sept. 25   A very warm morning. Frank is washing and I have been trying to patch his pants but my hands tremble like one with the palsy. Mr. Rhyne is fixing his wagon. Mr. Kerfoot traded his cattle for mules. The bothersome Indians have been around the wagons all day begging.

Sept. 26   Cool and clear. They hitched the Shanghai to our wagon but he got out of the harness quicker than they put him in. We started and came seven miles to Corn Creek, stopped watered and ate dinner. Mr. Kerfoot had to get some black smithing done. We came on ten miles and camped in a valley without water and but little grass. They drove the stock to the mountains to feed.

---

[11]We have been unable to identify a "Shanghai pony." Was it a mongolian pony used by the northern Chinese? There were hundreds of Chinese in the American West by this time. In the 19th century they used the term "Shanghai" for all kinds of animals, for they reminded the speakers of those huge shaggy-legged chickens (i.e. the Cochins) from China.

Sept. 27   Clear and cold. The horses were miles from camp.
We came 14 miles to Cove Creek, watered and fed. We
bought a bushel of potatoes at one dollar a bushel. We came
seven miles over very rough, rocky roads and camped on Pine
Creek. There is one man and his little boy living here. He is a
herder. They drove the stock over the mountain to grass.

Sept. 28   We came 22 miles over tolerable good roads except
two or three big hills we had to pull up. We are camped at a
town called Beaver on Beaver Creek. Little Jeff is sick. We
will stay here until Monday.

Sept 29   They have to get some blacksmithing done. Mr.
Kirkland and Mr. Rhyne are nailing horseshoes.

Sept. 30   Frank is making harness. Att traded all the cattle
off for mules and traded the cow for beef. Today has been very
windy. Mrs. Kirkland and I were baking light bread when
her dress caught fire and she was all in a blaze when I saw her
and would have been badly burned if it hadn't been for
Frank. He put the fire out.

Sunday, Oct. 1   Cloudy and windy. Frank and I are curing
beef and the others are at the same work. The Indians are
around the wagons wanting to trade. This evening is cold and
raining.

Oct. 2   Cold and windy. We have a fire in an old house to
cook by. They did not get through with their work. We will
have to stay today. It thundered harder than ever I heard it in
old Missouri. Little Jeff is very sick.

Oct. 3   Clear and cold. We all started again and came 20
miles over tolerable good roads. We are camped tonight at
Elkhorn Springs with very bad water and scarcely no grass.
There is one house here and the men who live here are
herders and were run on yesterday by the Indians.

Oct. 4   Mr. Kerfoot's horses are all gone. Mr. Kirkland, Att and us started. Att wanted to see a doctor for Jeffy. We came 20 miles over good roads and came through a little town called Red Oak Creek. The water is red and the houses are all built of sod. They are the color of brick. We are camped in Pairawine [Parawan]. and have no grass. They bought wheat chaff for the horses. Att took Jeff to an old lady for to doctor him. This is a pretty little town, two mills running from a ditch dug from the mountains. The houses are all brick and the town is laid off in squares and has been forted in. The women came to camp and begged for Annie. One of them offered a sow for her.

Oct. 5   We came 18 miles over rough roads and through some deep deep sand. We stopped in a little town called Summit to water and feed. We are camped in Cedar City and it is the prettiest little town we have come through yet. It is laid off in squares and has a row of cottonwood trees on each side of the street. They have no grass for the horses but turned them in a lot and fed them

Oct. 6   Mr. Kerfoot had to send back to Summit after his mule. We came six miles to grass and stopped to wait for him. Frank took the horses over the mountains and found plenty of grass for them.

Oct. 7   We started, came a mile and stopped in a little town for me to make some rose root tea for Jeff. We then started and came 22 miles over the rockiest roads you ever heard of. We came over one mountain called the Black Ridge. We all had to walk up. We are camped in a valley with plenty of grass and water. Here we caught up with a man who says he will go through with us.

Sunday, Oct. 8   We started again with the roads worse than ever, nothing but rock. No one can imagine how bad they are; only those who have travelled them know. This evening the sand has been awful. We had to double team to get through.

Mrs. Kirkland and I walked until we almost gave out. We came through a town called Cottonwood. We got here about night, stopped and watered and filled our kegs, then came on. Frank had a balky horse in his team. We came to a sand hill and he stopped. They worked with him some time before they got him started. We were in the night getting to camp. We are camped in a valley with neither grass nor water.

Oct. 9   We are up by daylight. Our horses are all gone. Frank and some of the others went to hunt them and found them seven miles from camp going back. We came 22 miles over dreadful roads, over mountains and through sand. We came over one mountain with the road dug out of its side. On one side the rocks were as thick as they could lay and looked like they had been blown up and burned. On the other side a low valley looked scarry to look over and the road was so narrow. We came through a town, stopped and watered and filled our kegs. We then came on and passed through Saint George.[12] We had to stop here to get some water kegs. We started and took the wrong road. We had to pull through a sand bank after dark and had to double team when it was so dark we could not see the road and could just see the wagon before us. We had a creek to cross and one of our horses fell down. I thought the wagon would turn over. We are camped in a town called Sandy Clarrie [Santa Clara, Utah], right in the street is a molasses mill. They have to tie the horses to the wagons and feed them on molasses cane. It is very cold and windy.

Oct. 10   Still cold and windy. Mr. Kerfoot had a wagon tire to set. Mr. Kirkland and us started to go 14 miles to the

---

[12]Saint George is in Washington County, Utah, the very southwest corner of the state, in the Virgin River valley. It was named for George Adam Smith, counsellor to Brigham Young, the Mormon leader. Young maintained a winter home there because of the mild climate. It is now an historic site. Leigh, *op. cit.*, p. 84.

resting spring and wait for them. We came three miles, took the wrong road. The road we took was awful, with some hills that it was all four horses could do to pull one wagon up. We all got out except little Frankie, who was too sick. Mrs. Kirkland and I walked through sand over our shoe tops and carried the children until we gave out. We drove five miles and came to where the road went right into the cedars. We then had to turn and came back over the same road. The right road runs right in the bed of the creek. We crossed the creek ten times. We are camped between mountains by ourselves. The horses were driven over the mountains to grass.

Oct. 11   We were up early and Frank and Mr. Kirkland went for the horses. Two Indians came running to camp with their guns to eat their breakfast. We started up the creek over the rock. I am sick from my walk yesterday. I thought jolting over the rock would almost kill me. We came over some of the awfulest hills. Frankie and Jeffy are both in the wagon sick. About 10 o'clock we got to the resting spring, turned our horses on grass to stay until morning. This is an old camping ground. The rocks are covered with names of persons that have camped here. We had not been here a half hour until about 15 Indians were in camp. They stayed until sundown begging for something to eat, then told us if we gave them a pint of flour from each wagon our horses would be all right in the morning.

Oct. 12   Cool and clear. We started on the thirty miles of desert and have to haul water for the horses and ourselves. We travelled up the bed of the creek, with nothing in it but rock and the high mountains are on each side. What an awful looking country. We travelled up that ten miles and then up a steep hill into a deserted-looking place with nothing growing on it but desert wood. It is a bush that grows straight up about 15 feet high with long, sharp leaves. About 8 o'clock at night we came to a creek called Beaver Dams. We stopped and watered there. There are several families living here in tents. We started on to the camping place. It was so dark we could just see the leaders' teams. We came to the Rio-virgin river, crossed it three times after dark. I was frightened almost to death, lumbering over rocks and plunging into the river. We got to camp at half past nine all tired out.

Oct. 13   We started down the Riovirgin river, through sand just as much as four horses could pull the wagon through. We crossed the river 26 times. We came down the bed of the river most of the way. We came 22 miles and were within a mile of the camping ground when Att came to our wagon and told Frank to drive out to one side of the road for Jeffie to die. He died about six o'clock.[13] Mrs. Kirkland dressed and laid him out. Frank made a coffin for him and we put him in the coffin at 11 o'clock at night.

Oct. 14   We started through the sand and heat. The sun shines as hot as it ever did in old Missouri. We came 25 miles, crossed the river eight times. It was quick sand. Mr. Kirkland's wagon got stuck three times and the men had to wade in and push it out. We had a very steep hill to pull up after sundown and had to double team to get up. We are camped in the valley with sand up to our shoe tops. It was after dark when we got to camp. We could not find wood to get supper with. We are going to take Jeffie to the next settlement to bury him.

Sunday, Oct. 15   Clear and warm. We came five miles through sand deeper than ever. We came to the Riovirgin hill, turned the horses on grass and will try the hill in the morning. We all have to cook enough to last three days.

Oct. 16   We all started up the hill early. It is the awfulest

---

[13]See introduction above for information about Jeffie.

hill you ever did hear of. It is two miles long, winding around the mountains. They only got five wagons up. The men and horses broke down. They had to put six and eight teams to a wagon and the men at the wheels. There are two places the horses had to jump up on a rock about three feet high. The men lift the wheels up. If they had gone ten inches out of the way they would have fallen down a mountain hundreds of feet.

Oct. 17   Frank was sick all night, completely broke down. Little Frankie and Annie are both very sick. They have four wagons to get up this morning. About 12 o'clock the last was up and the men and horses broke down. We then had to drive 15 miles to water, over awful roads, rock and sand. The Virgin river water is very bad water. It is perfectly red and thick with sand though it was all we had to use while we were on it. We got to camp about 9 o'clock. Mrs. Kirkland and I walked through the sand until I just gave out and had to get in the wagon. We are camped in a settlement called the Muddy, mostly Indians. When we drove up there were about 25 Indians around the camp fire. Frank is sick and hardly able to be up. Mary Rhyne is very sick.

Oct. 18   We will stay here today to rest the horses and to bury Jeffie. We could not bury him any sooner on account of the wolves. They would have dug him up as soon as we buried him. The Indians have been so thick we could hardly walk for them. We have been baking bread for the 60 miles of desert.

Oct. 19   Clear and warm. Frank is rested and feels much better. We came 15 miles over the worst roads, with sand so deep we could go only a few steps till we had to stop and rest the horses. We all walked, who could. We came out into a rocky canyon with just enough room for the wagons to pass between the mountains. We came down one very steep, rocky

hill and met a freight wagon. The men had to stand on the
wheels to keep it from turning over. We are camped in a
valley on the Muddy.[14] The Indians followed us all day and
they are thick in camp.

Oct. 20   We were up early for breakfast. The Indians were
so thick I could not eat my breakfast. They were pulling at
my dress, pointing at my bread with their arrows and begging
for every mouthful I had. We filled our kegs with water and
started on the sixty miles of desert. We came 20 miles,
stopped, watered and fed and then started out for the night.
We drove until midnight, stopped and fed and had a cup of
coffee.

Oct. 21   The roads we came over last night were very rocky.
Frank's team is almost worn out. We stopped at 6 o'clock and
fed. Frank has to take one of the horses out. We got to the
Virgin at ten o'clock. Six Indians followed us across. This is
an Indian settlement and they got them to hold the horses for
two or three biscuits. There are two or three white men living
here, a Mr. Jones from Shelby. Mary Rhyne is very sick.

Sunday, Oct 22   A very warm morning. Mary is no better.
We started, came three miles to a big spring, stopped and
filled our kegs with water for the horses and started on. We
came 22 miles over the most awful roads, rock and sand. We
came within a rocky canyon that was [unreadable word] and
the horses broke down. There were high rocky mountains on
each side. Just as the moon went down, Mr. Kirkland had one
of his wagon tires come off. The others went on and left us
there alone. It was so dark we could not see the road before we
got to camp. We went tumbling over rock and could hardly
sit in the wagon. We are camped at Cottonwood Springs, a
low, swampy valley with a few cottonwood Trees.

---

[14]The Muddy River rises out of a group of warm springs and today flows into Lake
Mead. This Nevada valley was named "Muddy" in an attempt to pronounce a Piute
Indian term. Helen S. Carlson, *Nevada Place Names* (Reno, NV, 1974), p. 174.

Oct. 23   The sick are no better. We started again, with the roads worse than ever. If you could see them you would say it was impossible for a wagon to pass over them. Frank had to take his tools out and put them in the freight wagon. Four of the horses gave out and we only came 12 miles. We got in camp at the Mountain Springs just before sundown. I feel more discouraged than ever.

Oct. 24   Clear and cool. The Indians had 5 horses hid out in the mountains. They told the men they would get them if they would give them some flour. They agreed to and they had them up in a few minutes. We filled our kegs with water for the horses and started on the 50 miles of desert. We drove six miles and stopped to stay until morning. They turned the horses on grass and found a little spring in the mountain. It took four men until midnight to water the horses.

Oct. 25   Very cold and windy. Frank stayed out all night with the horses and said he liked to freeze. We saw where the Indians had killed and cooked two or three horses. Att bought another span of mules. We started, travelled the most of the day through sand. We stopped, ate our supper   fed, watered and started for the night. We travelled until midnight and stopped to rest. Annie is very sick.

Oct. 26   Very cold. We came six miles to the Winston Springs, turned our horses out and will stay for two or three hours rest. Then we ate our dinner and baked bread for the night. Started at 4 o'clock, and travelled until midnight, stopped and ate and had a cup of coffee, then came on. Frank went to sleep and lost his whip.

Oct. 27   We stopped at daylight to feed and started on. We travelled all day through sand which in places was so very deep. The sun shone very warm and the horses almost broke down. Mr. Kerfoot had to leave one of his horses on the desert to die. The water here is alkali and the wells just like a [two unreadable words]   This is a dry, sandy looking place and there is very little for the horses to eat.

Oct. 28   We filled our kegs with the alkali water and travelled on the 35 miles of desert. We travelled 15 miles through sand and up hill all the time. It was very warm and dry. We had to take one of Att's horses to work. We got up to the top of the hill just at dark. We then went almost straight down for about fifty feet and then gradually down hill all night. We travelled down the canyon with the high rocky mountains on each side. You have no idea [three unreadable words] through the snow. We got to Camp Soda just as the morning star was rising. We were almost starved. We have been without provisions, except bread, for three days.

Sunday, Oct. 29   There are two soldiers living here. They gave us a piece of pickled pork for breakfast. They bought a beef and we all liked to foundered. Here we came to the Mohavia [Mojave] River.[15] Little Annie and Mary Rhyne are very sick. Annie acts like she was crazy and we can do nothing for her.

Oct. 30   We started again through the sand down the Mohavia and only came sixteen miles to the fish ponds.[16] Mr. Kirkland's horses gave out, so we stopped with him while the others drove on. They left us just after we stopped some freighters who were going to San Bernardino. They let Mr. Kirkland have a span of mules to work in.

Oct. 31   We were up before daylight, got our breakfast and started. We passed our other wagons, some of their horses

---

[15]They are now traveling through the Mojave, a major desert of some 15,000 square miles.

[16]Fish Pond was a general store operated by one Lafayette Meacham. Here they could buy all kinds of supplies both for themselves and for their animals. They could also have blacksmithing done. It was located on what is now the Marine Corps Depot of Supplies between present Barstow and Daggett. Erma Peirson, *The Mojave River and Its Valley* (Glendale, CA, 1970), pp. 23, 155-56.

being gone, then came 20 miles through sand. The sun shone very warm, and we camped at the cottonwood trees. Frank bought some milk for Annie at 50¢ a gallon.

Nov. 1   We started early and came 20 miles through sand and dust, up to the Mohavia river. We crossed the river two or three times, coming two miles through a thicket of cottonwood trees as thick as could stand. This river runs under ground, then comes up in places and runs for a few miles and sinks again. We are camped at Mr. Allens, on the river. Att wanted to get something for Annie to take, but the doctor is not at home.

Nov. 2   Cold and clear. Little Annie died this morning just before daylight.[17] She died very hard. She was teething and had the diarrhea. We could not get any medicine on the road for her. Mrs. Kirkland and I washed and dressed her. We will take her to San Bernardino to bury her. This morning one of Att's horses was mired down in the quick sand and died this morning. Today we have to cross the San Bernardino mountain.[18] We came up hill till three o'clock. At the going down place they locked both hind wheels and started down. The road is dug out in the mountain. There is just enough room for the wagons get through. We came two miles and a [unreadable words] and a bend of the river. We are camped tonight at a ranch between the mountains, which are straight up and down with a space almost 50 feet [unreadable word] between them. The river runs between them and there is no water in the river. [Three unreadable lines.]

Nov. 3   We started again down hill, the road being very

---

[17]"Little Annie" was the daughter of the Gatewoods.

[18]They will cross the mountains over the famous Cajon Pass. One of the best descriptions of the problems in traveling through this access route to San Bernardino is to be found in Erma Peirson's book, *op. cit.*, pp. 71-75. The pass lies between the San Gabriel Mountains on the west and the San Bernardino Mountains on the east. The "down place" is at an altitude of 4,195 feet.

rough and rocky with rocks of all sizes and colors. Some of them are striped red and white with the stripes about a foot apart. We came six miles to the toll gate, where we had to pay $1.50 for the wagon. We stopped and bought barley and feed. There is one family living here right on the creek between the mountains. We came twelve miles, then stopped at a ranch to water [two unreadable lines] show. We then came on twelve miles over good roads to San Bernardino. The ground was covered with prickly pears. Some of the men stopped and got some of the pears to eat. This is a valley surrounded by mountains. We are camped on Warm Creek at an old bachelor's by the name of Eldridge. We are very much dissatisfied with the looks of the people and the country. They turned the horses on grass. We expect to stay here to rest and then go on to Los Angeles.

Nov. 4   A beautiful morning, clear and cool. Frank is making Annie a coffin. We took her out of the wagon and laid her in the house. She will be buried this evening at three o'clock at the grave yard in this place. One of our freighters that came in with us brought us a handkerchief full of grapes to eat.

Sunday, Nov. 5   Cool and pleasant. We all feel more homesick than ever. I feel like I could cry my eyes out. The people came around the wagons all day to see what we look like. One of the mules are gone, Frank has gone to hunt for it.

Liverpool to Utah in 1866
by Sailing Ship and Prairie Schooner
ᛜ Caroline Hopkins Clark

INTRODUCTION

This diary was written by Caroline Hopkins Clark as she crossed the Atlantic by sailing ship, traveled to the Missouri Valley by train and river boat, and crossed the plains by the Platte River route to Utah. She was born on May 15, 1831, at Sutton Coldfield, a suburb of Birmingham, England. She heard missionaries of the Church of Jesus Christ of Latter-Day Saints preach and she became a Mormon on December 12, 1849. Her conversion resulted in rejection by her family.

Soon after being baptised she met a young man named John Clark, also a new convert to the Mormon faith. They were married on May 31, 1852. John had been born on May 14, 1833, in Lincolnshire. They spent their first years of marriage in Birmingham. Seventeen children were born to them over the following years. Three of the children died in infancy.

The official "Third Generation Records" of the Mormon Church list the names and birth dates of the children, eight of whom emigrated with their parents to Utah in 1866:

William Roland	b. Dec. 5, 1852
John	Aug. 25, 1854
Harriet	Mar. 23, 1856
Orson John	Dec. 12, 1857
Herbert Henry	Sept. 20, 1861
Samuel Lorenzo and Edwin Francis (Frank) twins	Sept. 6, 1863
Martha Eliza	Apr. 17, 1865

Throughout the overland journey Caroline Clark was pregnant with another child, but she says not a word about it in her diary. The party arrived in Coalville, Utah, and soon thereafter Ada Emiline Clark was born on October 11, 1866. Five more children were born to them through the years following according to the official church records.

John Clark farmed for a living. He was ordained a High Priest of the Church in May 1879, and a Bishop on May 14, 1882.

Caroline Clark died on Oct. 30, 1900, in Upton, Summit County, Utah. John's death was also in Upton on March 23, 1909.

This diary was published by the Daughters of Utah Pioneers in *Our Pioneer Heritage*, X (Salt Lake City, 1967), pp. 43-49. It is with the permission of that organization that we publish it here.

THE DIARY

Monday, April 30, 1866—ship *John Bright*[1] sailed from Liverpool, England, with 747 Saints under the direction of C.M. Gillett[2] and landed in New York, June 6, 1866. We left Liverpool at four o'clock on the afternoon of April 30, 1866

May 2nd—Martha is seasick. We went upon deck. It is a grand sight to see the waves roll mountains high. Herbert seasick, and Roland poorly. Sister Staples is very kind in helping with the children. John is busy attending to the cooking, but all together very comfortable.

3rd—We have just been up on deck to see a steamer pass. A

---

[1]John Bright, for w1om this sailing ship was named, was a prominent member of the House of Commons of that day.

[2]Collins Moore Gillet was a Mormon leader who had spent the previous three years as a missionary in England. It was while crossing the plains with this group of immigrants that he took sick and died on August 20, 1866. *Latter-Day Saint Biographical Encyclopedia* (Salt Lake City, 1971), vol. IV, pp. 634-35.

hailstorm has commenced and the vessel is rocking. It is about time for prayers.

4th—The ship rolls very much. Martha and I went up on deck. A wave dashed over and gave us a ducking. We saw five large fish. Their heads resembled those of horses.

6th—We are feeling a little better. Martha said she dare say you would be wondering what we were having for our dinner. We had a Yorkshire pudding. Just as it was done, the captain ordered us up on the deck, so we had to stand outside and eat it the best we could. We also had boiled potatoes and peas. They had to stand in the water about one hour after were done, before we could get to eat them. Evening, we are on the top deck, and the winds are very high. Little Frank is afraid he will fall over. We wish you were all with us, particularly Tom Green. He would make a little fun out of it, to see us tossing to and fro.

7th—We are all sailing very swiftly today. I wanted to find what time it was, and Jack said I was to ask Mrs. Barlow.

8th—John has to work very hard in the cooking department.

10th—The sea is very rough. None of us are able to stand on our legs. I fell down and hurt my leg badly, and John has had many falls, in fact we all fall more or less. The tins are rolling about, the victuals are tossing about, but we cannot help laughing.

11th—Dare say you have heard people say they could go to sleep with rocking, but we cannot go to sleep with rocking. We had plenty last night. Talk about a swing boat, why bless your life, it is nothing compared to being rocked on the sea. We can hardly keep in bed. We had to get up and turn our heads where our feet should be, or we would not stay in bed at all. The tins and boxes were rolling about. The slop buckets upset. The sailors said it was as rough a night as they had ever seen, and it continued so all day.

12th—Saturday night, 6 o'clock. We have just finished dinner. The sea still remains very rough, but we are not at all afraid for we feel we shall get to New York quite safe. The reason I tell you of these things is because I told you I would send you the truth of how things were. We have plenty of music and dancing on board. Mr. Cox is very tolerable.

15th—A beautiful fine day. We had a concert and dancing on deck. At night we went up on top deck to see the sun sinking in the west. It is the grandest sight we ever witnessed. It is impossible to describe, but if you would like to see it you will have to do as we have done. It is my birthday today.

18th—A very rough day, and we were driven back some distance. We have had to keep to our bed because we could not stand up. Sometimes we were almost upright in bed. There was much confusion with the boxes and tins, as many were smashed all to pieces. John has had several falls, but the rest of us are well now.

20th, Sunday—We have had two good meetings during the day. It is very foggy. John is boiling potatoes for our supper.

22nd—We expect to be given notice in about a week to quit the *John Bright*

23rd—Every few days they stove the vessel out, so we have to go up on top deck. We thought if Brother Greene and some of the Birmingham boys had been with us, it would have caused rare fun to see us gypsying in the sun and to see the big fish trying to catch the little ones. We have had three births but no deaths. Herbert, Frank and the baby have the whooping cough.

24th—Very foggy. We cannot see far, and we dread the banks of Newfoundland, where whales were seen this morning.

25th—We wonder if our "company general" went to have his bread and cheese. We would like to have some We have to drink water and vinegar with a little sugar in it for our drink.

26th—We fully expect the pilot in tomorrow to take us to Castle Gardens.[3] Our health is very good.

30th—The sea is very rough. Little Frank and Roland were seized with a blight in their eyes. We had to be smoked out again, so we took our dinner on top deck. We can see many fishing smacks so expect we are nearing land.

31st—Quiet and cold as winter in Birmingham. The vessel is quite at a standstill.

June 1st—Much warmer, many fishing smacks about. The second mate and two more men went out in a boat and brought a turtle which caused a great deal of fun on deck. Little Frank seized with the measles.

2nd—The vessel goes as much backward as forward, so you see how fast we are sailing. The baby and I have the bowel complaint.

3rd—About one o'clock we saw a boat coming along which proved to be the pilot. There was great shouting for joy. Sorry to say, the baby keeps very ill. Little Frank is some better.

4th—Smoked out again. Great preparations were made for the inspector to come and look over the ship. Martha, in a great hurry to come down stairs, came down all at once, but has not hurt herself much.

5th—The tug has just come to take us to New York. It is the grandest sight I have ever witnessed; to see things as we go up the river. We have just gone up on deck to pass the doctor. He took no notice of any of us, so we passed first rate.

6th—We are still on the ship in much confusion. They have taken our berths down. We expect to go into Castle Gardens today. Sam and Emma Pike came to see us.

7th—We were taken into Castle Gardens today about 12

---

[3]This locale preceded Ellis Island as an immigration center for the United States government from 1855 to 1890.

o'clock. We had to stay there until twelve o'clock at night. During this time we went into New York, and found some bread and cheese and a little something else. We had to pay at the rate of a pence for a small loaf. Martha[4] and I bought a hat for traveling. They are one yard and three quarters around. If you take a piece of string and measure with it, you can see how far it was around our hats. At ten o'clock we had to walk about two miles to a steamboat. The lame, old, and children had to have cars, so we fell in with that number. We had to sit in the boat all night, so you can guess how comfortable we were.

8th—At break of day we were hurried out to go to the train. We rode all day. It is a pleasant country. It is impossible to describe the acres of land that lie uncultivated. Riding in the train is very tiresome. It is something like a galvanic battery, and much faster than we go in England.

9th—We are still riding by rail. We went through British Canada. We were stopped on the road and searched by soldiers for firearms. We had to change trains at Montreal. Mr. Wheeler, the cab man, met with an accident. He had to have his foot taken off. We saw some beautiful waterfalls on the road. The houses are mostly built of wood. The people dress fine about here.

10th—Still continue on by rail. We got some new suits, which were quite neat. Things are very cheap in Canada. Meat is one half shilling a pound and everything else according. The eggs are five pence a dozen. Things have raised on account of the war. Soldiers are stationed every short distance along the road.

11th—We are still journeying by railway. We had to change

---

[4]This Martha was a grown woman. She seems to have been a servant in the employ of the Clark family. We have no further information about her. She should not be confused with the family's baby girl.

cars and drop over a river into the United States. There we got refreshments and started again on our journey. The baby[5] remains very ill.

12th—It is very tedious, riding by rail so long. The country looks well. We have passed by nice villages. Herbert is seized with the measles.

13th—Very sad news to tell of today's journey. Mr. Cox was taken worse during the night, and remained so until about nine o'clock, when he died. The name of the place was called Michigan. He was taken on to Chicago. We stayed there during the night. Sorry to say baby keeps very ill. Little Frank has the bowel complaint.

14th—Today's journey is a sad one to us, on account of the death of our own dear baby. She died at the place where Mr. Cox was buried. John stayed behind to bury her. She died with the same complaint as my other three children. We left Chicago and proceeded by train to Quincy [Illinois]. We changed trains, and crossed the river.

15th—We took the train and proceeded to St. Joseph, [Missouri] and stayed all day and night there. We inquired about Mr. Burr from Birmingham, and found him. We had a very hearty breakfast, dinner and tea. We had for dinner, a leg of lamb, green peas, and new potatoes. They wanted John to stay with them. He would get from four to five pounds a week. A gentleman got out of his carriage and wanted Martha to stay. He said he would give her four dollars and her board a week. The servants have not much work to do.

16th—Then we took a boat and went up the Missouri River. The water is very dirty with undercurrents. We saw Indians on the bank.

---

[5]This was the Clarks' youngest child. She had been born on April 17, 1865, and given the name Martha Eliza. Church of Jesus Christ of Latter-Day Saints, Third Generation Records.

17th—We still keep going up the river. We have to be on top deck. We can lie and see the moon and stars shining upon us.

18th—We are still on the river. It remains very hot, and the water keeps very muddy all the way.

19th—Arrived in Wyoming [Otoe Co., Nebraska], very early in the morning. The heat is very oppressive. You should see the children, they are blistered with the sun. Little Frank's arm is very bad. We can see something like sparks of fire. They are small insects. There are not many houses. The teams came to the river for our luggage and took it on to the grove.

20th—We pitched our tent at night, then a heavy thunder storm came up and we all got wet through. We had to take the children into a shed and keep them there until we dried their clothes.

22nd—Another lot of teams have joined us. We do not know how long we will stay here.

23rd—We are still in the shed. We saw Mrs. Yates from Birmingham.

24th—We do not expect to leave for four or five weeks, then we will start with the Birmingham Saints.

26th—The London Saints arrived this morning. Mary was confined this morning. She has a girl and doing fine.[6]

27th—We had more friends come to see us. One gave us about two pecks of flour and other things which came in very useful. Brother Bean came and showed us how make our bread for the plains.

29th—We went over to Nebraska [City] today. It is very rough riding. Sometimes we went up, down and sidewise with our ox team. The teamsters said that was nothing to what we would have to go thru before we got to Utah.

---

[6]We don't know the identity of this "Mary."

July 3rd—Still remains very hot. We had another thunder storm but escaped getting wet. We do not know when we leave here.

11th—Left Wyoming five miles, and then we joined Captain Chipman's trains.

16th—We traveled very slow. Today we were crossing a creek, when the cattle turned, I went to get down out of the wagon, and Mr. Stonehouse went to help me and we both fell and hurt us very bad. John went to stop the brake, and got a bad foot sprain. He isn't able to sit up with his. The weather is very hot. The children are getting fat.

22nd—We passed Tree Creek and Beaver Creek today. We reached the Platte River. John's foot is better, he can walk again.

25th—Yesterday was the anniversary of our people who first entered the valley. We traveled about half the day, then we had singing and dancing, and all enjoyed ourselves. We are journeying by the Platte River. A young deaf and dumb girl died in our camp.

30th—We are still by the Platte River. There are small mountains on one side, and moutains on the other. We passed Cotton Tree [Cottonwood] Creek, and there were many soldiers camped there on account of the Indians, There were two more deaths in our camp.

Aug. 1st—We crossed the Platte River. It was very deep, and in places took the wagon up to the covers. We all got over safely, but our clothes were wet.

6th—We left South Platte (a distance of fifteen miles.) You should have seen the mountains we went down. It looked impossible for any persons to go down them, let alone with wagons and oxen. We are among the Indians.

10th—We passed Chimney Rock. It is a rock that can be

seen many miles off and forms a chimney. We passed high rocks. All things are going well with us.

14th—We passed Laramie, Wyoming; the soldiers stopped our train to see what firearms we had. They told us the Indians had killed a hundred or more and robbed them. I guess you would like to know how we live on the plains. We do not get any fresh meat or potatoes, but we get plenty of flour and bacon. We have some sugar, a little tea, molasses, soap, carbonate of soda, and a few dried apples. We brought some peas, oatmeal, rice, tea, and sugar, which we had left from the vessel. We bought a skillet to bake our bread in. Sometimes we make pancakes for a change. We also make cakes in the pan, and often bran dumplings with baking powder. We use cream of tartar and soda for our bread, sometimes sour dough. At times Roland goes to the river and catches fish and sometimes John shoots birds. We get wild currants and gooseberries to make puddings. All together we get along very well.

18th—Today we had trouble with the Indians. We suppose they followed us. We had just corralled, and begun to cook our dinners, when the alarm came that the Indians were driving our cattle. The boys followed them, but they got away with ninety-one head and wounded three.

20th—We passed Deer Creek. The same day the Indians took our cattle, they took all the possessions of two homes, killed the people and burned their homes. A telegraph message has come to tell us Brigham Young is sending us some mule teams and provisions to help us.

22nd—We crossed the [blank] bridge. There were many soldiers there on account of the Indians.

24th—This morning we were just starting when four of our men drove in about one-hundred cattle that they had taken from the Indians. We found the train they belonged to and we gave them back.

26th—We passed the Devil's Gate. Jack wanted to know if the devils lived there. John has been appointed captain of the guards. We have been forced to have men guard our trains back and front.

29th—Today we saw the first mountains with snow on them. At noon we came to some springs called, Iced [Ice] Springs. It is very cold. We can scarcely keep ourselves warm.

Sept. 1st—We passed South Pass. The cold has been severe. We dined on the leg of an antelope. It sure was a treat.

3rd—The mule teams have met us and brought provisions. They have gone on to meet the ones that waited back.

6th—We crossed Green River and Ham's Fork River. Today was the twins' birthday. We had a hare and a half, so we are not starving. Little Frank keeps very thin, but seems pretty well in health.

9th—We passed muddy station. They say we are just a hundred miles from the Valley. We had another birth, and three children have died. We are still able to see snow on the mountains. Mr. Gillett, captain of our vessel, has died on the plains. He was just a young man and highly respected.

12th—We have reached Coalville.[7] John and Bill went on early in the morning and found Tom and Frank. They brought a team and took us from the train to their house where they made us very comfortable. I would like to have gone on to the Valley, but I began to feel very unwell and thought it best to stop. Little Frank was worse as well.

23rd—Today we had more trouble on account of the death of

---

[7]This is the county seat of Summit County, Utah, at the confluence of Chalk Creek and the Weber River at the upper end of Echo Reservoir. The name derives from the fact that there are coal veins in the surrounding area, the first to be developed in Utah. Rufus Wood Leigh, *Five Hundred Utah Place Names* (Salt Lake City, 1961), p. 14. The Third Generation records indicate that through the following years the Clark family resided in four other Summit County towns: Henefer, Echo Canyon, Kamas, and Upton.

dear little Frank. He got worse every day after we got to Frank's and died on September 23. He suffered a lot with pain. He has never been well since he had the measles. His little body just wasted away. He was very merry on the journey and was often singing until the last two days. He had plenty to have done him good. Some people brought me eggs, new milk, a fowl for him, plenty of fresh butter, biscuits, and plenty of milk for getting, so we are not starving.

California to Texas in 1868

◊ Ruth Shackleford

INTRODUCTION

What with all of the discouragements of their westward journey (see pages 87-150 above) and evident dissatisfaction with California, after a stay in that state of some three years, Ruth and William Frank Shackleford decided in April 1868, to go back to Missouri. They planned to travel the Butterfield Overland Mail Route across Arizona, New Mexico and Texas. There seems to have been some thought concerning the possibilities of stopping off in eastern Texas. They had relatives living in the little village of Center Mill, Hood County, Texas, which is what they did. They finally decided to make Missouri their destination and settled in Roscoe, St. Clair County.

The reader should peruse the introduction to the Shacklefords' westward overland trip (1865) above, pages 87-90, for more information about these remarkable diaries and also about the family.

THE DIARY

WEDNESDAY, April 8   This morning we left San Bernardino for Texas after bidding farewell to many of our friends. We started and had considerable trouble with the wild horses. We came three miles to Matthews Mill and bought 600 pounds of flour at four dollars a hundred. We came on then to the Santa Ana river. It being very deep and running swift we had some trouble crossing with our wild horses. Mr.

Kirkland's horses got tangled up in the harness and he had to jump out in the deep water to straighten them. We came on two or three miles and camped at the foot of a hill, where Mr. Hamilton's and Mr. Garton's families were waiting for us. Some of our friends came with us to see us safely in camp the first night. We turned our horses out and got supper.

April 9   Cool and cloudy. We were up early fixing to start. Mr. Curtin and Mr. Airfoot came to camp and stayed all night with us. After breakfast they harnessed up to start and had some fun with the bronco horses. They kicked the harness off as fast as they put it on. We came twenty miles over tolerable good roads, to the San Jacinct [Jacinto] river, an ugly stream, and a bad crossing, with a steep bank coming down to the deep water. The horses being wild and unruly, we were some time crossing. Mr. Kirkland's team stalled and Frank had to pull out with his mules. We drove up a few yards from the river and camped for the night in a low flat place with weeds and grass knee deep. They turned the horses out and prepared for the night in a low flat place with weeds and grass knee deep. I feel very much discouraged and would rather turn back.

April 10   Still cool and cloudy. Two of Mr. Hamilton's horses are gone and two of the boys are going back to hunt for them. We came 15 miles over very good roads but there was very little to be seen except mountains and mesquite brush. About ten o'clock it began to rain and we had a very disagreeable time. We are camped tonight at the foot of the big hill near a ranch where there are big rocks piled one on top of another. It was so rainy and bad weather I could not get out of the wagon. Frank had to get supper. They tie the horses and feed them.

April 11   Still cloudy and rainy. It rained very hard last night but we all kept dry in our wagons. We had a big time this morning getting up the big hill. Frank had two wagons to pull up with his mules besides his own. We stopped at a ranch and got some cheese, then came on. The roads were very slippery. We stopped at a little town called Temakely [Temecula][1] and got some brandy, then came on, up hill and down with the roads so slippery the horses could hardly stand up. We crossed the creek three times. Two wagons got stuck and they had to double team. Then the men waded in the water and dug and pried the wagons out. We then came a few miles through a doleful looking country and camped on Oak Flat with plenty of wood, water and grass. Today has been cold and rainy. We came only twenty miles.

Sunday, April 12   We will stay here today. It is still raining and very disagreeable. Our train consists of thirteen men, four women and fifteen children. They are: John S. Hamilton and seven children, one grown daughter and two grown sons and four small children and Charley Coply, a young man he has with him; Abraham K. Kirkland and wife and three small children and Henry Coggans with him to help drive his team; John Barton and wife and two small children, Henry Birdwell and old Mr. Crowden with him; A.B. Gatewood and three children and George Ridgway with them, and our own family and John Smith with us to drive one wagon. We have seven wagons and fifty-six horses in our train. Today we have been baking light bread, boiling hams, cooking beans and stewing fruit and ironing. Mrs. Kirkland and I and Mrs. Hamilton went in an old house and stayed out of the rain. The men have been sitting around talking. None of us spent

---

[1]They now joined the Butterfield Overland Mail route. The "little town called Temakely" was Temecula *rancho*, which was the site of the Butterfield station there in Riverside County. They passed over the site of the present-day town of Temecula. Erwin G. Gudde, *California Place Names* (Berkeley, 1969), p. 334. Roscoe P. and Margaret B. Conkling, *The Butterfield Overland Mail, 1857-1869*, vol. II (Glendale, Calif., 1947), pp. 244-45. Gudde says that the meaning of the word, Temecula, is unknown.

the Sabbath as we ought. The boys got back from hunting Mr. Hamilton's horses but did not find them.

April 13   Clear and cold. The boys went back after the horses again. We all started again, came sixteen miles up a canyon with roads very bad, up hill and over rock. We all started again, and got along very well except Frank, who had his wagon broken. We are camped tonight at Oak Grove, on the banks of a creek on the other side of which are high bluffs covered with cedar trees. They turned the horses loose on the grass.

April 14   We have to stay here today. Frank has an axle to put in Mr. Barton's wagon. I have been baking light bread and cooking all day. Mrs. Kirkland is doing the same. Jane Hamilton is washing and some of the men have gone hunting. The children are enjoying themselves fine. My babe is sick from being out in the sun and smoke today. Frank got another hand to go with him. George C. Deacon.

April 15   Clear and cool. We came fifteen miles over very rough, muddy roads. Frank's wagon got stuck and we had to unload and dig it out. We passed several ranches and crossed the creek four times. We are camped tonight at Warner's Ranch.[2] They turned the horses out on the plains. Wood and grass are scarce. After supper an old squaw came in camp begging. Mr. Coggans whipped her away.

April 16   Clear and pleasant. We came two miles to a blacksmith shop and stopped for Frank to get his wagon mended. The blacksmith charged him three dollars and fifty

---

[2]This was the establishment of Jonathan Trumbull Warner, called by the Mexicans Juan José Warner, who had come overland to California with Ewing Young's trappers in 1831. The ranchhouse is now an historic landmark. In the 1850s the road from Warner's Ranch to Yuma was declared a public highway. Warner sold the ranch and moved to Los Angeles in 1855. Joseph J. Hill, *The History of Warner's Ranch and Its Environs* (Los Angeles, 1927); Kenneth L. Holmes, *Ewing Young, Master Trapper* (Portland, Or., 1967), pp. 61-93; Lorrin L. Morrison, *Warner, the Man and the Ranch* (Los Angeles, 1962).

cents for mending it. We all sat around the balance of the day, some cooking, some washing and so on. Wood is scarce. They have to go to the mountains after what they burn. Another man, George Beck, came into the company. He is going with Mr. Barton.

April 17   Clear and warm this morning. Old Mr. Cowden started back. He thoiught he could not stand to cross the plains. We came fifteen miles over good roads, passed one ranch and stopped at eleven o'clock to stay until tomorrow. The men are firing off their guns and fixing them up for the Indians. Frank went out and killed two rabbits. We are camped tonight in San Philippe [Felipe] valley with wood and water scarce but claw brush so thick we can hardly get about. Mrs. Kirkland and Mrs. Barton are washing.

April 18   Clear and warm. We started and came ten miles over rough roads through a valley surrounded by the [Vallecito] mountains, then over an awful rocky hill and down into the canyon. We all had to walk over the hill. We came four miles through the canyon to the [?   ] hill. It looks almost impossible to get down with the wagons. The wind is blowing very hard and it makes our little wagons look like they were going over all the time. It took two hours to get down the hill. They had to tie the wagon wheels with ropes, then the men at the wheels to lift them over the big rocks that are in road, if it might be called a road. The only way we could tell the road was that we could see where the wagons had run against the big rock. After we got down the hill we came four or five miles over a tolerable good roads and camped at Vicetah [Vallecito].[3] They have a little store and stage stand here but a doleful looking country all around.

---

[3]Vallecito was near present Palm Springs. The word means "Little Valley." The Conklings describe is as "a veritable oasis in the desert to travelers over this route," *op. cit.*, pp. 229-34.

April 19   A very warm morning. Some of our horses are gone this morning. We didn't get a very early start. We came 18 miles through very heavy sand and nothing to be seen but the high brush. We are camped tonight on Carsons [Carrizo] Creek,[4] one white man living a ranch here. We are camped on the bank of the creek in a dirty, sandy place with no grass nor wood. We have to tie the horses and buy hay for them.

April 20   We were up before day and got ready to start early across thirty miles of desert. They had some trouble with the broncho horses before they would stop jumping and kicking in the harness. We came eight miles up a sandy wash, then up a big hill out into the sand and it is as much as the horses can do to pull the wagons. We are camped tonight near a ranch at a big pond with wood and grass scarce. We got in camp at six o'clock, all very tired. The Indians are in camp wanting to herd the horses.

April 21   The herders drove up the horses and two of Mr. Kirkland's horses are gone. They started to hunt them and met the Indians coming with them. We had to give them two dollars and some flour to get them. We came 18 miles over sandy roads through a doleful looking country with nothing to be seen but sand and dust. We are camped tonight at a ranch on dry creek. We got in camp at three o'clock, all very tired, and had to draw water out of a well to water 53 horses. The women are all cooking. Indians are in camp with fish to sell. Mrs. Barton bought some and gave me some for supper. Frank has to go on guard tonight.

April 22   Very warm and windy. Frank and Mr. Gatewood got lost last night at midnight when they started to camp from herding and walked two hours before they found camp. I heard them halloing in the night and thought the Indians

---

[4] Carrizo Creek Station was an ideal stopping point for the stages. The little creek was some three feet wide. It was very clear and palatable. Conkling, *op. cit.*, p. 227.

were coming. We came fifteen miles through very deep sand. The wind was blowing very hard and we thought we were going to have a sand storm. The sand in the desert is in piles almost as big as a house, caused by the storm. We stopped at one o'clock to get dinner and and feed and then go on across 20 miles of desert but the wind continued to blow so we have to stay all night. We are camped at Alamere [Alamo Mocho] Station,[5] put the horses in the corral and buy feed at three dollars for the night. The whole earth has been overflowed by the Colorado river and it is nothing but a sand bed.

April 23   The wind blew very hard all night and this morning is cool and cloudy. They harnessed up to start and one of Frank's horses kicked the harness off twice before he would start. We came nine miles to an old ranch over tolerable good roads with sand and dust a foot deep and nothing to be seen but sand hills and brush and prickly pear. We stopped at the Seven Wells and watered and fed, then came on seven miles through sand and dust to Cook[e]'s Wells, where we camped for the night. We got in camp at six o'clock, bought hay at five cents a pound for the horses. There is plenty of wood and water. We got our supper and went to bed.

April 24   Warm and windy. We started early, came ten miles over very bad roads and through a thicket of mesquite trees to a slough, where the Colorado river is backed up. We passed some of the awfulest sand hills. They are piled up higher than a house. It is the most desolate looking country we ever did see. Frank and I came on before the other wagons and when we got there the Indians gathered thick around the wagon. I was a little frightened. They would keep asking if there were any more coming. They proped up the wagon beds four inches with blocks and then started across the slough.

---

[5]This was probably Alamo Mocho (Stump of the Cottonwood) Station, on the bank of the Alamo River. Conkling, *op. cit.*, pp. 221-23.

We had a very bad hill to come down into the water. We all crossed very well except Mr. Kirkland. His team would not pull in the water. The men had to wade in up to their waists. Frank had to take his mules back to pull the wagon out. The Indians are as thick as can well be. They are watching us cross, some up in trees or anywhere that they can get to see. After we got across we came six miles over good roads and through the prettiest place we have seen in a long time. The willow trees and brush were so thick we could not see through it. We are camped tonight at Pilot Rock [Knob] one mile from the river, with plenty of wood and water but no grass. We put up the horses in the corral and bought hay for them. This evening another young man, William More, came in with us. He is going with Barton.

April 25   Warm and windy. We came up to the ferry but the wind is so high we cannot cross. We are camped at Ferryman's ranch. They have to take the horses two or three miles from camp to grass. Frank is one of the herders. We are all going to wash   after that got dinner. The boys took us out to learn us to shoot. We all fired three or four rounds at a board. Some of us hit it and some did not. Lottie fell off the wagon this evening and cut her leg to the bone in the brake rack. We have plenty good mesquite wood to cook with.

Sunday, April 26   Still very warm. We all crossed the river this morning in a flat boat. They could only take on one wagon and six horses at a time. They charged us forty two dollars for crossing. We all get across by two o'clock. We saw some steamboats while we were at the river. We came six miles through sand [several unreadable words] in a low flat on the river, with Fort Yuma [Arizona][6] on the side and the

---

[6]Fort Yuma was on the north bank of the Gila River. The town of Yuma grew up on the opposite side of the stream. Edwin Corle, *The Gila, River of the Southwest* (New York, 1951), *passim*.

city on the other. The boat landed while we were there. We stopped in town a few minutes, then came on nine miles up the Hila [Gila] river and camped on its banks with no wood nor grass. We had to tie the horses and feed them on barley.

April 27   Cloudy and windy. We came 26 miles up the Heely [Gila] river with roads very rough and dusty, up hill and down. Sometimes we could hardly get along between the river and hills. One of Mr. Gatewood's horses got mired in the river and he got some Spaniards to pull it out. We are camped tonight at Mission Camp [Arizona].[7] Have plenty of wood, water and grass. They are trying to elect a captain but have considerable contention and no captain.

April 28   Clear and warm. We came sixteen miles over rough, sandy roads up the hill and passed one ranch. We are camped tonight at Antelope Peak in a flat on the Heely. We got in camp at three o'clock and have plenty of wood, water and grass.

April 29   A very warm morning. We came fourteen miles over rough roads to Mohawk Station, where we stopped and got water, then came eleven miles over rocky plain, through miserable looking country with nothing growing on the plain but cactus. We came down a big rocky hill into the bottom and camped for the night with good grass but have to carry wood and water some distance. Mr. Kirkland took Dick Delay, a young man from Arizona who wants to go to Texas, in with him.

April 30   Clear and warm. We came four miles through deep sand to Stanvick station and camped for the night. We have no grass for the horses. They were tied and fed barley.

May 1   Cool and windy. We came fourteen miles over tolerable good roads to [Patrick] Burk's Station[8] but there is

[7]Yuma County, Arizona, was on the south bank of the Yuma, some 4½ miles northwest of Wellton. Conkling, *op. cit.*, p. 190.

[8]Named for Patrick Burk, the first station keeper. Conkling, *op. cit.*, p. 181.

no one living there now. We stopped and turned the horses out to grass and got dinner. Dick Delay gathered Mrs. Kirkland some mustard green for dinner. She divided with me, which was quite a treat. After dinner we started and came eighteen miles over very rocky roads. We came up one awful rocky hill onto a rocky plain with nothing growing on it. The wind is blowing the dust so we can hardly see. It is the awfulest looking country we have seen. As far as our eyes can see we can see nothing but the sand and dust blowing. We travelled a few miles and came to the top of the hill where the Oatman family was murdured by the Indians. Frank was on ahead hunting grass. I felt miserable when we got here and did not see him. They had to tie the wagon wheels with ropes to get down the hill over the big rock. After we got down we came out on a low flat and passed the graves of the Oatman family.[9] They are laid by the side of the road seven in one grave, the father, mother and five children. We are camped tonight in Oatman Flat, two men living on a ranch here. There is no grass and we have to buy hay at 25¢ a head for 53 horses. The wind is blowing so hard we had an awful time getting supper. We had to hold our plates to keep the wind from blowing them away while we were eating. I think we will get our peck of dirt.

May 2   Clear and calm. We started and had a steep hill to

---

[9]This is named for the attack on the Oatman family in 1851 by Apache or Havasupai Indians. The family's father, Royse, and mother, Mary Ann, were killed as were children, Lucy, age 17; Royse, Jr., 10 or 12; Charity Ann, 4; and Roland, 18 months. Lorenzo D., 16, was left for dead, but he recovered. Two girls, Olive Ann, age 14, and Mary Ann, 7, were taken captive by the Indians and later traded to the Mohave Indians. Mary Ann died a year later; but Olive Ann lived. She was rescued some five years later by a white man, Henry Grinnel, and a Yuma Indian, named Francisco. A minister, The Rev. Royal B. Stratton, got to know Olive Ann and Lorenzo, and wrote their story in a book, *The Captivity of the Oatman Girls*, which gained national attention. A succinct treatment of this subject is in Dan L. Thrapp's *Encyclopedia of Frontier Biography*, vol. III (Glendale, Calif., 1988), p. 1071.

pull up. Then we came out on a rocky plain, the most miserable, desolate looking place, the rocks looking like they have been burned in a fire furnace. We came on over the plain a few miles, then down into a rocky canyon, through it and out on a flat and good roads with thickets of mesquite trees on each side of the road. We came fourteen miles to Canyon Station, stopped and watered, then came about two miles and camped by good grass to stay until Monday. Frank is on guard tonight.

Sunday, May 3   A pleasant morning. We are camped under some nice cottonwood trees. Mr. Delay is very sick. Today some have been cooking, some washing, some fishing and shoeing horses. Frank has been shingling Mrs. Kirkland's hair.

May 4   We started and came thirteen miles to Suttons ranch, where we stopped and turned the horses out to feed. The kegs were filled with water, we got dinner, then started on the forty five miles of desert. We travelled until eleven o'clock, stopped and watered the horses and took a cup of coffee, then started and travelled until two o'clock, when we stopped, turned the horses out and slept till daylight.

May 5   We got our breakfast and started over the dry alkali plain to Maria Copa [Maricopa] Wells.[10] We turned the horses on salt grass until until midnight, then fed them up and bought hay for them. Wood was scarce and the water not good. There is a company of soldiers stationed here. Some of them have their families here with them. It is a miserable place for a white man to live. They have a store or two and some other houses. John Smith went to sleep and let someone steal his revolver out of the holster.

---

[10]Maricopa Indians, a Yuman tribe. Col. Philip St. George Cooke of the Mormon Battalion was supposed to have dug the wells in December 1846. Conkling, *op. cit.*, p. 169.

May 6   Clear and cold. We started out with the Indians as thick as they can be. When we pass their wigwams the little naked Indians come swarming out like a swarm of bees. We came twenty five miles and camped at a ranch on the Heely river. Just as we drove in camp Mr. Barton's horses got scared and started to run but done no damage. They have to carry wood about a mile.

May 7   Cool and clear. We started this morning through the long dreaded Apache country. We came twenty five miles through a doleful looking country with very good roads. We are camped tonight at a ranch on Blue Water.[11] They have to draw water out of a well sixty feet deep to water the horses. They have to take the horses a half mile from camp to grass. It takes eight men to guard them. Frank is one of the guards.

May 8   Coyotes raised such a howl just before daybreak. They scared us as we thought they were Indians. A man is buried here who was killed by the Indians a few days ago. We have all been cooking today for the desert. It is now one o'clock and they are watering the horses to start on the forty six miles of desert. We started at two o'clock and travelled until 11, stopped, fed and took a cup of coffee, then started over very sandy roads and travelled until 7 o'clock. We got in camp all warn out and some of the horses were completely broken down. We came through a place where the Indians had killed two men and took a drove of cattle. We saw the horses lying dead on the roadside. The grass and weeds were flattened as if a log had been rolled over the place but we saw no Indians.

May 9   Clear and warm. They put the horses on grass and will rest this morning. We got our breakfast, then the men all slept. Mrs. Kirkland and I have been washing and baking

---

[11]Pinal Co., one of several change and water stations established by Butterfield in 1858-59. Conkling, *op. cit.*, p. 165. They have left the Gila River.

light bread. We have to be at something to keep our eyes open. We are camped at a ranch on a wide open plain eighteen miles from Tuscon [Tucson]. Two men live here and keep the stage stand.

Sunday, May 10   We started and came 18 miles to Tuscon, over hilly, rocky roads. We passed through town and camped about one mile from town at a mill in a thicket of mesquite bushes. We have plenty of good wood and water but poor grass.

May 11   Clear and very warm. We will stay here tonight to wash and clean up. The men have to go to town to get feed for the horses. They stayed in town all day. They bought some lettuce, onions and beef so we had quite a treat for supper. Mr. Delay is still sick.

May 12   Clear and cool. We started and came by a town. We saw the walls of an old Mission house that is 160 years old. We came thirty miles over rough roads to Seneca Creek. We crossed the creek eight times. We are camped on the creek in a bottom with plenty of grass and water, though a very dangerous looking place to camp. Frank is on guard tonight.

May 13   Cool cloudy. We started over the awfulest roads, up hill and down, over pole bridges, across branches and over rocks. We had one hill to come down that they had to tie all the wheels with ropes; then the wagons slide along sideways. We came seven miles and Mr. Barton broke his wagon. We had to stop to get it mended. They put the horses on grass. Mr. Barton took four men and went back five miles to get a stick for an axel. They got back at four o'clock. Frank went to work on it and worked until dark. The guards who were out today said they saw Indian breastworks, made of rock, which they hide behind and shoot at travellers.

May 14   Cool and windy. We were up early. Frank had the wagon fixed by 9 o'clock and we started, came twenty eight miles over tolerable good roads to San Pedro. There is good water but no wood or grass. They turned the horses out and fed them. There is a stage stand here and twelve soldiers stationed here to keep it. They say the Indians make a raid once in a while trying to get the stage horses. The wind is blowing so hard we liked never to have gotten supper.

May 15   Still very windy. We have to stay here until eleven o'clock so we can make a certain drive on the thirty five miles of desert. They put the horses on the mountains and herded them until 11 and then came in to start. We filled our kegs with water and started thru deep sand. We came through one dangerous looking canyon with just room enough for the wagons to pass through high mountains on each side. We had to look straight up to see the tops of them. We came out of the canyon onto a plain, came 20 miles and camped with no wood, water but plenty of grass. The wind is blowing so hard we can hardly stand up.

May 16   We were up before daybreak, took a cup of coffee and started. We came fifteen miles to the Sulphur Springs, stopped, turned the horses on grass and got dinner. We had no wood to cook with and there was so much alkali on the ground it looked like snow. After dinner we filled our kegs and started through the wide open plain, came within a few miles of the Apache Pass[12] and camped for the night with no wood nor water but plenty of grass. Frank is on guard tonight. We can see the Indian fires all around.

Sunday, May 17   Clear and warm. We were up before daybreak, got breakfast and started thru the Apache Pass, over awful roads, up hill and down. We had to tie the wagon

---

[12] A narrow passageway between Dos Cabezas and Chiricahua mountains. Often used by travelers in that part of Arizona. A post office had been established there on Dec. 11, 1866, with George Hand as postmaster. Will C. Barnes, *Arizona Place Names* (Tucson, 1988), p. 23.

wheels with ropes, and then in some places the men had to stand on the wheels to keep them from turning over. Every man who could leave the wagon had to take his turn and go on guard through the pass. We passed the place where there had been sixty persons killed by the Indians and saw their graves. We got through by eleven o'clock and were camped at the foot of the pass between the mountains, near a station where there is a company of soldiers. The Indians are very bad. They ran a herd of stock off from here a few days ago. There is plenty of grass and wood here but water is scarce. The soldiers are thick in camp. Gatewood sold four horses to them. We have not spent the Sabbath as we ought.

May 18   Clear and warm. We have to stay here half the day for Mr. Barton to get his wagon fixed. He got it fixed by 12 o'clock, then we filled our kegs with water and came 18 miles over tolerable good roads, to Sansimore[13] and camped for the night on the wide open plain with no wood nor water and poor grass. Two of the boys went to hunt water and came running back to camp and reported the Indians close by. We could see their camp fire and we didn't know but what we would be attacked before day.

May 19   We had quite a fright last night. The guards shot at a wolf that came in camp. We thought the Indians were coming. Every man was out in a minute with his gun ready for a fight. It liked to scare Mrs. Barton to death. She began to scream and jump and throw the children in the wagon out of the way. We started, came 17 miles through Doubtful Canyon,[14] with tolerable good roads, and through a doleful looking place with high mountains on each side. We stopped

---

[13]San Simon, Cochise Co. According to Will C. Barnes, *op. cit.*, pp. 386-87, San Simon boasts that it is the only town in Arizona that owns and operates a public bath house. An artesian well furnishes water and keys to the bath house are distributed to all citizens.

[14]Or Stein's Pass, a very hazardous part of the journey, Conkling, *op. cit.*, pp. 128-29.

at Stine's Peak to feed the horses and get our dinner. The wind is blowing so hard we liked never to get dinner. We fried bread for dinner and had about as much sand as flour. There is water and grass but no wood. There is an old deserted ranch here. The herders saw the Indians over the mountains. It is a good place for the Indians to hide. We started at four o'clock, came fourteen miles over good roads and camped on the open plain with plenty of grass but no water or wood. We had to dig a hole in the ground and cook with weeds. The wind is blowing very hard. Frank is on guard tonight.

May 20   The wind blew very hard all night and is still blowing, so we can hardly stand up. We came fifteen miles to Burney's Station and stopped to let the horses graze. We have to water out of the nasty, muddy pond. We rested two hours, then filled our kegs with the muddy water and came on twelve miles and camped out on the plain for the night with plenty of grass and no wood or water. We have to cook with weeds and the wind is blowing very hard.

May 21   Still very windy. We came about ten miles over rough roads to the Soldiers' Farewell,[15] stopped and watered the horses, then came 18 miles over good roads to Cow Springs,[16] where we camped for the night, with grass and water but no wood. We have to cook with weeds and grass. There are deserted ranches at all these places.

May 22   Cool and cloudy. It looks very much like rain. We started and it began to thunder and rain. It rained very hard for a few minutes to the Rio members [Mimbres][17] and camped with plenty of grass and water and wood enough to cook with. There is a settlement here with mostly Spaniards

---

[15] Between Soldier's Farewell and Cow Springs they passed over the continental divide at an elevation of 4,900 feet. Soldier's Farewell is also called Soldier's Grave. Conkling, *op. cit.*, p. 124; and Barnes, *op. cit.*, p. 414.

[16] *Ojo de la Vaca.*

in it. They say the Indians are very bad and they have to herd their stock all the time.

May 23   Cool and cloudy. It rained and the wind blew all night. We moved up onto better grass this morning and will stay until Monday. We have all been washing today. Three of the men went out hunting last night but got no game. Frank is on guard tonight and will be half of the night.

Sunday, May 24   Clear and warm. Three of Mr. Gatewood's horses were stolen last night by the Indians. They cut the ropes, took off the hobbles and run them off. He and four other men have gone to hunt them. We all feel much disheartened. We can't tell how long we will have to stay in this awful place.[18] A man came running into camp from town and told us the Indians were coming. We started after the horses, women and all, and soon got them all tied up close to the wagons. Then every man got out around them with guns but saw no Indians. We have been baking light bread today. I have baked six big loaves. Mrs. Kirkland four. Dick Delay is still sick.

May 25   Clear and cool. Mr. Gatewood got back last night but didn't get his horses. They saw where the Indians had taken them into a canyon where it was not safe for five or six men to go. We started and came through town to get some corn for the horses. They have a very nice looking stone hotel and a few doby [adobe] houses. There is nothing very interesting here. Nine of the Spaniards started and say they

---

[17]Grant Co., N.M. Conkling describes the station thus: "There were great groves of cottonwoods here and also a beautiful variety of willow from which the river derives its name. Although the Mimbres belongs to the peculiar class of the southwest desert streams, that flow and sink into their beds to reappear and flow again at some distant point, there was a permanent flow of good sweet water in the river at this point...Old inhabitants in the valley recall that grass in some sections stood waist high." *op. cit.*, pp. 119-20.

[18]It is hard to believe that she is writing about the same locality as she describes on May 22, above.

want to go to Texas with us. We came eighteen miles over tolerable good roads, except five or six miles where they were very hilly and rocky. We are camped tonight at Fort Cummings[19] with plenty of water but wood and grass are scarce. We had to buy grass at two cents per pound for the horses. A company of Negro Soldiers are stationed here.[20] They have a nice fort and the nicest looking buildings we have seen since we left Tuscon. We had a hard time getting supper. The wind was blowing hard and we had to cook with weeds. We made a fire by some big rocks and managed to cook a little.

May 26   Clear and windy. We have to stay here until twelve o'clock to get ready to start on the sixty miles of desert. The herders got into our bacon and beans last night and helped themselves to what we had cooked. We started at twelve o'clock and travelled until sundown, stopped, took a cup of coffee and then travelled until one o'clock. We then stopped and tied the horses until daylight, then came on over good roads, except in a canyon which we had to come through. We had a very bad hill to come down, over rock. I thought the wagons would be broken all to smash, but we got through safely.

May 27   We started at daybreak, came about twelve miles and stopped for breakfast and let the horses eat. We are out in the open plain with no wood, no water and very little grass. I

---

[19]Luna Co., at Cooke's Spring, 6 miles northwest of Florida, N.M. This fort was designed by General George B. McClellan for protection of travelers on the Butterfield Overland Mail in 1863. It was permanently abandoned in 1891. T.M. Pearce, *New Mexico Place Names* (Albuquerque, 1965), p. 58.

[20]On July 28, 1866, Congress approved the formation of two regiments of infantry and two of cavalry composed of "colored men" to serve on the frontier for the purpose of building roads, serving as escorts, and fighting the Indians. These were the "buffalo soldiers." They were so-called by the Indians because the texture of their hair reminded them of the hair of the great animals. John M. Carroll, *The Black Military Experience in the American West* (New York, 1971), *passim*.

broke Frank's favorite jug getting water out of it after breakfast. We came on over tolerable good roads, except three or four miles in very deep sand, to Mercatch [?], where we will cross the river. We are now standing at the Rio Gande waiting to cross. We all bought some eggs at 20¢ a dozen. We got across by sundown and had to pay 50¢ for crossing. One of Mr. Barton's horses fell off the boat and they pulled her out with ropes. We came one mile down the river thru deep sand and camped with plenty of wood and water but poor grass.

May 28   Clear and warm. We will stay here today to wash and fix the wagons. Some of the boys are going hunting. Frank and Mr. Kirkland went uptown to see if they could get a shop to set three wagon tires. After we got through washing and fixing the things in the wagons, Mrs. Kirkland and I baked light bread, cooked some bacon and eggs, stewed some apples and grapes. There are thirteen Spanish plows running here all day. They have oxen and a long pole with an iron spike on the end of it to stick the oxen to make them go. Their plows are a forked pole with a piece of iron on the edge. They just scratch up the ground a little.

May 29   We started and came two miles through sand to a little Spanish town. Frank bought some peas at one dollar a gallon. We then came on ten miles over very sandy roads to Los Crucius [Las Cruces], and passed some pretty wheat fields. Los Crucius is a considerable sized town. They have a nice Catholic church and other nice buildings for this country. We stopped in town awhile. They bought horse feed at four cents a pound. Frank met a man who gave him some cooked pears. We came on five miles from town and camped with plenty of wood and water but grass scarce. We came through Fort Filmore [Fillmore].[21]

---

[21]Named for President Millard Fillmore. It had been established in 1851 by Colonel E.V. Sumner for the protection of travelers. Pearce, *op. cit.*, p. 58.

May 30   There were five more men who came into the
company with us this morning: Mr. Shirley, Mr. Roberts,
Mr. Meeks and two Belcher brothers. We came fifteen miles
to Cottonwood Bend [Texas] and camped to stay until
morning on the banks of the Rio Grande out in the hot sun.
We got in camp at one o'clock, with wood and grass scarce.
We are waiting for Mr. Hamilton and Mr. Barton who stayed
back in town.

Sunday, May 31   Cool and cloudy. We had a very bad
accident in camp this morning. Only four or five of us were
up. I was at the back of the wagon mixing bread for breakfast
and Dick Delay was getting up. He had his shotgun within a
few steps of where I was, by his side. He accidentally stepped
on the lock and the gun went off, knocking me down and
shooting Mr. Ridgway in the chest. He seems badly hurt.
They put him in our little wagon and took him to Franklin[22]
to a doctor. We started and came fifteen miles over very
rough rocky roads. We are camped on the banks of the river
under a big cottonwood tree, with plenty of wood but no
grass. I have been sick all day from the shock I got this
morning. I am not able to get supper. Frank is on guard
tonight.

June 1   Clear and cool. The stage passed last night and
scared the horses. They all started to run with their hobbles
on. We thought the Indians were after them. We came fifteen
miles over very hilly, rocky roads to Franklin and got to town
about two o'clock. We found Mr. Ridgway able to travel.
The doctor did not take the shot out of his chest. We passed
through town and camped. It is a very nice looking place with

---

[22] Franklin was one of the earlier names of *El Paso del Norte* (North Pass), the Spanish
name given by 16th century conquistadores. It had grown out of several early settlements.
The name Franklin was given for Franklin Coons, who was named postmaster in 1852.
Fred Tarpley, *1001 Texas Place Names* (Austin, 1980), pp. 76-77.

the nicest looking doby buildings I ever saw. There is no grass for the horses. We have to tie them and buy hay at a cent and a half per pound.

June 2   A very warm morning. Frank has to get the tongue put in his little wagon this morning. They charged him fifty cents for the iron. We started and came 24 miles over very rough, bad roads. We came through three Spanish settlements and are camped in one tonight with no wood or grass but plenty of muddy water. Our horses are all getting sick. One of Frank's is too sick to work. Henry Coggens has the chills.

June 3   Warm and windy. We came fifteen miles through deep sand and over rocks, passed through one little Spanish settlement, stopped and bought some onions at 25¢ a dozen. Mr. Hamilton bought some apricots. We are camped on the banks of the Rio Grande with plenty of wood but no grass. We had quite a wind storm about sundown with an appearance of rain but it all blew over.

June 4   We started and came fifteen miles through deep sand most of the way and then rock. We are camped tonight in a nice cottonwood bottom on the Rio Grande, which is very comfortable and refreshing to the weary travellers, after travelling all day in the hot sun and sand. There is plenty of wood but no grass except salt grass and that is not good for the horses. We have several sick horses in our train now.

June 5   Clear and warm. The mosquitoes lost no time last night. They came in swarms and kept us fighting all night. We came 24 miles through deep sand to Pierpont's ranch, where we are camped for the night with plenty of wood and water but no grass, except that which they buy at a cent and a half per lb. One of Frank's mules is sick. Frank is on guard tonight.

June 6   Very warm. We have to stay here a few hours so they can send across the river to buy corn for the horses. One or two families are living here in this awful looking place. I can't tell how anyone can content themselves to stay here. We have all been washing. Mr. Gatewood and Mr. Beck went across in a ferry boat to get horse feed and had to pay three dollars a hundred for it. We started at eleven o'clock and came fifteen miles through awful sand and the sun was very hot. It makes our horses look very bad. We are camped tonight by a slough with plenty of wood and water but scarcely any grass.

Sunday, June 7   We came eight miles through sand and alkali dust to Fort Quitman[23] and saw the Negro soldiers marching around with their white gloves on and their faces as black as ink. We passed through the fort and saw two negroes astraddle of a high pole because they had been drunk. We came a mile and a half below the fort and camped on a slough that is backed up from the Rio Grande river. The locusts keep up such a fuss they almost deafen us. We have plenty of wood and water but very little grass. We had quite a wind and rain storm this evening.

June 8   Cool and windy. We will stay here today to set wagon tires. We have three very sick men in our train and many of our horses are sick. Frank is on guard tonight.

June 9   We had a very hard storm last night with rain, hail, and wind. It blew very hard for about half an hour, then it seemed as if a water spout had bursted and the whole bottom was covered with water in a few minutes. We all had to gather up our things in a hurry and expected to be washed away but the water was only about two inches deep where our wagons stood. We have to stay here today on account of the mud.

---

[23] Another lady traveler wrote in her reminiscences in 1893, telling of her visit to Fort Quitman in 1869, "When we sighted the Rio Grande, five miles below Fort Quitman, a sense of relief took the place of my recent uneasiness and fear; and when we drove into the forlorn and tumble down adobe built fort, I wanted to greet everybody as friend and brother. The troops stationed here were colored. . ." Carroll, *op. cit.*, p. 106. Carroll's reference is to Lydia Spencer Lane, *I Married a Soldier* (Philadelphia, 1893), p. 186.

Frank and Mr. Barton went up to the fort to get corn for the horses and had to pay five cents a pound for it. We have all been drying our beds, cooking, patching and so on. Our sick are no better and the locusts still keep up their songs.

June 10   Clear and warm. We started and came six miles through a miserable looking country to where we will leave the river. We stopped and stayed until three o'clock, then filled our kegs with water for the horses and started on the thirty miles of desert, with some of our horses so sick they can hardly walk. We came eight miles through a rocky canyon, roads very bad, and as luck would have it we found water and had to stop on account of our sick horses. We are camped in the canyon with tolerable good grass.

June 11   Clear and warm. One of Mr. Gatewood's horses died last night, one of Frank's mules and one of Mr. Hamilton's horses are down and can't stand up and several more of the horses are very sick. We will stay here today and see if they get better. We are all very much disheartened.

June 12   Warm and windy. Mr. Hamilton's horse is dead. Our poor mule is still lying suffering. We have to leave her. We started and came four miles through the canyon and over rocky roads. After we got out of the canyon we came six miles over tolerable good roads. We all stopped to rest the horses but Mr. Gatewood drove on. We turned the horses on grass and rested two hours, then started. One of Mr. Kirkland's horses died. Just as we started we met a train of Texans going to California. They say we are going the wrong way. One of the men promised Frank that he would shoot his mule that he left in the canyon. We came ten miles over good roads, found water and camped for the night in a valley between the mountains with plenty of wood, water and grass. Mr. Gatewood was here waiting for us. It is thundering and lightning with the appearance of a storm. Frank is on guard tonight.

June 13   We came fifteen miles to Eagle Springs and camped in a canyon between the high Rocky mountains. A company of Negro soldiers is stationed here. Water is scarce and what we have is nasty, muddy water, hardly fit to drink. We have tolerable good grass but have to take the horses over the mountains to get it. There is no wood. We have three men in our train who some say have the smallpox, which has caused great excitement. Orders were sent on ahead not to let us stop at any of the stations.

Sunday, June 14   Cool and cloudy. We will stay here until two o'clock to cook for the sixty miles of desert. We all baked light bread, stewed fruit and boiled some bacon and beans, then filled our kegs with the nasty, muddy water and started. We had a shower of rain just as we started which revived us very much. We came eight miles and found water enough to water the horses, then travelled till sundown, when we stopped, turned the horses on grass and got supper. We rested two hours, then travelled until eleven o'clock over rough roads, then stopped, turned the horses on grass and went to bed.

June 15   We started early and came ten miles, then got breakfast and rested two or three hours. We then started and travelled until sundown through the sand and dust. We passed one lone grave on the desert. Our horses almost gave out when we got to water. Frank's mule was almost crazy for water. They could hardly hold her to get the harness off. We have plenty of water and grass but no wood. We have to cook with weeds.

June 16   A very warm day. We have stayed here all day to rest the sick horses. Another of Mr. Gatewood's died to day. We have all been washing a little and trying to cook but we have a hard time out in the hot sun cooking with weeds. We have to stand over the fire to put on weeds all the time to keep it from going out. I have a sick headache from being out in the hot sun and smoke all day. This is Frank's night to go on guard but I was so sick he did not go.

June 17   Cool and pleasant. Our horses were stampeded last night and ran to the mountains before they got them stopped. They thought they were gone but they soon got them back. We do not know what scared them. We started and came seven miles to Dead Man's Hole, to get water. They didn't want us to stop because we have smallpox in our train but we stopped and stayed two or three hours, got dinner and filled our water kegs. The Negroes are building them a stone house at the foot of the mountains. There is no timber growing here, Nothing but mescal catclaw brush and rock in abundance. We came eight miles over good roads and camped out on the plain with no wood, water nor grass. They tied the horses and fed them. The wind is blowing very hard and it is thundering and lightning with the appearance of a storm. I still have a headache very bad. Frank has the cooking to do.

June 18   Very windy. It rained some last night. We came ten miles to the Barrel Springs and are camped here between the mountains. There are more Negroes here and they seem to enjoy themselves. Grass, water and wood are scarce. There is a large train of Texans here, going to California. Our sick men are not much better.

June 19   Cool and clear. Although we had a very hard rain last night we started at eight o'clock and came twelve miles over good roads, through a nice oak grove to a spring in the mountains, where we found enough water for us all to drink but none for the horses. We stopped and ate dinner, resting two or three hours, then came ten miles over good roads to Fort David [Davis], a tolerable nice looking place. Soldiers, white men and Negroes, are stationed here. They are putting up some very nice looking houses and have three or four stores. Frank bought some coffee at 50¢ per lb., sugar at 40¢, flour at 10¢. We drove thru town and camped, tied the horses and fed them.

June 20. Clear and warm. We will stay here until evening for the train to buy horse feed. They bought six hanigars of corn at four dollers a hanigar [hanaper]. Frank bought 25¢ worth of soap and two pounds of soda at 40¢ a pound. He met with a friend who gave him three or four pounds of coffee and nine or ten lbs. of bacon. Mrs. Kirkland, Mrs. Hamilton and I went up to the store and got some calico to make a bonnet. We had the doctor come to camp and see the men with smallpox. He says it is not a smallpox. He vaccinated all the children except ours. We moved up two miles and camped to stay until Monday. There is a train of Texans camped here going to California. There is plenty of grass, wood and water. Frank is on guard tonight. They have to take the horses to the mountains to get grass.

Sunday, June 21   Cool and pleasant. They bought a beef this morning, killed it and we had quite a treat. The Texas ladies came up to camp. They try to discourage us all they can by abusing the country. We have been cooking all day. Frank bought some salt from a Texan at 3¢ a pound.

June 22   Cool and windy. We started. Frank has a broncho that is doing his best in kicking and jumping and rolling over the wagon tongue. We came through a very hilly, rocky canyon with rocks hundreds of feet high, perfectly round and straight. We all had to get out and walk. We came about ten miles and it began to thunder and rain, blow and hail. We stopped and unhitched the horses from the wagons. We thought we were going to have a hail storm but it only lasted a few minutes. We then came five miles and camped for the night in the canyon close to a creek but there was no water in it; plenty of grass and wood. Frank took his little wagon and they all put a water keg in it and went up the creek to a hole of water and hauled enough for the train to cook with. Another train of Texans passed us bound for California.

June 23   Clear and cool. Last night the water came down the creek a booming, bringing the rocks and brush before it. A water spout bursted in the mountains. It made a big lumbering when it came and we have plenty of water this morning and it is as cold as ice. We came ten miles over rough roads to Gorrila [Barilla] Station. Negroes are stationed here. They wanted to keep us from passing. They said we had smallpox. We passed on by them, drove up to a big pond and turned the horses out and got dinner. There is another big train of Texans going to the land of gold, they think. We filled our water kegs with water and came five miles and camped for the night out on the plain, with plenty of grass and wood.

June 24   Clear and windy. We came about five miles over rocky roads and found water in Gorilla [Barilla] Creek. We stopped, turned the horses out and will rest awhile. Here is another train of Texans with a big drove of cattle on the way to California. We stayed two or three hours to eat dinner, then started and came about ten miles and made a dry camp on the plain, with tolerable good grass but no wood. We had to cook with weeds and the wind was blowing so hard we could hardly stand up. It blew our fire away as fast as we could build it. Our wagons rock and shake like they would go over. Frank is on guard tonight. He is complaining very much.

June 25   Frank had a chill last night at midnight as he came off guard and is still very sick. We started before sunup and came five or six miles, stopped and got breakfast at a dirty, muddy pond that hundreds of cattle have ran through the last few days but it is all we have to cook with or drink. After breakfast we came on over good roads to the Leon Holes. We got here at one o'clock. This is a dry alkali place with no wood and very poor grass. The water is so salty we cannot have good coffee or tea. There is a stage stand here with three or four white men and some Negroes living here. Frank is still very sick. We got dinner and filled our kegs with the salt water. They say those waterholes have no bottom. We came four or five miles and camped for the night. Grass and wood are scarce. The wind is blowing our dresses around the thorny brush and tearing them to pieces.

Friday, June 26   Clear and warm. Frank is better. We came nine miles over good roads to Fort Stogdon [Stockton]. There we had to stand in the hot sun two hours. They said we could not go through town because we have smallpox in the train but the boys have all got about well at last. We started, came through town and stopped one mile from town. They have a considerable sized town and fort. We got dinner over. Some want to go across the desert and some the southern route. They talked about it until evening and all concluded to go the southern route, which is 150 miles farther, so we all started and nearly to town then backed out. Frank, Mr. Kirkland and Mr. Gatewood will try the desert. Mr. Hamilton and Mr. Barton will go the other road. So we parted here. Frank and Mr. Kirkland and Mr. Gatewood took the little wagon and went into the fort to get corn and water barrels for the desert. They got four barrels from two to four dollers apiece. They got corn at 8¢ a pound. We have fifteen men with us and Mr. Hamilton has eight. Henry Coggens went with him. We filled our kegs with water for the horses and came five miles, when we camped out on the plain with plenty good grass but no wood. We have to cook with little sage brush. The wind is very high. It is almost impossible to cook at all.

June 27   Clear and warm. We came eleven miles to Antelope

Springs and stopped to get dinner and water is so salty we can hardly cook with it. Mrs. Kirkland and I tried to boil some beans but could not boil them soft. Our coffee was so salty we could scarcely drink it. The grass is so dried up with alkali that it cracks under our feet as we walk. The whole country is covered with mesquite brush and muscat. After dinner we started, came ten miles over good roads and camped for the night out on the plains in a very pretty place for this country with good grass but no wood or water. Dick Delay is very sick again.

Sunday, June 28   Very pleasant this morning. We came 12 miles over very good roads through the mesquite brush to the Horse Head Crossing on the Pecus [Pecos] river, a nasty, dirty, muddy, ugly stream. Everything within two or three miles around is burned up with alkali and the dead cattle lay thick on the banks of the river. We dip up the water and put it in the barrels for the dirt to settle to the bottom, then use the water for cooking and drinking. They have to take the horses two miles from camp to get grass. Frank is one of the herders. Dick Delay is still sick. Mrs. Kirkland is complaining very much. The boys killed a beef this evening for us to cook for the desert. There are about 2,000 head of cattle on the other side of the river, just off the desert.

June 29   Warm and windy. The mosquitoes lost no time last night in keeping me company. The boys around camp had to sit up all night with blankets wrapped over their heads and keep smoking to keep them from eating their eyes out. The guards had to smoke their pipes and even then were almost eaten up by them. The horses are covered with knots where they have been bitten. Today we will cross the river. Mrs. Kirkland is very sick, though she and I have to cook all day in the hot sun for the desert. There is not the least bit of shade to put our horses under the little children are crying because the sun burns them and they can't get out of it. The men are crossing the wagons then tie ropes long enough to reach across, then tie one end to the wagon tongue. Then the men swim and pull the wagons over. They tied four water barrels together, put the decking plank on them and took most of our loads over on them. Some would pull and some swim after and hold them. There are a company of negro soldiers stationed here. Mrs. Kirkland, I and children crossed in a skiff boat there. The negroes brought the boat down where we were crossing and helped us to get the balance of our load over. They got everything across by four o'clock. The men are all very tired and half sick. They have been swimming the river backward and forward all day long. We are camped on the banks of the river between the river and a big alkali pond with just enough room for our wagons to stand between them. The herders have to swim back across the river to herd the horses.

June 30   Warm and very unpleasant where we are. Mrs. Kirkland is very sick. We reloaded our wagons and filled our water barrels with nasty, dirty water. We can see the dead cattle floating down while we are dipping up the water and see them lying on the banks all over. This is all we will have to drink for 87 miles. There is a man in camp now telling us there are three thousand dead cattle in a canyon we have to go through this evening. This is not very pleasant news to the worn out travellers and half of them sick. Mrs. Kirkland and I prepared our camp fire to kill the smell. The herders drove in the horses and swam them across the river and we all started on the long desert at one o'clock. We came 15 miles through a doleful looking country with alkali dust three or four inches deep. Every now and then we would pass a pile of dead cattle seven or eight in a pile and it being a very warm evening it was not a very pleasant trip I tell you. We came through the long dreaded canyon but did not have half as much use for our camphor as we expected to. There were about 300 dead cattle from the river up instead of 3,000. The canyon is three miles through and very rocky. We stopped at 8 o'clock and ate supper and rested the horses two hours. We then started and traveled until two o'clock, then turned the horses out and slept until daylight.

July 1   Warm and windy. We started at daylight, travelled until 8 o'clock, stopped and got breakfast. We then travelled until one o'clock through a lonesome looking country with nothing but the wide spreading plain to look at. We stopped and got dinner and fed the horses and rested until three o'clock. We started again, met a drove of cattle going on past a place where there has been a ranch. Then we travelled until sundown over good roads, stopped and fed the horses and came on until one o'clock. We stopped and fed at Chiny Pond[24] but there was no water. We are now out of water for the horses or to drink ourselves.

July 2   We got to the Cancho [Concho] river this morning, just as the sún was rising. We are all very tired and worn out from lack of sleep. I have not slept more than three hours since we started on the desert. While we were watering our horses there were four Texas boys camped close by. We heard them singing like Indians and that they were, so we drove up to a stone wall and prepared for fighting them but soon found our mistake, which made us feel much better than if we had gone to fighting the redskins just after getting off the long and tiresome desert. We drove in to camp, turned the horses on grass and got breakfast and rested while the Texas boys brought some beef up to swap for bread. They had not any bread for four days. When we gave them the bread they

---

[24]Wild China Ponds. This was a good watering place along the way. It was named for the china berry trees which flourished here. Conkling, *op. cit.*, vol. I, p. 371.

whooped and yelled "Hurrah for Texas." After breakfast we came four or five miles and stopped on the banks of the river in a thicket of mesquite brush. Another train of Texans was here with a drove of cattle on their way to California. Frank sold his water barrel to them to hold water on the desert. We stayed there until 4 o'clock, then came up one and a half miles to a picket station and camped for the night. Have to take the horses across the river to grass. Frank is one of the guards. There is a company of white soldiers stationed here, the first we have seen since we left except the officers of the negroes. Frank bought some flour and bacon here.

July 3   Cool and cloudy, having the appearance of rain. We travelled till 12 o'clock and camped on the Concho river to stay until morning. Plenty of wood, water and grass, with pecan trees on the river. There is no other timber except mesquite. The boys have all gone fishing.

July 4   Raining and very disagreeable. We like never to get our breakfast. The rain would put out the fire as fast as we could kindle it. We had a nice mess of fried fish. We came six miles through a hilly country having no timber but mesquite. It began to rain so hard that we had to stop at the foot of a big hill, turn the horses out and make up a big fire. The boys have all gone fishing for their Fourth of July sport. Mr. Ridgeway was sitting on the bank fishing when he looked up and there was a panther just fixing to jump on him. They shot at it but did not kill him. We started on at 2 again and came five or six miles and camped for the night in a thicket of mesquite brush.

Sunday, July 5   Still raining and the roads are very muddy. We came twelve miles through the open plain and happened upon some wild cattle. We stopped and killed a nice fat cow, took what we wanted and left the balance lying on the road side. Camping at 2 o'clock, we stayed until morning and

cooked up some of our beef. Grass and water were scarce, the
water having to be carried some distance. Mrs. Kirkland is
washing and I have been cooking as hard as I could ever since
we stopped. Frank is on guard tonight.

July 6   A warm and cloudy morning. We travelled about
twelve miles and stopped for dinner, crossing the river just
once. As we finished dinner it began to rain and rained for a
few minutes as hard as I ever saw it rain in my life. After the
rain was over the frogs began to croak so that we thought it
was a big drove of sheep up the river. We started, came four or
five miles to a stage station and thought we were going to have
a hail storm so we camped for the night near the river. The
boys all went fishing and caught all the fish they wanted.
There was plenty of wood, water and grass.

July 7   Clear and windy. We started, crossed the river and
came several miles over muddy roads to Fort Concho,[25] a
very pretty place. Seven or eight hundred soldiers are
stationed here. They would not let us stop in town, so we
drove on through and stopped for Frank and Mr. Kirkland
to go back and get provisions. They got some coffee and
bacon, but could not get any bread stuffs. Coffee and bacon
were forty cents a pound. We then came out three miles fom
the fort and stopped for dinner. They let the horses eat grass
two or three hours, then started and took the wrong road and
travelled twelve miles over a beautiful plain to a corral on the
river, built for the purpoose of catching wild horses, we
supposed. Next we drove out close to the river and camped,
with plenty of water and grass, wood being not so good. We
have plenty of fried fish but bread is scarce and what little we
have must be saved for the children.

July 8   Clear and warm. We started out, travelled on through
the plain till 8 o'clock and came across some nice fat cattle.

[25]Present San Angelo.

We stopped and killed a beef, took what we wanted and left the rest. Those were cattle that had been lost from droves as they are going through. We travelled on and happened to see a train of Texans going to California with a drove of cattle, so we got on the right road again. One of the men gave Frank a bushel of meal, which we were very glad to get. Continuing on for the three miles we stopped for dinner and fed the horses. We rested till 2 o'clock, then came ten miles over good roads and camped out on the plain at a pond of water, with plenty of wood and grass and plenty of fried fish for supper. Frank is on guard tonight. I washed until 10 o'clock.

July 9   Clear and cool. We travelled till 12 o'clock over very rough roads and stopped for dinner on the banks of the river. The boys are all fishing. Mr. Meeks gave me four nice catfish, the smallest one is over a foot long. Travelling on till 4 o'clock we crossed the Concho river for the last time, filled our water kegs with water and drove about five miles and camped for the night out on a beautifal plain with plenty of good grass and wood. Frank is on guard in the place of one of the other boys, who is sick.

July 10   Clear and pleasant. Five of our Texas boys left us this morning for home. They think we are out of Indian danger and they want to get home. We came on two miles to the Colorado river in Texas.[26] We had two very steep hills to pull up. Frank's broncho pony started up hill jumping and kicking and stopped the wagon when they were about half way up. Then they had some trouble getting up. I thought they would kill the pony before they got up. We then came three miles to Spring creek. There are some cattle drovers living here. We then came six miles to Elm creek, stopped

---

[26] Here the Shacklefords, the Kirklands, and the Gatewoods left the rest of the party and the Butterfield route. They would join the Butterfield Trail at Sherman, Grayson Co., on September 7.

and watered the horses, and then took the wrong road for three miles. We then took out across the plain to find the road, which we travelled about two miles and came to the road, where we stopped and got dinner. After dinner we continued three or four miles up Panther creek, stopped and watered the horses and filled our kegs. Driving farther on six or seven miles we camped for the night out on the plain. Grass and wood are scarce.

July 11   We came seven miles to Home creek, where several families are living. It is a lonely looking place to live in. We stopped to buy some meal or flour, but they had none. They give some of the boys all the corn bread they had baked. That is all the kind of bread they have now. We came on three miles and stopped for dinner under some shade trees, which seem very pleasant to us who have not had the pleasure of sitting under one for a long time. Mrs. Kirkland is sick, so we rested till 2 o'clock, then came twelve miles through some beautiful country, with pretty, fat cattle all over the plains. We are camped on the plain by a branch but very little water is in it, and what is is green as grass. Plenty of wood and grass. Frank is on guard tonight.

Sunday, July 12   Clear and warm. We have to make our breakfast this morning of beef and coffee, which is very poor living. Mrs. Kirkland is better. We came twelve miles over very rough roads. We crossed the creek and camped under a big tree. There is a field of corn here just in roasting ears. We got what we wanted, eating them in place of bread. We got dinner over, then they concluded to stay till morning. Frank bought some corn meal at one dollar and twenty-five cents a bushel. We have what buttermilk we can drink. Two more of our Texas boys left us this morning to go home. There are a good many living here raising cattle for their living. They turned the horses out without herders.

July 13   We started, passed five or six houses and stopped at all for milk. We got our kegs filled with buttermilk and bought butter at a bit a pound. Coming on eight miles, we stopped for dinner in a pretty oak grove, rested two hours, then came ten miles more and camped for the night on the plains. Just as we drove into camp it began to rain and rained very hard for about half an hour. There is good wood and grass at this place. They turned the horses out with herders. Mrs. Kirkland and I did not get out of the wagon to get supper. The men have made up a big fire and are all standing around it nearly crazy because they are out of tobacco. Some of them have chewed sticks till their teeth are sore.

July 14   Cool and cloudy. We came ten miles to a little settlement called Commanche [Comanche], where there are a few houses and two stores. We stopped and bought some things at the store. Tobacco was the first thing some of the men bought, coffee next. We came out one mile from town and camped on Squaw creek to stay till morning. Two more of our boys stopped here. They are going back with a drove of cattle. We have only four men. It is rather lonesome in camp now. We had a very hard thunder shower this morning.

July 15   We have stayed here today to rest the horses and to wash. Mrs. Kirkland and I have been washing all day. Frank and Mr. Kirkland went up town and got some corn. The people want them to stop here very bad, they think they have not seen enough of Texas yet. Had another hard rain this evening. Frank traded his broncho pony off for a horse that was no better.

July 16   Warm and cloudy. We came ten miles to the Leon river over very rough, sandy roads and stopping for dinner and to rest the horses after dinner. We came on, crossed the river, had a very steep hill on both sides. We all got over very well, then came five miles over rough roads and camped at

Mr. Stone's for the night. Had a hard shower of rain just as we got into camp, which made everything very disagreeable. Mrs. Kirkland's little boy is very sick.

July 17   A warm morning. We travelled untill noon through a timbered country which was very sandy and very hard on the horses. We stopped for dinner and to rest the horses, in a place where there was plenty of grass. The horses were then turned out without herders and we had no trouble with them. After resting two hours, we continued on ten or twelve miles through deep sand and camped on a little creek.

July 18   Clear and warm. We came upon a little town two miles farther on called Stephensville, where the houses looked like those built when Texas was first settled. Everything looks like it was going to destruction. We stopped in town a few minutes and Frank bought some sugar at twenty-five cents a pound. Coming on through the town, we stopped at a little creek called Bosco and watered the horses, then came ten miles over very bad roads to the Indian water holes and stopped for dinner and to rest the horses. Just as we drove up the horses to start again, it began to rain and rained for about an hour as hard as it could come down. We then started out, coming five or six miles over very slippery roads. We had to cross the creek five or six times and banks were so steep and slippery that the horses could scarcely stand up. We all had to get out and walk over them. Our camp is at a Mr. Roberts, where we got some good buttermilk and roasting ears for supper. It is still cloudy and looks like rain.

July 19   This is a very warm and sultry morning. We waited until 9 o'clock before we started for the roads to dry some, then after we had started we had to cross the south fork of the Leon river. Which had very steep banks on both sides. We came on about three miles and crossed the same river again. There are several families living here where we got some buttermilk to drink. Then we continued on about ten miles over very bad roads. With the roads and sand and the extreme heat of the day, it made going very difficult for the horses. We had a hard thunder shower about 2 o'clock so we drove out under some oak trees until it was over, then came five or six miles and camped in a pretty oak grove near a settlement.

July 20   Still very warm and unpleasant. We came ten miles over tolerable good roads through some pretty country. Stopped at a place, we bought butter at a bit a pound. We stopped in a little town called Stockton and got dinner and rested the horses until 4 o'clock. We started, crossed the Brazos river, where the water is clear but salt to drink, and came on six miles through prairie to Center Mill[27] and camped for the night. Frank and Mr. Kirkland are very much dissatisfied with this part of Texas. It is hilly, broken country timbered with scrub oak.

July 21   We have stayed here to look around and see what they can do. There is a protracted meeting going on here. Frank went last night and said they had a good meeting. We could hear them shout a half a mile. This has been a very warm day and I have been doing some washing. Frank has gone to the meeting tonight.

July 22   Still warm. Mrs. Kirkland went to church today and saw a great many strange faces. We heard a good sermon, and saw one of the preacher's wives converted to God and heard them shout until they were perfectly exhausted. Mr. Kirkland met his brother today, whom he has not seen for a long time. Mr. Kirkland and Mrs. Kirkland have gone to church tonight.

---

[27]Here decisions would be made about whether to settle in Texas or to go on to Missouri where they had lived before their 1865 journey west to California. The Shacklefords and the Kirklands decided to go on to Missouri, where they settled in Roscoe, St. Clair Co.

July 23   Frank rented a house today at six dollars a month to stay in while the horses rested up. Mr. Kirkland moved into a schoolhouse close by. Frank can get all the work he wants to do. They have no vegetables nor wheat this season on account of the grasshoppers. They live on corn bread and beef.

July 24   Still very warm and unpleasant. Frank is fixing to repair an old buggy and I have been to the preaching again today. They are having a good Baptist meeting.

July 25   Nothing new today. Frank is working on an old wagon and I have been patching some. We are not satisfied with Texas yet. Where we are stopping there is a mill, one store and three dwelling houses. Here the men seem to have no energy to do anything save drive cattle.

Sunday, July 26   Very warm and unpleasant. Frank and some of the children have gone to church. The meetings will close tonight. I never heard how many joined the church. Jake Kirkland and wife came up today to see Mrs. Kirkland.

July 27   Clear and warm. Frank is busy at work on an old wagon wheel and I have been washing and ironing.

July 28   Still very warm and dry. Nothing new has happened today. Frank is still working on the wagon. Mrs. Kirkland came down and stayed all day with me. We have been sewing.

July 29   It is still too warm to be comfortable. Frank is working away on the wagon wheels. I have been stitching shirt bosoms for Mrs. Leadbetter, finishing four for which I got twenty-five cents apiece. This evening I went down to see Mrs. Burns.

July 30   Mrs. Kirkland and Mrs. Gatewood have gone to the sulphur springs[28] on a visit to see Mr. Kirkland's brother. Have been sewing for Mrs. Burns and Frank finished the wagon he was working on today.

---

[28]Not to be confused with the city of Sulphur Springs, much farther east.

July 31　　Today is my birthday. I washed this morning and iron this evening. Frank is working on a buggy. The old mill is lumbering away. They only grind on Friday and Saturday.

August 1　　Still very warm and unpleasant. Mrs. Kirkland and Mrs. Gatewood got back this morning some better pleased with Texas. I have been making sacks and handkerchiefs for the merchant here at ten cents apiece. The Methodists have preaching today and tonight at the arbor. Frank has gone tonight, leaving me and children at home.

Sunday, August 2　　Frank and some of the children have gone to meeting. The little ones and I did not go. After dinner we went up to see Mrs. Kirkland and stayed while Miss Oxer came home with them from the springs. We had a nice rain this evening.

August 3　　Some cooler after the rain. Nothing new today. We have all been sitting around not doing much.

August 4　　Warm as ever. Frank is working on an old buggy and I have been sewing for Mrs. Burns and Mrs. Ranking. Mrs. Gatewood took Miss Oxer home.

August 5　　Frank finished the buggy he was mending and Mr. Kirkland has been setting their wagon tires. I have been washing and packing up to start tomorrow. We had another shower of rain this evening, which livens everything up very much.

August 6　　Mr. Gatewood got back from the springs today in the notion to marry, so they all been sitting around camp. Frank wrote a letter. There is preaching today in the arbor. We have concluded to stay two weeks longer, and we had to move our in camp since Mr. Ranking wanted the house we are in. We are camped under some oak trees close to the schoolhouse where Mr. Kirkland is camped. It rained very hard just after we got into camp.

August 7   Warm and windy. Frank has another buggy to repair. I have been making Mr. Gatewood a fine shirt, which is not very nice work out in the wind and dust

August 8   Nothing of importance happened today. Frank is working on the buggy and I have been washing and ironing and sewing some.

Sunday, August 9   We can hear the sermon without going. Also there is singing in the schoolhouse this evening, where Mr. Kirkland is camped.

August 10   Today is Frank's birthday. There is nothing new and it is still very dry and warm.

August 11   Frank is working on an old buggy. I went to the creek and done my washing this morning. This evening I have been sewing for Mrs. Burns.

August 12   The weather is still very warm and disagreeable. Frank is working a little. They have to go twice every day and get up the horses and feed them corn. Mrs. Kirkland and I have been ironing and fixing to go to the Masonic dinner tomorrow.

August 13   Very warm. We all went nine miles to the Masonic dinner and saw a great many people but did not enjoy ourselves at all. I had a sick headache and did not get any of the dinner or hear any of the speaking. They had plenty of baked beef, goat meat, corn bread and coffee for dinner. We stayed there until 3 o'clock then went nine miles up to the sulphur springs to see Mr. Gatewood get married.[29] He was married to Miss Oxer, after which we had a very nice supper but I could not enjoy it.

August 14   Still very warm. We all came to Jake Kirkland's and took dinner, then came seven miles to where we are

[29]Atwell B. Gatewood was the widower of Ruth Shackleford's deceased sister who had died on the trail west. We do not learn the full name of "Miss Oxer."

camped. There are a great many persons at the springs for their health. I think the water is awfully bad to drink.

August 15   Very warm. Frank is at work and I have been sewing all day for Mrs. Leadbetter. Mr. Gatewood brought his wife up this evening. She does not like the idea of going to Missouri. I have sat and sewed and listened to a good sermon.

Sunday, August 16   Preaching again today. Frank went over but I stayed in camp and heard most of the sermon. Mr. Gatewood took our little wagon and went down to get his wife's plunder.

August 17   Very warm. Mrs. Kirkland and I went down to the creek and done our washing. This evening I have been sewing for Mrs. Burns.

August 18   Raining and very disagreeable for those who have to camp out of doors.

August 19   Still raining and the roads are very muddy. We all stayed in the schoolhouse during the daytime and sleep in our wagons at night.

August 20   It is still raining. Frank finished the buggy he was repairing. Today he will get two cows and calves for it. He sold two of his water kegs for two dollars apiece and got sixty pounds of beef today at three cents a pound.

August 21   Still cloudy. Frank and Mr. Kirkland have been fixing to start. I have been tucking some skirts for Mrs. Burns.

Sunday, August 22   Clear and very warm. I thought I would faint cooking out in the hot sun. Jake Kirkland and wife came up from the sulphur springs to see her sister, Mrs. Gatewood. She went home with them to stay all night.

August 24   Very warm. The men are getting up their cows. Frank has two cows and calves, Mr. Kirkland one, and Mr.

Gatewood four. Mrs. Kirkland is washing. Frank has bought eight bushels of meal since we have been camped here, at seventy-five cents a bushel.

August 25   Clear and warm We were up early and got up the horses to start. One of Frank's cows got away and he had to hunt her, not finding her until about 9 o'clock. Then we all had some fresh beef brought to us so we have to fix that up. Then we got dinner and afterwards left Center Mill on Long creek, Hood county, Texas, where we have been camped for five weeks. We came ten miles through prairie most of the way. We had very little trouble with the cows. Now we are camped on Mustang creek, close to a farm, where we put the cows and calves in a pen. We turned the horses out on the prairie. We have as many peaches as we can eat.

August 26   It is very clear and warm. We started by crossing Mustang creek and came four or five miles, then crossed Deer creek. From that place we took the wrong road and travelled some out of our way. We met three men who told us the way, so we went out on the prairie to hit the right road and proceeded on five or six miles. At Sycamore creek we are camped for the night. It is in Tarrin county, Texas, at the edge of the cross timber. I have the sick headache very bad.

August 27   Very warm. I still have a headache. We came on ten miles through the cross timber and over very rough, sandy roads. We are camped tonight at Mansfield's Mills. One of Frank's calves got lost in the bush and he had to go back after it. There are some very pretty farms here in the prairie and a big stream mill that grinds all the time.

August 28   We started out and passed two or three pretty farms where the people on them look like they make a poor living. We then came out through a hilly broken country where we passed a few farms. We got as many peaches as we could eat. We came up one very steep rocky hill through a

little town called Cedar Hill. There is one store and a few
dwelling houses, which are all going to rack. Continuing on
three or four miles we came to a creek called Ten Mile, in
Dallas county. We got water out of a nice spring. The calves
were put in a pen and the cows and horses were turned out on
the prairie.

August 29   Clear and warm. We came thirteen miles
through the prairie and passed a few farms. Everybody is
drying peaches. We get all we can eat. Tonight we are camped
in Trinity River bottom. The timber is very thick here. The
calves are tied up and the horses and cows are turned loose.
The timber is so thick we can see but a few yards from camp
but the mosquitoes can very easily find us and they almost eat
the children up.

Sunday, August 30   Very warm. We will stay here today.
Two of the horses are gone and Frank and Mr. Kirkland
have gone to hunt for them. We have all been sitting around,
not enjoying ourselves at all. Frank and Mr. Kirkland got
back with the horses this evening about 3 o'clock.

August 31   Warm and raining. We crossed the river this
morning and got over very well, since the water was only up
to the wagon beds. They are building a steamboat to run on
the river next winter. We came on through Dallas, a tolerable
sized town with some very nice buildings. There are four
churches here and schools but everything seems to be going
down. We came two miles this side of the town and at Cedar
Grove on Turtle creek. Frank and Mr. Kirkland went back
to town to get provisions, bringing twenty pounds of bacon
at a bit a pound. Frank got a letter from Mr. Hamilton. They
have stopped in Hays county, Texas.

September 1   It is still raining and very disagreeable. Frank
and Mr. Kirkland have gone to get corn to feed the horses
while we are travelling. I have been writing a letter to Mr.

Hamilton for Frank. Gatewood sent his two boys back after a cow we left over the river and the soldiers took them up in town and made them pick up chips all day, and then took Wallace's coat away from him.

September 2   Still cool and cloudy. Frank and Mr. Kirkland are going on to Missouri and Gatewood will stay in Texas. Frank let him have his little wagon at one hundred dollars. We have two cows and calves that they got for working while we were in Hood county, Texas. Mr. Kirkland took one but we had to leave the others behind because we have no one to drive them. Mr. Kirkland has a young man with him. We came ten miles over prairie and stopped at a big well for dinner. A very hard shower of rain fell just before we stopped. After dinner we started and had another hard rain. Five miles farther we reached Spring creek, where the banks were so steep and slippery we could not cross, but had to camp in the road. We sure had a muddy time. The mud and clay would stick to our feet so that we could hardly get about. There is another family camped here where the women pulled off their shoes and stockings and waded the mud barefooted. We put our horses on the prairie, got supper over and go to bed.

September 3   We started at 9 o'clock, coming up over the hill very well, then came on eight miles over pretty prairie, thickly settled. We stopped on rock for dinner and afterwards passed through a little town called Plano. Then covering seven miles over very rough roads we came upon a toll bridge over a little creek, where we were charged thirty-five cents a wagon. We stopped and got water, then came out on the prairie one mile and camped for the night in Collins [Collin] county. Frank and Mrs. Kirkland bought some molasses at fifty cents a gallon.

September 4   Clear and warm. We started and passed

through McKinny, the county seat of Collins, which appears to be a very busy place and containing some very pretty buildings. Frank bought one bushel of meal at fifty cents, two pounds of butter at ten cents a pound. We came on through the prairie, passing some beautiful farms and nice houses and stopped at a peach orchard where we got some peaches to eat. After ten more miles we stopped for dinner and then continued six miles on, passing through a little town called Weston. There is one store and post office and a few other buildings. We crossed the river where the Cambelites were baptizing some persons. We are camped out on the prairie between two farms.

September 5   It is clear and warm today. Some pretty farms were passed in the prairie, then we came upon the little town called Farmington. A very few houses, one store, one church, and two or three horse mills were found here. We crossed the creek two or three times and there is very little water in it. Tonight we are camped at house under a big oak tree by a nice spring in Grayson county. We stopped at 2 o'clock. Mrs. Kirkland and I washed some.

Sunday, September 6   Still warm. We will stay here today to rest the horses. We have been sitting all day, very lonesome and tired. Frank wrote a letter to brother John.

September 7   We started on again and came four miles through prairie land to Sherman, which is quite a nice little town, the county seat of Grayson county. There seems to be a great deal of business going on here and Frank bought two yards of calico at seventeen cents a yard. We left the town after remaining an hour and came on four miles over tolerable good roads to a mill. Here Mr. Kirkland bought corn at fifty cents a bushel. We then came one mile over very rough, hilly roads to a little creek with very steep banks.

The End

The Gila Trail: Texas to California, 1868

Harriet Bunyard

INTRODUCTION

In the pioneer Savannah Memorial Park in El Monte, California, are three grave stones of particular interest to anyone who seeks information about the Larkin S. and Frances (Stewart) Bunyard family. The cemetery records list the following persons as having been buried there:

L.S. Bunyard	died 6-18-1889	age 77
Frankie Bunyard	died 1898	age 81
Hattie Bunyard	died 1897	age 51

Harriet (Hattie) Bunyard was the author of the following diary telling of their long journey from McKinney, Texas, to El Monte, California. One insight gained from the cemetery records is that she remained an unmarried woman all her life.

The best reference for the names of the Bunyard children is the 1870 census of El Monte Township, which reads as follows:

Mollie Bunyard	27 years old
James B. [Beal]	25
Hattie [Harriet]	21
Daniel	20
Josephine	15
Oscar	12
Fanny	10

The children's father was Larkin B. Bunyard. His birthplace had been North Carolina and date of birth November 11, 1812. The maiden name of the mother was Frances (Fanny) Stewart. Her birthplace was Tennessee. Harriet was born in Texas.

The story of the family was gathered up by the researchers of the Works Progress Administration (W.P.A.) in 1937. It is one of moves westward over many years.

They lived in McKinney, Texas, for a number of years. There the father had taught school. He also operated a cotton gin for a period. Upon reaching California, Larkin Bunyard became a farmer, and this was the trade he followed until a year before his death in 1889.

In the El Monte area the Bunyards settled on a tract of twenty-five acres just west of town. Although there were no improvements on the land at the time, they were able to purchase a three-acre tract just south of Main Street in El Monte, where a house had been built.

This was a deeply religious family of the Baptist faith. Politically they leaned toward the Democratic Party. They seem to have immersed themselves in community service and improvement.

The diary was kept in pencil. It was transcribed by Fanny (Bunyard) Lewis, another daughter. An undated clipping from an unnamed newspaper among the records tells how Mrs. Lewis was especially careful in copying the diary that it be done accurately. She did it with pen and ink. She said it was somewhat dim in places, but "with the aid of a magnifying glass, every word was completely identified." It was published in the *Annual Publications of the Historical Society of Southern California* (XIII, 1924), pp. 92-124.

Two persons have been particularly helpful in tracing information about this elusive family: The cemetery information was supplied to us by Hubert E. Fouts, Secretary of the El Monte Cemetery Association. Mrs. Sally M. Emerson of La Cañada used her expert knowledge of Southern California history to search out and supply us the information about census records and other materials. We are indebted to both of these persons and are grateful to them for work well done.

THE DIARY

April 29-30: Collin County, Texas, Have almost completed our preparations for the much-talked-of journey. Friends and neighbors have been so kind in assisting us. Long will they be remembered.

May 1st: Bid a kind adieu to my much loved Texas home. Although the road was very muddy we had a pleasant drive. long will it be remembered. Arrived at Uncle Stewart's in the evening, twelve miles distant. Will remain here until Monday, this being Saturday.

May 3rd: All in fine spirits. Started early—traveled fifteen miles; crossed the west fork of the Trinity and Little Elm. Had no trouble; camped on a high beautiful prairie. Passed over a broken, hilly country. Two men were hung near the camp the evening before and were said to be still hanging; were hung for stealing.

May 4th: Started early, traveled over a beautiful, sandy prairie, arrived at Pilot Point[1] about 12, stopped and ate dinner and purchased some necessary articles. Had some photographs taken. Fred Turner insisted that some of the girls should stay with him, said he had no companion but no one would take pity on him and stay. Left town about 3 o'clock. It was rather dusty, being sandy soil. Splendid water there. Crossed a small creek. The road was very rough but all made it safe through. Passed through the cross-timbers;[2] they have a picturesque appearance—part oak timber with

---

[1]Pilot Point in Denton Co., Texas, was named for a high ridge nearby that can be seen for some distance. The townsite had been platted in 1853. There is a big grove of post oak timber on the ridge that extends into the prairie. Fred Tarpley, *1001 Texas Place Names* (Austin, 1980), p. 163.

[2]A compact description of this feature is to be found in Albert Pike's *Prose Sketches and Poems* written in 1834, "These Cross Timbers are a belt of timber, extending from the Canadian River, or a little further north, to an unknown distance south of Red River. The belt is in width from fifteen to fifty miles, composed of black-jack and post

small prairies. Crossing was good across Big Elm. Camped
upon the prairie. 'Twas dark when we camped; everybody
tired. Traveled eighteen miles.

May 5: All ready—waiting for some immigrants who camped
on the other side of the creek. They are from Arkansas. Four
wagons, two hacks, 10 men—This is a lonely looking place,
seven miles, crossed Duck Creek, stayed to eat dinner. It is
very pretty stream, rocky bottom. Just ready to start when
Stewart's wagon tongue got broken, we made another, went
two miles, camped by a little branch near Boliner. Stayed one
day, went fishing with one of the ladies living near Boliner
[Bolivar?], caught some small fish. Would not like to live
here. Sold some things that we started with in order to lighten
our loads.

May 7th: Denton—Two more young men joined the train
making 22 men. Crossed Clear Creek, passed two vacant
houses, suppose the Indians were the cause of them being
left. Came to Denton Creek, there had a little bad luck, a
wagon turned over but no serious damage done. Went two
miles farther, and camped by a little branch, here the water
falls 15 feet from beautiful shell rock. Trees growing down
there with their tops just even with the level of the land. Such
a good place for Indians to hide. Passed two vacant houses,
they look very desolate. The country has a wild appearance.

May 8th: Quite a pleasant wind blowing from the east this
morning. Started early, traveled 21 miles over such a rough
road through very thick post oak timber. Came in sight of
government mills, there at a branch we found a broken wagon
loaded with very large cotton-wood log, pried the log off and

oak, with a thick layer of undergrowth of small bushy oak and briers, in places absolutely
impervious." We have used the updated edition edited by David J. Weber (Albuquerque,
1967), p. 8. See also the Letter of Louisiana Strentzel, in *Covered Wagon Women*, Volume
I, p. 251, footnote 2.

took the wagon away. Passed over in safety. Here are quite a number of small houses all made with the plank standing on one end also covered with plank. They are all close together and form quite a romantic appearance. Camped near by in the timbers. Stood guard tonight. Now I wish there were no wild Indians.

May 9th—Sabbath Morn: What are my friends in Collin doing this morning, going to church I will suppose. Started and drove two miles to water for the stock. Have camped in very nice place. Will remain until Monday. Every appearance of rain, all hurrying to get tents stretched and fixed before rain. One lonely looking little house in sight, the people that live there are part Indian. Eight more wagons with 10 men joined us this morning. They were camped at Decater waiting for company. Appointed Uncle Stewart captain of the train.

May 10th-11th: Rain prevented us leaving until Tuesday when we drove 14 miles, passed where there had been a little village but was but one family there. All left on account of the Indians. The country is very broken. High hills covered with large rocks that look like houses in the distance. I am now sitting on the hillside while the clear notes of the whipporwill is singing in the still twilight evening—a memory of the past comes o'er us.

May 12th: Came seven miles and camped in a small prairie surrounded with timber and high hills. We went to the top of one of the hills and found many curious rocks. The top was almost covered with level rocks while on the sides were great stacks that looked like they had been placed there by the skill of man. Crossed west fork of the Trinity—had no trouble crossing.

May 14th-15th: We are now camped by a nice, clear branch and good spring up on a hill. Splendid cold water. Jacksboro is in plain view. Federals quarters are nicest part of town.

Elm and Mesquite timbers, sandy soil with rocky hills is general appearance of the country. Mostly timber except small prairies. The people here are kind and accommodating. It is reported that there has been some Indians seen not far off, but we have not seen any. Some of the girls went up town today, others went fishing, but did not catch many. Two of the Federal officers visited our camp—nice looking men. They say if we stay here until the evening of the 16th that they will visit us with their brass band.

May 16th—Sabbath Evening: We have traveled about 15 miles today Passed through Jacksboro and over a very rocky road. It is quite a romantic looking country. High hills as far as I can see, covered with small timber and large rocks. Oh! how it did rain and blow last night. There is a very cold northwest wind. Several families from Denton County have overtaken us. There are now 45 men in this train.

May 17th: Two men passed by camp last night going after the doctor for some wounded men that had been in a fight with the Indians. There were 12 men out herding stock—no firearms but pistols and 50 Indians dashed down on them. Killed two men and wounded five. One of the wounded died this evening. Killed every one of their horses. This fight occurred five miles above where we are now camped. The men that were wounded are at a ranch about one mile from our camp. Several of the boys went to see them this evening. They suffered so much before they had any attention. Supposed the rest of the wounded will get well. The stage passes from Belknap to Jacksboro. the distance of 38 miles, and is guarded by five Indians of a friendly tribe. They look so Indian-like with two rings in each ear and beads strung all about them. Traveled 15 miles today over nice road and beautiful prairie.

Young County, May 18th: One yoke of oxen was missing this

morning, therefore we have moved only one mile to better range. An old vacant house here and very good water. Found the oxen but too late to go any farther so will remain until morning.

May 19th: Started late—traveled 10 miles. Passed Fort Belknap. The houses are very much delapidated here. Many chimneys standing alone. Not more than six families living there. It is a very pretty place for a town if it was only improved. Crossed Brazos river; it is a beautiful stream with no timber immediately on its banks. Live oak and mesquite and elm with sandy soil is general appearance of the country, with the greatest quantity and very good variety of wild flowers. Some of the most beautiful. Camped about three miles from town. It is 35 miles from Belknap to Fort Griffin.

May 20th: Detained again on account of stock. Some of the boys caught some very nice fish in the Brazos. Started after dinner, went six miles. Camped in nice place in small prairies, surrounded with post oak timber.

May 21st: Very warm and cloudy morning. Started early, made a drive of 17 miles; splendid road. Had nothing but branch water and it was warm, not clear. The Collin County boys killed an antelope this evening—the meat resembles that of a kid.

May 22: Camped one mile from Fort Griffin on east side of clear fork of the Brazos. It is a pretty stream with large pecan timber on the banks. I think we will get some nice fish here.

May 26: Will leave here this morning; passed away the time very well since we have been here. Sabbath morning we hitched up our ambulances and drove to the fort. Federals have very nice quarters there. The citizens' houses are very inferior, small log huts. Have splendid water here. Indians have caused more disturbance for the past five months than for several years. Little girl living here that the Indians took and kept eight months. Her friends bought her. Whilst they had her they picked a round ring of powder in her forehead as large as a ten-cent piece. It makes a black ring and cannot be taken away. Suppose they done it that they might know her again. They had her little sister but would not sell her. Her friends think they will sell her this year. The other little girl said that they were very kind to her. The Indians killed their mother when they captured them. In our drive Sabbath morning we went one-half mile from the fort to where were camped considerable number of Tonk Indians[3]—was but very few that could talk English. Their little huts were covered with hay and dirt and doors just big enough for one to pass through. They were all busy at work. We then called at Miss Campbell's. Spent an hour—went back to camp; here we got plenty of pickles and beans to do us through. We also had some fish from the river Wednesday morning. Will start this morning. Got late start but everything was rested and we traveled 18 miles over rough rocky road. We have splendid camping place this evening with fine range; our teams are in better order now than when we started. There is quite a number of emigrants near and with us now.

May 28th: left camps early; traveled over beautiful road; found some cranberries, the first I ever saw. They are splendid. Traveled 16 miles and camped by nice running stream and fine spring—cold water which is quite a treat. There is a grave near this spring—it has no inscription on it—therefore we know nothing of the inhabitants thereof. Some one perhaps that like us was in search of a new home. How I should regret to leave one of my friends along the roadside in a strange land. We have not passed a house since we left Fort Griffin which is 35 miles.

---

[3]The Tonkawa Indians were a small nomadic tribe in central Texas. They were later removed to Oklahoma, where 40-50 individuals live today.

May 29th: All is ready and started early when to our surprise about 30 Federals from Griffin rode up just as the last wagon was leaving camp. They halted the wagons and searched them for some carbine guns that some of the train had purchased. They did not find them therefore we had to stay at the same camp; came back and stayed there all day—The Federals camped on the other side of the branch and watched around all day. That night about 8 they came to our camp and arrested several and kept them all night. Ten guns were brought up that night—they were brought by a citizen at the fort—the sergeant had stolen them and given them to the citizens to sell. The sergeant was arrested and one of our men was taken back to testify against the citizen that sold them and the others that had purchased were taken next morning to the fort. Imagine our anxiety although neither father or brother had purchased a gun yet our friends in the train had. But as fortune favored us they did nothing but take their testimony and permitted them to return to camps next evening. This only detained them two days. They did not give back the money that the men paid for the guns. I am very glad as we were detained that we were at such splendid water.

May 30th—Sabbath Morning: Although we do not wish to travel on Sunday we will have to leave here today—as our stock are beginning to ramble. Camped again; traveled about 12 miles; passed Thornton's Hill—are but two houses there but many chimneys standing where houses have been—they look so lonely standing there. Country broken—Mesquite and Chaparall bushes with few scattered Elms, are the only timber. How strange it seems to travel all day and not any houses. We hear of Indians being seen at every foot but we do not apprehend any danger from them. It rained a hard shower this evening—some hail—which renders camping rather unpleasant. We miss our nice spring tonight as the water is not very good. Are camped tonight on a high prairie and in sight on another hill another large train is camped.

May 31st: Started early—traveled 20 miles. Came in sight yesterday of a high peak of mountains—was in sight all day and camped just opposite it tonight. It is noted place and is called "Indian's Pass." Here the Indians pass through the mountains. Some of the boys went to the top; they looked to be about one-half as high as they really were. A large rock seems to cover the top of the peak; it is on the left of the road—found some beautiful cedar trees here.

June 1st: Passed stage stand this morning. Traveled eight miles—most of the way with mountains on each side of the road. Had to camp here in order to have plenty of water—had clear running branch—very good water. Found some gooseberries and green grapes—made some pies of them.

June 2nd: Camped in sight of the mountain—yet been passing them all day—something resembling a grave was found on the top of one of the mountains—with a pile of rock by it with white cloth wrapped around the rock. We do not know what it was for. Found great many Buffalo hides near the camp; suppose that they had been stretched there last winter. Have not seen any Buffalo yet—seen some little prairie dogs today; they resemble a squirrel. Have not come to large town yet. Had some fish from the creek that was near the camp this evening. Have traveled about 13 miles today.

June 3rd: Started early—passed old Fort Chilltoueno[4]—was very much disappointed. I expected to find people living there but the only inhabitants were a few colored soldiers. One Mexican keeping stage stand. All of the houses that I saw were made of rock and there was some very nice looking

---

[4]She had a difficult time spelling of Fort Chadbourne. In this one entry she renders it in two ways.

dwellings here and it would be a beautiful place if it were only inhabited by nice people and some improvements made. It is 105 miles from Fort Griffin to old Fort Shaddron [Chadbourne]. Are still camped in sight of mountains. When I was at home I thought I liked the mountains, but they look so lonesome way out there where a bird is scarcely ever seen. We have had very cool, pleasant weather to travel so far; today has been warm and the road very dusty. Came about 15 miles today.

June 4th: Some stock missing this morning. Moved four miles; crossed Colorado river. Camped on the west side of it. It is very pretty stream—no timber on the banks as far as I can see—crossed so near the head that it is very small. The boys have caught some nice fish from the river. It is 30 miles from the Colorado to Fort Concho.[5] Some Federals camped on the river near our trains. Also another train of immigrants that was behind came up with us and camped on the right of the road while we were on the left. There are no immigrants ahead of us.

June 5th: Found all the stock and all ready to start early. Had light shower of rain yesterday evening and still cloudy with quite a pleasant wind blowing this morning. Made a good day's drive—had to leave the road one mile to get water sufficient to camp with and then it was not good.

June 6th: Oh, we have had such a splendid road—the most level prairie I have ever seen. Crossed north of the Conchip [Concho]. Passed through the Fort. It is a beautiful place for a town and there are some very nice looking buildings there, principally made of rock. Here we saw the colored troops standing around among the Yankees,[6] regardless of color or

[5]Present San Angelo.

[6]For the "Buffalo Soldiers" see Shackleford Diary, in this volume, 1868, footnote 20, May 25.

grade. North Conchip [Concho] is small stream; very nice timber on its banks. The main stream is considerable larger. Here we had some large fish and are camped near the bank tonight. We will travel up this stream 45 miles. It is 85 miles from Fort Conchip [Concho] to Fort Griffin. We are now 350 miles from home or McKinney. Is splendid spring not far where we are camped. Two or three company's of infantry soldiers are camped at this spring two miles from the fort.

June 7th: For the last two or three days we have had wild currants in great abundance. The little prairie dogs bark and run about as we pass their dwellings which are all subterranean.

June 8th: Nothing of interest passed today.

June 9th: Camped near the Concho. Been washing and rearranging things generally. Will leave here this evening— make short drive in order to reach the desert or the river in two more days. Here we found another large cold spring surrounded with willow trees. The cattle got scared, we suppose at a dog. Quite an excitement was raised in camps— we didn't know but what the Indians were about. Part of the boys went in pursuit of them while others tied horses to the wagons. They did not go more than a mile until they succeeded in bringing them back. No one was hurt. Will leave here this evening. We have two men in our train that have traveled the road before—this is a great advantage.

June 9th: Camped in nice place near the river. Had a shower of rain this evening which was quite an advantage. High hill near the camps and on the right of the road—not near so high as some that we had passed but it was near the road and myself with several others went to the top; there we found something that looked like a grave that had been there a long time; it had rocks piled around it. Have had very little sickness in the train so far. One man sick now; has been very sick; I hope he will get well.

June 10th: Camped again on the river [Concho]. We are not far from the head and it is getting small; 70 miles from where we cross the river and then strike the desert. Had another shower of rain this evening. All seem to think we will have plenty of water.

June 11th: Near the river again—found plenty of gooseberries but did not find very nice camping place—so many Mesquite bushes.

June 12th: Started very early—went 12 miles—camped in very nice place—will start across the first desert tomorrow. They say that we will have plenty of water most of the way. The sick man is improving; I think he will be well soon. I think this is beautiful country.

June 13th: Rained very hard last night which makes it very pleasant traveling this morning. Passed this morning where a United States soldier was buried, he started across the plains intending to overtake a train of immigrants that were going to California, but failed to do so and therefore starved for food. When he was found he had canteen with water in it by him. He was trying it seems to get back. Found plenty of water and camped early this evening. Mesquite bushes is the only timber in sight.

June 14th: Came four miles. Stopped by a pond of water—ate dinner—did some cooking—filled our barrels with water and started early after dinner. It is 35 miles to the Pecos which is the next water. We traveled until after midnight. Had beautiful and bright moonlight most of the time. Had very good grass—little bush for wood.

June 15th: All ready to start early this morning. Gave our horses water out of our barrels. They were not very thirsty. Arrived at the river early in the afternoon. Nothing had suffered for water. Passed through the Castle Mountains. They are the prettiest mountains I ever saw—not a bush can be seen—nothing but scatter grass; some of them resemble houses very much from a distance. Passed Central Station[7] yesterday—nothing but Negroes there guarding stage stand.

June 16th: The Pecos is narrow, deep and muddy stream with no timber on its bank   it is now level with the banks; very bad tasted water. There is a skiff that the mail is crossed in and we have permission to cross our things in it—commenced crossing as early as we could get all the stock to the ford—they would put the things out of the wagons into the skiff and then tied ropes to the wagons and crossed. One wagon came uncoupled in the river; another broke the rope that was on the tongue but those on the opposite side still had hold of the other ropes and the men swam in and brought all safe to shore. Got all the wagons and the plunder over about 3 o'clock and then commenced crossing the cattle and horses. Just about the time all the wagons were over, Brother Dan and Ed Stewart with several others jumped into the river to try their speed swimming; the current being very swift Ed Stewart cramped and was sinking the last time when they caught him. In trying to rescue Ed, Brother Dan came very near drowning being so near exhausted; the skiff was pushed to them and they got in and came safe. Mr. Bottoms had a mule drowned in trying to cross. The only thing that we lost. They kept crossing about 10 o'clock in the night. When anything would start down stream they would plunge in and bring them out. It is only a few places that the stock can get down to the water without going in overhead.

June 17th: Had but little trouble in crossing the remainder of the stock—got them over and commenced reloading about 12 o'clock. The men have labored faithful in getting across

---

[7]This would have been Centralia Station, which has erroneously been referred to as a Butterfield Station. The Conklings suggest that it was built by F.C. Taylor in about 1870-71. Harriet Bunyard's reference to it here would suggest that the Conklings were wrong, that Centralia Station was alive and serving the public in 1868. Conkling, *op. cit.*, Volume I, p. 362.

the river, that has been so much dreaded; all is safe and I am truly thankful. Will go seven miles this evening and camp again on the river. While we were loading the train that was behind came to the opposite bank. I can sympathize with them for I know that they dread crossing. This stream is kept full by melting snow from the mountains. It is 85 miles from Concho to Pecos River.

June 18th: Made long drive and camped in a beautiful place by a sulphur spring. The water is very cold but I do not like the taste. This is said to be a noted place for Indians as there is plenty of water here. There are some little Indian huts not far from camp. We are still among the mountains. The highest growth that is seen is a shrub called the Spanish dagger which is from four to six feet high with long blades, some two inches broad and three feet long, terminating at both ends. One end has very sharp point. It is 85 miles from Concho to Pecos.

June 19th: Drove over nice road and passed by some beautiful mountains. Are camped near a stage stand where is Negro guard. One white man there. We get water out of very good spring. A train of Mexicans and also one of Negro soldiers passed by our camp today. They are going to San Antonio.

June 20th—Sabbath Morning: Finds me in camp and will remain here until Monday morning. This morning is warm and cloudy. I wish we would have a shower of rain as the road is very dusty. It is 240 miles from where we now are to El Paso. When we get there we are half way to California. Spend day reading and talking.

June 21st: Rained some last night; is raining this morning. Had very hard rain ahead of us which makes the road pleasant and the air cool. We passed by a grocery. Camped near the fort. Mexicans live here but very few white people. Passed in sight of three farms; none of them had any fence around. There is large farm three miles from the fort. The

Negroes work it for the government. No timber at all here; they burn roots altogether for fire wood. I do not think that this is pretty country. Have fine springs here; the water is a little brackish.

June 22nd: Came nine miles today; found plenty of water and splendid grass; very good wood. Has been an old fort here. Mexican family camped with us tonight; they are going to Fort Janis, 60 miles from here. They travel by themselves and do not seem to be at all afraid. This is beautiful camping place and pretty surrounding country.

June 23rd: Cool and pleasant morning. All ready to start early. They told us that there was plenty water in about 12 miles from where we were. So we did not fill our barrels, only filled our small kegs. To our disappointment the water was all dried up and we had to go 25 miles in place of 12. So we had no drinking water all the evening. We found some water standing in a pond but not enough for our stock; it was then an hour after sunset but the moon was shining brightly so we camped and put all our stock in the corral without letting them eat any as they all wanted water—so we started next morning before breakfast and went eight miles to Barrella [Barilla] Springs[8]—here we found a cold, pure water well at the stage stand and a spring up in the mountains.

June 24th: Remained here until evening—filled our barrels with water and went short distance to better range. Ma is sick, has the flux; quite a number of the train has the same complaint.

June 25th: We are now traveling through a long and narrow

---

[8]Ruth Shackleford calls this Gorilla Station. It was on this day that the two diarists who were traveling the Butterfield route passed each other. Ruth Shackleford was traveling from west to east; Harriet Bunyard was moving from east to west. Neither knew of the proximity of the other.

gap through the Olymphia [Limpia] Mountains. Some places there is just space enough for the wagons to pass through. On the top of these mountains, some of which I suppose are near a mile from the level, we find low bunches of live oak trees. Rained hard last night. Found nice place to camp—plenty of wood but no water but we had water with us.

June 26th: Camped about 1 o'clock—found plenty of wood and water. Ma is some better. Part of the train went on this evening. Families remained here until morning as our trains need rest.

June 27th: Started early—passed some of the prettiest mountains. They are straight up about 50 feet with here and there a little bushes and vines running over them full of nice flowers. Branch running along the foot of the mountains and nice springs. Camped with mountains near on each side and spring on the left. The train that left are about three miles before us. Some of them are now six miles from Fort Davis. Ma is better this morning. Man passed camps last night and told us that four mounted Indians and eight on foot had taken all the mules and horses at stand at Barrella Springs Friday about 12 o'clock. The man was on his way to the fort after soldiers. They passed by last night going to recover their horses. Some moccasin tracks were seen in the road just ahead of us. This is their main passway they say. I do not think they will ever attack us; they will get their horses if they can. If I was at home I think I would go to church today. The time has passed much pleasanter than expected on the road; we will move short distance this morning to fresh grass for the stock. Camped in nice place by the side of high mountain.

June 28th: Will remain here today to wash as we have such nice clear water. There has been great deal of rain through this country, which makes the range fine. This pass through these Mountains is called "Wild Rose Gap" and it is very appropriate name as there are so many wild roses in the little valleys.[9]

June 29th: Passed through Fort Davis; it is pretty little place by the side of the mountains. The valley is wide here and the mountains small. Here are found vegetables very high, roasting ears ($1.50 doz.), butter ($1.00 lb.), eggs ($1.00 lb.). This is a beautiful valley. We have delightful camping place tonight. There is such a nice spring here and splendid water in abundance running out of the mountains about nine miles from Fort Davis. Several stores here; some white people and Mexicans and Negroes. There are 400 soldiers here. They played their band as we passed the fort.

June 30th: Are camped tonight at Barrella [Barrel] Springs, 18 miles from Fort Davis. Not very nice place to camp. Grapes not very good. We passed some nice grove of live oak trees today. Very little timber in this country. There is stage stand here. Negroes to guard it.

July 1st: Intended staying at Barrella Springs until tomorrow but there was train of Negroes from the pinery that were hauling lumber to Stockton and another train of Mexicans camped at the same place. They had whiskey and the Negro soldiers got drunk and began cutting up so we harnessed up and left when the sun was not more than one hour high. We traveled three miles and made a dry camp there. We found plenty of good grapes. We knew that they had the advantage of us, if we had killed any of them then we would have been detained some time if nothing more. These military posts are a great pest to immigrants.

---

[9]According to the Conklings, Wild Rose Pass is a mere three miles in length but is so narrow in some stretches that there is scarcely room enough for a road along the creek banks. The banks tower up on either hand nearly 1200 feet above the creek bed. They add, "No traveller could fail to be impressed by the rugged grandeur of Wild Rose Pass." *Op. cit.*, II, pp. 25-26.

July 2nd: Camped at Dead Man's holes[10] 13 miles from Barrella Springs. Is another stand here two miles from camp—good spring at the stand. There we get water to use. Water at camp for stock. This wide nice valley—no timber except some small brush.

July 3rd: Will remain at Dead Man's hole until morning. Have spent the day sewing and cooking. The train that was behind came up this evening. They will remain here few days as their cattle are lame and worn down. Our teams are all in good plight for traveling. We have had plenty of rain. Have shower most every evening, which is very agreeable.

July 4th: Started this beautiful Sabbath morning and will travel nine miles. Here we found plenty of good water in ponds. It has been many days since we was out of sight of mountains or in sight of timber of any consequence. We have beautiful level road all the time. To see the cactus and Mexican daggers you would think that there was no scarcity of timber.

July 5th: Several carriages, three wagons, one lady and several men passed this morning on their way to El Paso—from San Antonio. No wood here—not even small brush.

July 6th: Camped at another pond of rain water—better luck than we expected finding water. There is plenty of wood here. Passed Van Horn's[11] well this evening—could get no water. There is stage stand here. It is 32 miles from Dead Man's hole to Van Horn's well.

July 7th: Traveled all day and had to make dry camp. We had sufficiency of using water with us and they found enough

---

[10] According to the Conklings the name came from the discovery of a body of a dead man at the foot of a bold rocky bluff. They add, "In spite of the sinister sounding name, it would be difficult to find a lovelier or more romantic location." *Ibid.*, p. 33.

[11] This station was regarded as the best watering place between Limpia and the Rio Grande. *Ibid.*, p. 34.

water for the horses. Four of the men went ahead this evening to hunt camping place. They saw four bear. This is dangerous place for Indians. Has been moccasin tracks seen all about here. There was fire seen about 9 o'clock on the top of the mountains. Supposed it to be Indians camp. Tied all our horses to the wagon and never let the cattle leave the corral. We are camped in six miles of Eagle Springs.

July 8th: Started before breakfast and came to Eagle Springs. Here we found plenty of water for all the stock by dipping it with buckets. The spring is by the side of high mountain 19 miles from Van Horn's Wells to Eagle Springs. The train that is ahead did not get any water here. There was so many of them together. It is 35 miles from here to next water that we know of—if the other trains did not find water before they got there with their stock must have suffered greatly.

July 9th: The health of our little train is very good at present. We have 20 men—11 wagons—eight families with us. They say that we can see the river from the top of the mountains. The Negroes here have been very kind to us. The spring does not run off it uses and fills up as it is dipped out. There is quite a number of Indian Warriors said to live not far from Eagle Springs.

July 10th: Left Eagle Springs on the 9th about 2 o'clock—traveled until an hour by sun—made coffee and rested a while and started—traveling until 11 o'clock. Had splendid road and all went on without trouble. We passed through narrow canyon just sufficient room for a road. High mountains on each side. We arrived at river about 2 o'clock. Our cattle was very thirsty but all made the trip very well. I am proud to say that we are at the Rio Grande. It is said to be one-half way to California. The road is very dry and dusty now but every appearance of rain.

July 11th: Camped near the river. There is some timber on

the banks of the river—the first that we have seen since we left Concho except few scattered live oak. I do not admire this country. Has not been much rain here therefore grass is not very good. It is two miles from camps to Fort Quitman. Are in Texas and can see Mexico. Can see nothing but mountains and rocks. We will make short drives from now on so the stock can have time to recruit.

July 12th: Passed through Fort Quitman. Got some small June apples there. Didn't see any white women there. There were some Mexican women—some very nice looking— dressed very nice. Some nice looking white men. Beautiful grove of cotton wood trees around the fort. All the houses were perfectly flat. Camped by a lake near the river. Had very hard rain last night which was much needed. Came to this place Sunday evening. Will stay here until Tuesday morning.

July 13th: Started after supper and made nice drive by moonlight. The days are getting so warm that we cannot travel only early in the morning.

July 14th: Started this morning before breakfast and went to good camping place—had large cottonwood tree that afforded us nice shade. Started this evening about one hour by sun and traveled 12 miles—camped. The nights are pleasant for traveling. Mexicans brought some nice fish to camps for sale. Was little Mexican hurt near our camp. Plenty of cottonwood and Mesquite timber on the road. Roads are extremely dusty.

July 15th: Had shower of rain last night—makes traveling more pleasant. Started before breakfast, traveled five miles and stopped near the river. Will now get breakfast. We have fish for breakfast. Started near sundown—had not gone more than one-half mile when Mr. Coughram's wagon axle broke—took his load in other wagons and fixed his so it would travel and made drive of about eight miles. Passed by Mexican village. There are good many Mexican huts along the road. Found no grass therefore had to go to another camping ground.

July 16th: Started before breakfast and passed by stage stand. Did not find very good grass. The men are now very busy fixing the wagon. We will not have much more grass until we get to El Paso—as we passed by one of the houses last night was brilliantly lighted. It looked very nice from the road, white man with Mexican wife was living there. We started at 2 o'clock, went 10 miles, camped just at dark.

July 17th: Had nice shower of rain last night. We traveled near the river. Sometimes in three steps of the water; banks are very low and sandy. In one place the river runs where the road once was; road very dusty and warm. Traveling for some days past Mexicans—came to camps most every day. Some of them make a very good appearance while others ought not to appear at all. Where we camped yesterday was stage stand and several Mexican huts. One of the Mexicans had large herd of goats and cattle. They do not care as to houses—just so they have shade. Traveled short distance—bought some onions, pears and apples from Mexican.

July 18th: Have very nice place to camp. Started early— made long drive, passed through three Mexican villages. The road wound so that it was some distance from the place we went in at to where we left town. Their corn and gardens have no fence around them and therefore our loose stock gave us much trouble. We had to travel until dark to get where we could camp. Had hard rain this evening—very muddy camping. Eleven miles from here to Franklin. We have seen many buggies pass with nice looking white men in them. There are high sand hills through this country, nothing for stock to eat but weeds.

July 19th: Started before breakfast, went in seven miles of Franklin—stopped and got breakfast—passed through Fort

Bliss which is 15 miles from Socoro. Here is U.S. post and on short distance farther is Franklin. This is beautiful place—so many nice shade trees. Several white families living here. The town is near the bank of the river and just opposite this on the other side of the river is El Paso. So we stopped for some time in Franklin and purchased flour for the remainder of our journey. The merchants treated with wine and the children with candy. After making the necessary purchases we went one and one-half miles and camped at Mr. Van Poltersons. Here we were treated with great hospitality. He has 48 rooms. His wife is Indian. She is head of her tribe. They are very wealthy. They came to camps and we went to the house with them and they treated us with wine. He lives in a beautiful place near the river. We received letters from our friends in California—they write cheering news to us.

July 20th: We have had but little grass for our stock for several days. It is now nine miles to grass and water. We found very pretty place to camp and good grass. It is 95 miles from where we first struck the river to El Paso or Franklin. Total distance from Antonio to El Paso 654 miles. It is about 750 miles from McKinney to El Paso.

July 21st: Still at the same camp. Have been washing and baking light bread.

July 22nd: Still at same place. Left the old camp this evening. It was not pretty place to camp. Too many bushes. The Mexicans stole one pair of cows from Jim Stewart and run them across the river. The boys went across after them but failed to find them.

July 23rd: Started late in the evening and camped at a beautiful place with fine grass. It is 16 miles from here to El Paso. Made an early start this morning. Traveled until 12, stopped—rested a while and let the stock graze and ate supper. We then started and traveled by moonlight about 8 miles. Found very good grass.

July 24th: Started after breakfast and came to where Mexicans were living. They are very nice looking people—white as anybody. Us girls called in to see how the house looked, They gave us some apples to eat and were very kind. Their house so nice and clean inside; they have black Mexicans for servants. It is now 15 miles to where we cross the river. Got supper and traveled some distance—had moonlight to travel by. Camped in three miles of La Crusa, passed by an old fort. Some Mexicans were living there. The old fort looked very desolate.

July 25th: Passed through La Crusa [Las Cruces, N.M.]. It is very pretty situation for a town but the buildings are not pretty. The church bell was ringing as we passed through and the Mexicans were crowding to the chapel; they were all dressed very nice, with large bright colored shawls over their head and shoulders. They were carrying their musical instruments with them to church. We bought some cabbages and onions here. We arrived at the crossing of the river about 10 o'clock. The train that left us are camped five miles on the other side of the river. There is two families on this side; their captain's wife is very sick and could not cross the river, they forded the river. We intended crossing this evening, but alas, how little do we see of the future, it pains me to pen the incident. A young man that was with Uncle Stewart by the name of John Thomas accidently shot himself with his six-shooter; he was twirling it around and revolving it and it exploded. The bullet went on the right side through his breast and came out in his back on the same side. Oh! how it grieves me to think that anyone should happen to such an accident so far from home. He has not relatives in this train—has one brother in a train behind. Most of the men think his case hopeless, but I still hope. We have sent to town for a physician. The accident happened about 1 o'clock. He will have the assistance of our prayers. The captain's wife is very sick this evening. Sad, sad facts. Our friend died this evening between sundown and dark. He suffered greatly while he lived.

July 26th: Have dressed him very nice and sent him to La Crusa and had his coffin made and grave dug. The corpse left camp at 11 o'clock. His brother that was in the back train came up in time to see him buried. He was buried at La Crusa. We have crossed the river and came up with the train that had left us. We had no bad luck in crossing. All forded it; stopped after dark—rested three hours—started, traveled all night; came to water this morning; tanks have been made here for the purpose of furnishing water to immigrants. They sell the water at 10 cents a drink. Has watered two trains and one beef herd today. Has made near $100.00. It is 18 miles from here to river and about 30 miles to water ahead which is Crook [Cooke] Canyon. They say that this is the most dangerous place that we will have to pass. We crossed the river three miles below La Missella [Mesilla, N.M.]

July 27th: Started late in the evening. Traveled until about 3 o'clock; arrived near Fort Cummins [N.M.]. Here we find splended grass and water; it is called 35 miles from here to where we got the last water but we made good time and our stock did not suffer. Two large beef droves are camped here. Had nice shower of rain this evening which was very agreeable, for this soil is very dusty—no timber here—nothing but small bush to burn.

July 30th: Leave Fort Cummins this evening. Will drive through Crook's Creek this evening. Did not travel very late but the road was rough. We have traveled from Fort Davis to Franklin with families and 20 men. From Franklin to La Crusa we had only three families. The others stopped to wait for their friends. Overtook the train that left us at Fort Davis.

We did not join them at Cummins. Their train had to wait on account of sickness so five other wagons joined us and we went on. We now have 25 men. Dangerous road ahead.

July 31st: Are through the worst of the canyon and nothing has happened; camped at Membris [Mimbres] Creek. We left the town to our right as this is the best way. Membris is small, clear stream with cold springs along its banks. There is something over 7000 head of stock camped on this stream part going to California and some not so far. Is small train of immigrants camped here from Dano County, Texas; they traveled up the Pecos 300 miles and when they crossed they were attacked by 75 Indians. They lost one man who lived in California and had come after his friends. They have 600 head of beeves. The Indians wanted them—they have had a hard time.

August 1st: Left Membris this evening. We have five men. Traveled 10 miles most of the way after night. There was several men or Indians seen on side of the road; they left and we did not learn who they were. Every man had gun in hand for fight, but fortune favored and we had no fighting to do.

[August 2nd:] Will drive to water this morning. Did not find very much water here but enough to answer our purposes; rested a while; ate dinner and started on. We have 55 miles to go now without water for our stock. Camped tonight near the mountains, by no means a pretty place.

August 3rd: Passed an old fort—got some water to drink— plenty for the horses but none for the cattle.[12]

August 4th: Traveled last night—had beautiful road. This is a pretty valley. About 12 o'clock several Indians were seen on horseback. This frightened me some. No moonlight—

[12]This would be Cow Spring or *Ojo de la Vaca* in Luna County, New Mexico. This spring was at the confluence of all the early roads that traveled east and west and north and south. *Ibid.*, p. 122.

nothing but starlight—how quiet. The train traveled tonight. The Indians did not molest us. Camped about 2 o'clock.

August 5th: Have reached the place for water, Stevens Creek, but have to dig out the spring, so all went to work and the stock got some water but not enough. All had plenty of water by 12 o'clock and we will leave this evening. Our cattle suffered some but none failed. It is 35 miles to the next water. Is a peak of mountains here 300 feet high called Stevens Peak. Stevens had a fight at this place some time ago and hence its name. Had beans and pie for dinner. We had cool, pleasant time to travel the road that was destitute of water.

August 6th: Good luck—we found water one mile from the peak and did not have to drive so far. We were glad to find good grass and plenty of water without going so far. The train that we left behind came up this evening. One of Dr. Beaves children died last night. It had whooping cough and chronic diarrhoea; have been two deaths in that train. Another babe died with same complaint.

August 7th: Quite a number of beeves have come up to this place for water—some of them do not look very well they have done without water so long. Made dry camp tonight.

August 8th: Will pass through Apache Pass today.[13] There is fort and 300 soldiers here. The canyon is the deepest and longest we have passed through but the road is very good. Came just opposite the post and camped. Here is plenty of good water and very good grass. There is quite a number of graves here most of whom were killed by the Indians. They are digging gold here. They suppose that there are very rich mines here.

---

[13]This is a narrow passage between Dos Cabezas and Chiricahua mountains. It was used generally by travelers through southern Arizona. A community by that name was aborning and a post office established on December 1, 1866. The name was changed to Fort Bowie in 1880. Will C. Barnes, *Arizona Place Names* (Tucson, 1988) pp. 23, 59.

August 9th: Started very early this morning. Oh, what a rough road we came over this morning. Coming out of the canyon it seemed as if we would never get to the top of the mountain. We gained it at last and then had a nice road and beautiful valley—such nice green grass. There has been a great deal of rain here for the last few days. We started before breakfast and have now stopped to get dinner. It has rained very hard. How glad I will be when we get to Tucson—it is 110 miles from Apache Pass to Tucson. Traveled until near sundown. Made dry camp. Started this morning and had a good road.

August 10th: This is beautiful country. If there was wood and water here this would be desirable place to live. Arrived at Sulphur Springs[14] about 11 o'clock. Will water here and drive on. It is 25 miles from Apache Pass to Sulphur Springs where we camped last night. There was no wood at all here but we found surplus plank enough to cook with. Started about 5 o'clock—drove 10 miles. Started after breakfast on 11th—drove within four miles of the [San] Pedro River. Could go no farther after dark on account of the short canyon between there and the river. Arrived at the river in due time—the road was narrow and rough but short. Here we found good grass and water. Small mesquite for wood. The Pedro is small shallow stream. Sandy banks. There was beef drove camped here yesterday. Some of the men that were with the drove had a difficulty and a man was killed. I do not know his name nor any of the particulars. We see his clothes and his grave near our camp. We will stay here for a few days to recruit our stock. There is two beef droves camped here. Was two beeves killed yesterday by lightning during hard rain. It is 35 miles from here to Sulphur Springs.

---

[14]This was the site of two springs impregnated with sulphur. In spite of the presence of the chemical this was a favorite stopping place because of fine grazing. *Ibid.*, p. 429.

August 13th: Moved our camp to a better place. The evening we moved it rained very hard and next morning where our old camp was covered two feet deep with water so we just moved in time. The river was overflowed. Three families with a beef drove have not crossed the river.

August 14th: Started this evening at 2 o'clock. Made nice drive—camped on high nice place—rained all night. I think it has rained on or in sight of us for two weeks. Passed through short canyon.

August 15th: Is still cloudy with every appearance of rain. Will start early this morning and make good drive as the road is hard and level. Went four miles from the river. Here we rested and got dinner. We then drove 10 miles. Camped in nice place—had plenty of wood and water. Stand with a number of soldiers stationed. The road is surrounded with mountains.

August 16th: Camped in one mile of Muscal[15] Springs. Here the Anienza swamp set in. The road is muddy and bad. Crossed the River Cienaga several times. It was swimming yesterday but is not very deep today. It is three miles through this swamp. Had steep, hard hill to pull up this morning. Got through the swamp about 10 o'clock. Stopped to rest and get dinner. Thirty-one miles from San Pedro to Cienaga Creek. The Cienaga is small, swift-running stream with some cottonwood timber on its banks. We crossed it four times today. The bottom is gravelly and good crossing. Came over some more bad road this evening. The hills that we came over today have pulled our teams harder than any place that we have every crossed. Camped before sundown.

August 17th: Oh, what a hard rainfall last night and what vivid lightning from every point. Only one tent left standing

---

[15] Mescal is a Spanish term for the agave plant. *Ibid.*, p. 272.

so we had to dry our beds today and therefore we will not leave here before 12 o'clock. This is high dry place to camp. Fifteen miles from here to Tucson.

August 18th: Started after breakfast. Arrived at Tucson about 3 o'clock. Camped on east side of town. Did not find good water nor much grass. This country is thick with mesquite bushes. We will stay until morning. There is quite an excitement in town about a silver mine that has lately been discovered near this place.

August 19th: Passed through Tucson. Got some nice watermelons. This is a beautiful place; some nice houses here. Goods are much cheaper than I expected to find them. Groceries are dear. Received a letter from friends in California at this place. They are in fine spirits. I am getting impatient for our journey to come to an end—yet it cheers me to think that every day finds us nearer our destination. It is 500 miles from here to the City of Los Angeles. Drove about eight miles from town. Found good grass and water; running stream and nice spring. Will stay here until morning. This creek is called Lon Creek. It is said to be the richest ever found. Sheep ranch here and few Mexican huts.

August 20th: Drove nine miles today, found good water but not much grass. It is 28 miles to the next camping place so we will travel tonight. The sun is now an hour high and they are fixing to start. The weather has been extremely warm for a few days past. The round cactus trees that grow here are quite a curiosity to one that never seen them before. These Mexicans will be very friendly but if they get a chance to steal they are sure to use it. Left camp at sundown, had good road and beautiful moonlight to travel by.

August 21st: Came about seven miles last night. Found pond of water sufficient for our stock and some grass but not the best. Plenty of wood and plenty of place to camp. Remained here until late in the evening. Traveled until after midnight.

August 22nd: Camped at a high peak (called La Catcha)[16] that can be seen 15 miles the other side of Tucson. It is 45 miles from here back to Tucson. There is pond of water here but our stock will not drink it. Farther there is more water said to be better than this. It can't be worse. This is warm and cloudy morning. Found plenty of water and grass. Three Mexican wagons camped here. Two women with them. They said there is great danger from Apache Indians here. Three men were killed near here three weeks ago. There is high mountains on each side. Nine miles further will find us out of danger of Indians so we will travel tonight. Was hard rain ahead of us this evening so did not travel very late.

August 23rd: Did not turn our stock out of the corral as there is no grass here. We want to go to grass early. Traveled three miles and found some grass. Passed blue water wells, the water was cold and good but the grass was scarce and in bunches. Started at sundown and came to plenty of water and some grass better than what we had. There is stand at Blue Wells, some groceries here to sell but they are very dear.

August 24th: Are camped near another stand 12 miles from the Blue Wells. There was Lemore[17] Indian here today. He had his face painted and long strings of beads in his ears. He was very friendly but all he wanted was a chance to steal our stock. We have found some good grass and plenty of rain water standing in ponds.

---

[16]Picacho is a high mountain in Pinal County. The name means "peak" or "point." It is sometimes called Saddle Mountain. *Ibid.*, p. 330.

[17]Here we face the difficulty when an English-speaking American tries to communicate with an Indian. Paul H. Ezell says that the Pima Indians of the Gila River area had special names for their separate bands. He quotes Franciscan fathers who had labored among the Pima as listing these names, two of them being *Comari* and *Bamori*. It is undoubtedly one of these that Harriet Bunyard renders as "Lemore." "The Hispanic Acculturation of the Gila River Pimas," *American Anthropologist, LXIII,* No. 5, Part 2 (October 1961), p. 115.

August 25th: Started late and come six miles and stopped.
The days are very warm but the nights are pleasant so we lay
by in the day time and travel at night. It is six miles from here
to the river.

August 26th: There is no more grass here so we will go on to
the river. Arrived at the river about 12 o'clock. Found some
grass but it is short and salt grass so it is not good for our
stock. There is a white man here. Says he will show us where
there is good grass in the morning. This place is called
Sacatone Village.[18] Here is where you first strike the Gila
River. This river is swift running stream—muddy—plenty
of willow and cottonwood timber along this stream. Lemore
Indians are thick here. How detestable they are—all the men
riding and the women walking and carrying all the load.

August 27th: The men have found splendid grass one and
one-half miles from camps on opposite side of the river so we
will remain here until Sunday. We reached here on Wednesday. It is 36 miles from this place to La Catcha Canyon. We
have found very little grass since we left La Catcha. We have
very good well water to drink. The pond water down this
river is more or less alkali. We will travel down this river 275
miles. The Indians are passing by here all the time. Some of
them ride nice ponies. Most of the men ride and the women
walk and carry the load. How detestable they are. I will be
glad to get out of sight of them.

August 29th: Left Sacaton late in the evening. Traveled 11
miles. Passed many Indian huts. Camped in one mile of
Lemore Village this morning. Is steam mill here; postoffice
and huts all around. Came to Maricopa Wells before we had
breakfast—distance of 12 miles. There is store here and two

---

[18]Sacaton was a very old Indian settlement on the Gila, now the seat of the Pima and
Maricopa Indian Agency. It had been made headquarters for the military district of
Arizona in 1867. Barnes, *op. cit.*, p. 372.

or three companies of soldiers. Oh, what warm weather. We are camped one mile from town. There is very good grass here—mostly salt grass. Pond water most of which is mixed with alkali.

August 31st: Is quite a pleasant wind blowing this evening and indications of rain. They are fixing to start. Will not get off from camps before sundown. We have to go 45 miles now without water so we will travel most all night. Maricopis Indians brought some melons and few roasting ears to camps today. They are an ignorant, silly looking people.

September 1st: Did not get to travel last night. Was a pony missing so we came one mile on the road west of town and camped. Here we found good grass and very good water. This is everything but a pretty place. It is suited only for Indians to live in. We will start about 3 o'clock this evening as it is cloudy and not very warm.

September 2nd: Had very pleasant time to drive and made good ride of it. We drove 20 miles, stopped three hours before day, rested and slept. Got breakfast and started. Drove about 10 miles, stopped to rest until the cool of evening. We have found no grass of any note since we left Maricopa Wells. We have nice shade to noon in today. We will drive to water tonight.

September 3rd: Did not get to water last night. Drove in three miles of Gila Bend—the watering place and as it was very late they concluded to wait until morning to drive to water. Arrived here very early. The stock had not suffered much. Is ranch here. Three American women living here. It is brushy, ugly place. There is no grass here but they tell us that there is plenty in three miles of this place. It is 45 miles from here to Maricopa Wells. This we came without water or grass.

September 4th: Left Gila Bend this evening. Drove five

miles. Here is a good well—cold water. Several white men living here. We stayed here on account of some stock that we lost on the desert. The boys have gone to hunt them. There is some grass here. We have not seen any Indians since we left Maricopa Wells. I would not be sorry if I never did see another one.

September 5th: The road was very dusty last night. There has been much rain here lately. There is plenty of Mesquite and cottonwood timber here. They do not have any cold weather here. The gentleman that is living here is making preparations to make a crop. He intends planting in three weeks from now. He is prepared to irrigate. He started to California last year—got this far and both his daughters married and he stopped here. All the people that live here seem to have plenty of money. But money would be no inducement for me if I had to live here. Man and his wife that was in this train stopped here to stay a while if not all the time. Their anticipations of California are not so great as mine or they would never have stopped here.

September 6th: Several young men that were in trains behind passed by here this evening. They are going horseback. Found all the stock so we will leave here this evening. Left camps at sundown. Drove nine miles. Stopped for the night.

September 7th: Came to water in two miles. Found pretty place to camp and some grass. This place is called Kunion's Station.[19] Seventeen miles from Gila Bend. Mexicans live here. We have to use the river water. Our teams and stock in general look very well.

---

[19]This was her mis-spelling of Kinyon's Station which was named for Marcus L. Kinyon, a director of the Butterfield Company in 1859. It had previously been called Murderer's Grave. The reason is told by the Conklings: In 1856 a young man had killed his guardian at this place. A newly arrived wagon train drew up just in time to observe the killing and "meted out summary punishment of the crime by executing the young assassin on the spot." Vol. II, *op. cit.*, p. 174.

September 8th: Drove ten miles. Made dry camp. Found splendid grass—let the stock graze a while. We would have liked to stay here day and night with this good grass but there was no water there; so we came on to Oatman Flat. We took right hand road and came to Pike Road. Is just room between the river and the mountains. For the road has been dug in the side so as to be safe. Is 14 miles nearer than the one that went around the mountain and then that road is very rough and hard on oxens feet. Had to pay light toll. This is the warmest place that I ever saw.

September 9th: Started from the station at sundown and I think that we had the worst road that we have ever had. But it was not very long. We came six miles and found plenty of good grass but our stock did not have much benefit of it there being no water here.

September 10th: Started early and came to Berk's Station. Here we found plenty of good water and very good grass; white people living here. Twenty-eighth of July this station was burned. Caught by matches; three times it has been burned and twice destroyed by water from the mountain and river. The weather is so warm here that matches kept in the shade will catch on fire unless kept in something that will not burn.

September 11th: Left Berk's station in the evening. Is another stand in five miles of this place. We did not stop there, we came on to Stanwick's Station very early this morning. Stanwick's is pretty place. Gentleman keeping batch here.

September 12th: Did not leave here last evening as some of the stock were missing so will leave this morning.

September 13th: Made a drive of 11 miles, found good grass and plenty of water. Is no station here. Passed an old station yesterday but it was uninhabited.

September 14th: Started late. Passed Texas Hill Station, 16 miles from Stanwick's. Very good well water here. Filled up some kegs with water then drove five miles to grass. Pond of salt water here. Will stay here until morning. Got late start again. Came five miles to river, nooned here. Was no grass here at all.

September 15th: Started in the evening. Passed Mohawk Station in the night. Had very good road. Seventeen miles from Texas Hill to Mohawk Station. How glad I will be when we cross the Colorado River.

September 16th: Had heavy sand road to pass over today. We made dry camp last night. Arrived at Antelope Station about 11 o'clock in the morning. We are camped near the river but there is no grass here; is some grass two miles from here. Will have to drive the stock to it. There is mountain just opposite the station that is 300 feet high. Nothing growing on it at all.

September 18th: Intended starting last evening but the cattle got away and we did not get all of them so we are still at the same camp. The weather here has not been so warm for the last few days. Stationers all keep whiskey along here. Four men that belong to the beef herd were so much intoxicated today that they knew not what they were doing. They charged and pitched around a while. Shot at the station keeper and then left without doing any damage to any one. Sixteen miles from Mohawk to Antelope.

September 19th: Found all but three of our stock so we will leave Antelope Station this evening. Started before sundown. Went to Mission Camp tonight, 16 miles. The night was pleasant for traveling but the road was extremely dusty. This morning was like winter and I am so glad to see the change.

September 20th: Have to drive to grass this morning, that is if we can find any. Drove three miles, found some grass and cane for the cattle to graze on. There are wagons passing the road all the time hauling to the stations, we have deep heavy sand most of the time since we first struck the river and will continue so for 75 or 100 miles farther.

September 21st: Drove in two miles of Gila City last night. An old stand here. Passed Gila City today and came six miles farther. Found no grass. Bought hay to feed the cattle. We have lost good many cattle now and I fear we will loose many more as grass is scarce. Nothing at Gila City but one station, it is now 14 miles to Fort Yuma.

September 22nd: Drove in one mile of Fort Yuma last night. Had splendid road. Passed through the town today. The fort is beautiful place on high hill that commands full view of Arizona City. The fort is on the other side of the river and Arizona City on this side. Goods and groceries are cheap here. Very few pretty houses in the city. Disappointed several times when I got here. First we got no letters, then we are expecting to get vegetables when we got here but there are very few here. They are expecting three boats every day that will bring vegetables.

September 24th: Camped six miles from town at the crossing on the Colorado. Found some grass and cane for the stock. Very pretty place to camp. The Colorado is 150 yards wide. I suppose muddy but it is good tasted. There is no timber on the banks here. Very thick brush and high weeds all the way from town down here. Boat come up but brought no vegetables. The Gila passes into this river just at Fort Yuma. The mosquitoes are very bad here. We next have a desert of 40 miles without grass, so will stay here several days. Our stock did not look very well when we got here. I do regret having to lay by when we get so near. We have traveled down the Gila river 228 miles. It is 320 miles from Arizona City to Tuscon and is 250 miles from Arizona to Los Angeles.

September 29th: We have now been camped at this place

eight days and have had so much trouble with the stock since we came here. The brush and weeds are so thick that they cannot ride through it. We will cross the river today. There has been Indians here every day since we came to this place. They bring little melons here to sell.

October 1st: We are in California at last. Is stand here and American man and lady lives here. This side of the river looks no better than the other, nothing but mountains and sand and brush. Some of our stock that we could not get that we will have to leave on the other side of the river as there is no grass here to graze on. There was a death in camps on the 30th. An infant 10 months old of Mrs. Collins. They are from Arkansas. They buried it near the station under a tree. Poor little child. It is now at rest. We bought some nice apples, onions and potatoes from a gentleman that is just from Los Angeles. He gives favorable reports of that country.

October 2nd: Left the river about 10 o'clock. We will have no more grass of any consequence for 40 miles. Our feed for our cattle cost $30 what time we stayed at the station. We drove six miles and came to Mexican ranch, here they told us that if we would drive six miles that we would find grass. So taking their word with Indians for pilot we drove about four miles and found some grass and water but it was so boggy that we could not have watered and the Indians were numerous. What could we do. Nothing but turn around and go back to the Mexican ranch. So we started back about one hour high and made the trip safe back not long after dark. Here we bought green corn to feed with. Had some water-melons today. There is sand hill after hill to be seen in the west with nothing at all on them. We are most ready to start again. We will travel tonight. The little Indian huts are thick. I will be glad when I get out of sight of them. They burn all their dead and if they chance to have a horse it has to be burned alive when the body is burned. They eat the horse and reserve a portion for the spirit that is gone when it returns.

October 3rd: We came to a station 14 miles last night. Had heavy sand road most of the way. This is the most destitute country of grass that we have ever traveled over. We will not feed at this stand but will start in the morning and go to the next one—distance of 17 miles.

October 4th—Sabbath Morning: We traveled most all day, reached the stand in the evening finding plenty of barley and hay to feed with. Remained here until next evening. We went to the next stand that night. Fed with hay and barley.

October 5th: We reached new river. This river is caused by the rise of the Colorado. It is not running now but there is ponds that is sufficient for the stock. There is well here but the water is not good. Here we found plenty of mesquite beans and dry grass for the stock. The first they have had since we crossed the river. There are few goods and groceries here. It is 45 miles to crossing of the river. We have found plenty of water on the desert.

October 6th: Will leave this evening. Fifteen miles to the next stand. Here we find dry grass and beans for the stock. Plenty of Lagoon water. Some better than the last we had. Remained here two days. Leave this evening.

October 8th: We now have 30 miles to go without water. We will go 13 miles tonight. There we will find some grass.

October 9th: Had heavy sand road last night. Got here about midnight. Will start at 3 o'clock this evening and drive to water tonight. The nights are very cool and pleasant. We will soon be across the much dreaded desert and we found the road much better than we expected. If you ever do travel this road you need not believe half that the people tell you.

October 10th: Reached the water about 3 o'clock in the morning but very little grass here. Bought hay to feed with.

Beautiful little running branch here. Groceries to sell here. It is eighteen miles to grass. We will go there tonight.

October 11th: Arrived at the stand just after sunrise. Traveled all night. Found good grass and plenty water. One American family living here. Twenty-five miles across the mountains. There is settlement of Americans, first settlement that you come to. It is on the San Diego road.

October 13th: Have rested two days. We will leave for the next stand this morning, 18 miles from this place. We will go there tonight. They say that we will have no more bad water to use. I think we have used our full share of it and we are now done with the dust and sand. There has not been any rain here this summer.

October 19th: I have not opened my journal for some time and have nothing to give as a reason neglecting my writing. We had pleasant camp at St. Philippi [San Felipe] with plenty of grass and water but we had some rough road to pass over before we got there. Stayed there two days. It is small valley. Mountains all around. Heavy timber on the sides and top of the mountains. Mexican family living. Some white men—groceries and few goods. Fifteen miles from here to Warner's ranch.[20] Is very pretty place. We have had plenty of potatoes and cabbages since we came here. This is the best grass that we have had for 300 miles. We have also had some large apples and delicious grapes. Had few sprinkles of rain this morning and it is still cloudy. Left Warner's ranch after dinner. Drove nine miles and found fine camping place. Passed through beautiful valley.

October 21st: Camped by a nice little stream of water—had very good grass.

October 24th: We have been camped two nights and two days

---

[20]See footnote 2 to Ruth Shackleford's 1868 diary, herein April 15, for information about Warner's Ranch.

near a stand called Oak Grove. Here we have splendid grass but not very good water. Two of the boys have gone on horseback to the Monte[21] to make a selection of places. We shall leave this morning. Are expected to meet our friends. Are camped tonight in a pretty place. Two families of Negroes live here. We got plenty of nice cabbage. The largest heads of cabbage—very cheap. These Negroes are wealthy. The boys met our friends and one of them came back. Met our sister and brother today. Oh, how glad we all are to meet again.

---

[21]Monte was the town name that would later be changed to El Monte, which is Spanish for "thicket." Erwin G. Gudde, *Californai Place Names* (Berkeley, 1969), p. 101.

INDEX